THE MOTOR CAR LOVER'S COMPANION

BY RICHARD HOUGH
A History of the World's Sports Cars
First and Fastest

BY RICHARD HOUGH AND MICHAEL FROSTICK
A History of the World's Classic Cars
A History of the World's Racing Cars

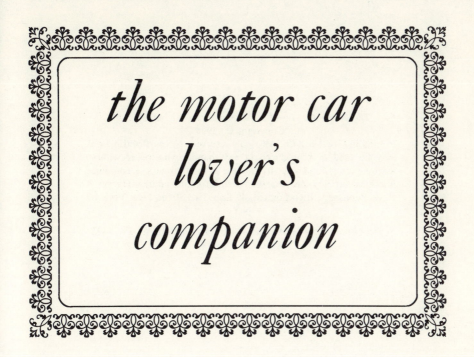

the motor car lover's companion

EDITED BY

RICHARD HOUGH

HARPER & ROW, Publishers
NEW YORK AND EVANSTON

TO LAURENCE POMEROY
M.S.A.E.

Acknowledgments

I would like to thank D. B. Tubbs for suggesting the charming Voisin couplet and Michael Frostick the Godley poem at the end of this book; L. T. C. Rolt for reminding me of the supremely evocative piece from Sir Osbert Sitwell's *Great Morning*; and David Higginbottom who shares my enthusiasm for Patrick Campbell but knows his work much better than I do.

In addition, acknowledgments are due to Messrs Macmillan and Co. Ltd. and David Higham Associates Ltd. for permission to reproduce the extract from *Great Morning* by Osbert Sitwell; Edita S.A. of Lausanne, Switzerland, publishers of *Automobile Year*, for permission to reproduce *Ford: the Car that Changed the World* by M. L. Dees and *Renault: the Cloth Merchant's Son* by Jacques Ickx; Messrs Cassell and Company Ltd. and W. W. Norton Inc. for permission to reproduce the extract from *Jaguar: a biography* by Lord Montagu of Beaulieu, and Messrs Cassell and Company Ltd. for permission to reproduce the chapter entitled 'The Jam Factory' from *Lost Causes of Motoring* by Lord Montagu of Beaulieu, and the extract from *Motor Cars and their Story* by Frederick A. Talbot; The Hutchinson Publishing Group for the extract from *W.O.: the Autobiography of W. O. Bentley*; New Directions and Messrs William Heinemann Ltd. for the extract from *The Air-Conditioned Nightmare* by Henry Miller copyright 1945 by New Directions, reprinted by permission of New Directions; Patrick Campbell for the story 'Speech from the Dock' from *A Long Drink of Cold Water*; The Temple Press Ltd. for the extract from *From Veteran to Vintage* by Laurence Pomeroy and Kent Karslake, and the article by Laurence Pomeroy from the issue of *Motor* dated July 18, 1962; John Murray (Publishers) Ltd. for the extract from *A Victorian Diarist: later extracts from the Journals of Lady Monkswell* edited by the Hon. E. F. C. Collier; Cable Publishing Company Ltd. for the extract from *Motor Racing Memories 1903–21* by W. F. Bradley; the extract from *Moonraker* by Ian Fleming reprinted with permission of Jonathan Cape Ltd. and the Macmillan Company, copyright by the Macmillan Company; 'The Journey' from *Those Barren Leaves* by Aldous Huxley, copyright 1925, 1953 by Aldous Huxley, reprinted with the permission of Harper and Row, Publishers Incorporated, and Messrs Chatto and Windus Ltd.; the Oxford University Press for the poem 'Motor Bus' from *Fifty Poems* by A. D. Godley. Finally, special thanks are due to Iliffe Marketing Company Ltd., publishers of *Autocar*, for permission to reproduce these extracts: 'Wedding', 'The End-to-End' by Henry Sturmey, 'Northward on a Rolls-Royce', 'The Controversial Rolls-Royce', 'The Olympia Show, 1906', 'Your Choice in 1914', and 'First Day at Brooklands'.

Contents

LONELY WHEELS
The Turn of the Century

Wedding

LAST WEEK a marriage was celebrated between the Hon. Eleanor Rolls and the son of Lady Margaret Shelly, at Ennismore Gardens Church. We need hardly say that the bride is the sister of the Hon. C. S. Rolls, who is well known throughout the autocar world as an enthusiastic follower of the latest form of recreative locomotion. Therefore, it is not surprising to hear that Mr Rolls drove friends to the church in an elegant motor victoria, and also in the procession afterwards back to the residence of his family at Rutland Gate, where a reception attended by some four or five hundred guests was held. So far as we know, this is the first time (though it certainly will not be the last) in which an autocar has been used by people of independent position in connection with a wedding of any note. Of course, the autocar has been requisitioned more than once at a wedding, but we believe in each case the bride or bridegroom was indirectly interested financially in the carriage of the future.

An Editorial Note from an 1898 The Autocar

Speeding into the Sunset

BY OSBERT SITWELL

This is surely the purest verbal distillation of early motoring, when there was a special piquancy, now, alas! gone for ever, in the first taste of independent, individual movement, without effort, and to wherever fancy took one. Only the very old today savoured it to the full. All too soon it was lost amid the fumes and stresses of crowded arterial road and super-highway. 'No other generation had been able to speed into the sunset'; and none was to do so again, at least with such an easy heart and mind.

This superb evocation of 'turn of the century' motoring is from the third volume of Sir Osbert Sitwell's autobiography, Great Morning.

JUST AS the swell had driven his tandem, so the nut essentially belonged, as much as a snail to its shell, to the fast, open motor of those days. This vehicle, so modern and of its time, induced in the young man a sense of being heir of all the ages, lord of all he passed by. For the sense of speed flatters the sense of power, raising the rich, and even the humbler lorry-driver, to a new and god-like level, as the houses rush past them, a peep-show, though filled with living people. In this matter, at least, the twentieth-century world had advanced upon the Roman (how greatly would the Romans have enjoyed rushing down their straight roads to the infinities of their Empire). Moreover, mine was the first generation in which the young men were allowed to take their sweethearts for drives—only fastest of fast actresses had ridden in tandems. . . . They would sit together, the two of them, the man at the wheel, the girl beside him, their hair blown back from their temples, their features sculptured by the wind, their bodies and limbs shaped and carved by it continually under their clothes, so that they enjoyed a new physical sensation, comparable to swimming; except that here the element was speed, not water. The winds—and their bodies—were warm that summer. During these drives, they acquired a whole range of physical consciousness, the knowledge of scents, passing one into another with an undreamt of rapidity, the fragance of the countless flowers of the lime trees, hung like bells on pagodas for the breeze to shake, changing into that of sweetbriar, the scent of the early mornings, and of their darkness, of hills and valleys outlined and tinged by memory; there was the awareness of speed itself, and the rapid thinking that must accompany it, a new alertness, and the typical effects, the sense, it might be, of the racing of every machine as dusk approaches, or the sudden access on a hot evening of cool waves of air under tall trees—all these physical impressions, so small in themselves, went to form a sum of feeling new in its kind and never before experienced. Even the wind of the winter, at this pace snatching tears from their eyes, and piercing through layers of clothes, was something their fathers had not known. The open car belonged to that day. No other generation had been able to speed into the sunset.

From *Great Morning*, 1948

Motoring Dress for Ladies

BY LADY JEUNE

According to Lady Jeune, and to many women whose memories go back to 1902, motoring even with the protection of a veil was impossible without the complexion losing its 'soft, peach-like bloom'. The lady automobilist indeed paid the price for the glorious sensation of the winter wind 'snatching tears from their eyes'. Until the coming of the closed carriage, and for long afterwards for those who continued to prefer open motoring, the problems of protection were serious and engaged the close attention of the clothing trade.

MY SIMPLE task in this volume is to discuss that side of the question which affects women very deeply: how to dress and equip themselves so as to be warmly and comfortably clad with as little disfigurement as possible. The fact that women should motor—if a verb may be employed—and care for it as much as they do is a great tribute to their lack of personal vanity, for, try as hard as they can, it is almost impossible to make the dress they have to wear a becoming one. In most of the sports and pastimes of women the dress they assume is arranged with a view to adding to their charms, and in nearly every case it can be both pretty and serviceable. In croquet, lawn tennis, skating, hunting, driving, or bicycling, the dress worn by women may be excessively becoming, as it can be made to show off the figure, and the hat or head-gear is generally a delightful frame of the face—indeed, the fact that the athletic costumes of women are so picturesque is possibly one of the reasons which have made out-door sports so popular among them.

In the case of motor driving or riding there are two things only to be considered: how a woman can keep herself warm in winter and not be suffocated by the dust in summer without making herself very unattractive. Dress must be regulated to a great extent by the speed at which she travels, and it is quite possible to wear a smart hat and pretty clothes if the pace is a comparatively slow one, such as is usual in the Park or in the streets of London. This chapter, however, has to deal with the more serious side of the question, how a woman should dress who goes on long journeys in every kind of weather, and at a high rate of speed.

The first consideration must be to keep warm, and the second—a no less important one—what head-gear must be worn that will keep on the head, and not be blown off by the first gust of wind. The question of warmth must be considered from every point of view, and plenty of suitable clothing is absolutely essential. A warm gown should be adopted, made of a material that will not catch the dust, and it is also important to wear warm clothing under the gown; for unless such jerseys and bodices are worn, the wind

penetrates, and it is quite impossible to avoid feeling chilled during a long day. The fatigue which is inseparable from many hours in the open air, and is also intensified by the rapid speed at which one travels, becomes greater as the day passes; with the increase of that fatigue a feeling of cold arises, so that unless a sufficient amount of warm clothing is worn the sense of exhaustion becomes very trying.

The best material for excluding the cold is leather, kid, or chamois leather; the latter may be recommended for lining the coat, and kid for the outside covering. This has, however, the disadvantage of being heavy and stiff, while chamois leather is softer and gives the figure more laxity. A coat lined with chamois leather and fur is the most successful of any, and the outside cover can be made in any pretty waterproof material.

The best coats that I have seen for motor car driving are some which come from Vienna, and are both cheap and comfortable. The fur employed for the lining is opossum, which is both light and thick; they are to be had of any length, they button up the front, are double-breasted, and have two warm pockets placed crossways in front. The coat of which an illustration is given is excellent for the purpose, but it is more elaborate. It has, however, the leather waistcoat or undercoat attached to it, and is extremely comfortable. It can be made in any cloth or material. It has heavy fur which, while it looks smart, is a sure means of catching and retaining dust, and the great object to be aimed at in motor travelling is to find something which will not collect dust, for if coats, rugs, etc. get dusty it is almost impossible to get rid of it. The longer a coat is the better, for it is round the extremities that the cold is felt as much as anywhere. Therefore a coat should be made loose enough to wrap round the figure and fold well over the knees. It is quite impossible to keep warm in a rapid motor journey except by using fur rugs, and they should be backed with leather, which mitigates the trouble of beating the dust out of them at the end of the day.

Difficult as it is, however, to keep warm and fairly clean as regards the clothes which should be worn, the real problem is how to keep a hat on. The head must be warmly covered and the hat small, for anything large or wide offers too much resistance to the wind, and gets quickly blown off. After many experiments I am satisfied that the blue Glengarry cap is the best head-dress for the motor car. It is pinned in one or two places to break the hard, straight outline, and to give a little height to it. It is light and warm, and with a long gauze veil, which covers not only the hat but comes over the ears; the wearer is as comfortable as possible. The veil can be varied from gauze in summer to a long grey Shetland cloud in winter. Grey is the best colour, as it shows the dust less than any other. The illustration shows the veil covering the face, and protecting it if the wind is too strong and cold. The material for making the veil must be not less than two yards long, and three-quarters of a yard wide. It should be drawn well up in front, and pinned to the bonnet, then pulled down over the ears, and crossed behind, bringing the ends to the front, where they can be fastened in a bow under the chin; two or three pins should be put in behind to keep it in its place, and it will, if properly pinned, remain perfectly tidy all day. It is necessary to have the veil sufficiently wide, so that there should be enough to fall down over the face if it is wanted. A long grey Shetland cloud is the best and most comfortable veil to wear in winter. The yachting cap has some advantages, but it is hard and heavy to the head. The best gloves to wear are white knitted worsted. These are warm and easy to wash.

There is one point interesting to every woman on which a few words are necessary, and that is what the effect of long days in the open, and the rapid passage through the air, must have on the complexion. It certainly does not improve it, but there is not much use in trying anything, except wearing a veil, to mitigate its evils. Many people use powder and grease to prevent the skin from getting red and hard.

Alas! if women are going to motor, and motor seriously—that is to say, use it as a means of locomotion—they must relinquish the hope of keeping their soft peach-like bloom. The best remedy is cold water and a rough towel, and that not used sparingly, in the morning before they start. There is one other, the last, but perhaps the hardest concession a woman can make if she is going to motor, and that is that she must wear glasses—not small dainty glasses, but veritable goggles. They are absolutely necessary both for comfort and the preservation of the eyesight; they are not becoming, but then, as I have tried to point out, appearance must be sacrificed if motor-driving is to be thoroughly enjoyed. Those who fear any detriment to their good looks had best content themselves with a quiet drive in the Park, leaving to the more ardent motorist the enchanting sensation of flying along the lanes and roads of our lovely country.

From *Motors and Motor Driving* in 'The Badminton Library of Sports and Pastimes', 1902

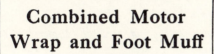

Combined Motor Wrap and Foot Muff

A Novel Gift Suggestion

DC 84—Covered with **Jap Silk** and filled with best quality Down. Light in weight, very warm and comfortable. Made with footmuff, hand-muff, and small pocket for handkerchief. In navy blue, brown or green. Other colours made to order in a few days .. **£5.5.0**

Motoring dress down the years

Chauffeurs' Clothing

The Capricious Motor Car

BY THE HON. C. S. ROLLS

These useful tips and hints, originally entitled 'The Caprices of the Petrol Motor', are contributed by one of the great figures of early British motoring. The Hon. Charles S. Rolls was sportsman, balloonist and aviator, as well as pioneer British automobilist and canny co-founder of the Rolls-Royce Company. Rolls's social connections, considered by some as perhaps a shade 'fast', proved their value in building up the sales of the cars which bore his name, until his death at the Bournemouth flying meeting in 1910, the first Briton to die in an airplane.

Not all Rolls's advice to the motorist is relevant today; but heed can still be taken with advantage of some of his 'don'ts' at the end, especially that relating to the hand or parking brake.

THE INTENDING owner of a motor car will often say, 'What in the world should I do if the thing were to break down on a country road?' and the object of this chapter is to enable the novice *en panne* quickly to recognize the symptoms of his case (so far as the engine is concerned) and then at once to 'spot' the probable cause and remedy.

In order to make these remarks complete, I have been compelled to enumerate a very long and somewhat formidable list of evils, and lest a glance at this should frighten off any would-be motorist, it must be clearly understood that the list comprises *possibilities* as distinct from *probabilities*.

What is here said should therefore be looked upon in the same light as a veterinary surgeon's book on horses, and readers must not think that if they purchase cars all the troubles here mentioned would necessarily occur to the motor any more than they would imagine that all the diseases described in a horse-doctor's book would happen to a newly-acquired horse. Many cars have been run by amateurs for thousands of miles without the occurrence of any trouble. In proof of this may I observe that a member of the Automobile Club recently stated that, although he had previously no engineering experience, he had run his car ten thousand miles without having to effect any serious repairs, and had experienced no trouble whatever except on two occasions, when the slight repairs necessary were done in a very short time.

The chapter is divided into two parts, the first dealing with the difficulties in starting, and the second with troubles on the road.

PART I

THE MOTOR WILL NOT START

A petrol engine will generally start most easily with all the cold-air inlets closed, the usual procedure being to shut these air-holes or taps, then let a little petrol into the carburettor, shake the float needle (if there be one) or inject petrol into the induction valves or through the compression tap on top of the cylinder, if such exists; then, the ignition tubes being red-hot, or the electricity switched on, the ignition retarded, a few turns of the engine should suffice to set it going; if however, it will not start, the trouble must lie in one of the following sources: 1, Ignition; 2, Carburation; 3, Compression; or 4, Moving Parts.

1. *Ignition.* Having satisfied yourself that the ignition is in perfect order, the fault must be in one of three sources remaining.

2. *Carburation.* Let us first take the carburation. There are many little things which may militate against a healthy explosive mixture reaching the cylinders, and we will first enumerate the principal causes in brief as follows:

(*a*) Wrong proportions of air and gas.

(*b*) Carburettor flooded.

(*c*) Carburettor starved.

(*d*) Cold weather.

(*e*) Stale petrol.

(*f*) Handle not turned fast enough.

To deal with these more fully:

(*a*) The mixture of hot air, cold air, and petrol vapour should be varied in every possible way—see that an excess of air is not being drawn in through a crack in a pipe or a loose coupling.

(*b*) Too rich a mixture may be caused by the presence of too much petrol in the carburettor; if this is so, turn off the petrol supply for a time and revolve the engine again with all air inlets wide open until the first explosions are obtained.

(*c*) Perhaps the cylinder cannot get any petrol vapour, owing to the nipple (in a float and jet type carburettor) being stopped up. This nipple can be taken out with a special key and cleaned by passing a fine needle through it, taking great care not to enlarge the hole in the least degree. Possibly there is no petrol in the tank, or you have forgotten to turn it on, or the tank is almost empty and the car tilted by standing at the side of the road; push it over to the other side. One can tell if there is any petrol in the carburettor by the position of the float needle, and the novice should provide himself with a diagram of his carburettor.

(*d*) In cold weather, if the car has been standing idle for some time, considerable difficulty may be experienced in starting up. Petroleum spirit will of course vaporize far less readily at a low temperature than at a high one. Artificial heat is therefore the remedy, and this can be most easily applied by taking out the mushroom-piece in the carburettor (if there is one) and warming it over the burners or otherwise; or warm petrol may be squirted into the cylinder or induction pipe or valves. In obstinate cases it may be necessary to warm the carburettor underneath by means of a little cotton waste soaked with methylated spirit. There may be a slight flare-up, but this will assist the carburation, and there is nothing to fear from it so long as the main supply cock has been carefully closed.

(*e*) The petrol remaining in the carburettor may lose its strength if the car has been standing a long while; it should be emptied out and refilled. A good plan when about to put away the car for some time is to stop the motor by turning off the main cock, so letting it use up the last drop of petrol in the carburettor.

The petrol in the main tank may also become heavy in course of time, especially if free access of air is allowed to it. A small instrument called a densitometer is sold for determining the specific gravity of petrol; the best specific gravity for starting is ·680; if your petrol when tested shows heavier than sp. gr. ·700 it should be changed or the tank shaken up.

(*f*) Perhaps there is nothing wrong after all, except that you do not turn the starting handle fast enough to cause proper vaporization. Remember that a few smart turns with the whole of your energy will be more likely to start an engine than hours of slow 'grinding'.

3. Having now ascertained that neither the ignition nor the carburation is to blame, if the motor still will not go we must look for the failure in either the compression or one of the moving parts.

Compression is the life and soul of a modern high-speed internal combustion engine.

When the engine is in proper working order, and being turned by hand, a considerable resistance should be felt at the alternate back stroke of each piston; this back pressure should require a considerable effort to overcome when the handle is being turned slowly. If the compression of any cylinder leaks, that cylinder will not give off its full power.

How to locate a leak of compression. If there is a loss of compression, a slight hiss will generally be audible when the handle is turned. In order to find out where the leak is, a lighted taper may be held over the cylinder in different positions, while the engine is being turned slowly; the flame will be turned on one side on meeting the leak; or soap and water may be painted about the cylinder head, and bubbles should soon indicate the presence of the leakage.

Possible sources of leakage. (*a*) A leakage will generally be found at the junction of such fittings as the ignition tube, induction valve, valve cover, sparking plug, compression tap, or other attachment connected with the interior of the cylinder or combustion chamber—probably a washer blown out or a loose nut will be the cause.

Should, however, the leakage not reveal itself under the above tests, it is probable that:

(*b*) The exhaust or inlet valves are 'pitted' or coated with deposit, and consequently permit a loss of compression past their seating; if this is so, they should be taken out and ground on their seats with fine emery powder and oil, or paraffin, till they bed properly; the engine may then have to be run for some time before the leakage ceases. See also that the valve springs have not grown too weak.

(*c*) There is a possibility of the compression also blowing past the piston-rings. This can generally be detected by listening attentively with the ear close to the cylinder at fault, and turning the starting handle or fly-wheel slowly—a gentle hissing will be heard at intervals. The cause of this is generally the sticking of the rings in their grooves. The remedy is to wash out with paraffin so as to free them for their whole circumference. If they still leak badly, the piston should be taken out and new rings fitted, especially if the engine has been over-heated at any time, in which event:

(*d*) the cylinder-head joint, if there is one, may have warped and the compression may be escaping from one cylinder to the other, and into the water space; water in turn will probably find its way into the cylinder, and being converted into steam, will interfere with the working of the engine and rust the valves. Little spots of rust on the valves will indicate what is happening, and the cylinder-head joint will then have to be re-made—a matter for an expert.

No compression at all. If on trying to start the motor no compression at all is felt on one cylinder, there may be a valve stuck open through a breakage or gumming (see later), or else the ends of the piston-rings may have by chance arrived opposite one another, thus allowing the compression to slip through the spaces. When this occurs, the rings should be freed by letting in paraffin and running the engine a bit on the other cylinder or cylinders if possible; the rings will probably soon change their position—they are purposely allowed (in most engines) to move round so as to wear evenly.

Apparent excessive compression. There may, especially on a cold morning, appear to be so much compression that the engine can hardly be turned; this stiffness is really due to the drying of the oil on the walls of the cylinder. To avoid this a copious dose of paraffin should always be injected when stopping the car after a day's run, and a few turns given to the engine by hand.

Note. It is most essential for every motorist to insist on having proper and convenient means fitted on his car for washing the cylinders with paraffin or petrol, both to facilitate starting up and to keep the piston-rings in good order.

Back firing. I have said that a considerable resistance should always be felt when turning a motor slowly by hand; sometimes, however, the innocent motorist, when endeavouring to put his engine into motion, receives something considerably more than a mere resistance. He may get a kick from the handle which will give his arm a nasty jar, or possibly sprain his wrist. These 'back fires' are the result of what is called 'premature ignition', and therefore belong strictly speaking to the chapter on 'Ignition'. I may merely remark that they are due to the spark-timing gear being too much advanced, the platinum tubes being too long, the burners being too close in, faulty opening of the induction valves, overheating of the motor, or ignition tubes being too hot; in the last case the burners may be turned down to allow the tubes to cool momentarily and turned up again when the motor starts. In the other cases the remedies are obvious.

4. *Moving Parts.* Having exhausted the possible causes of refusal to start except those consisting of some mechanical fault, we will now see what moving parts could go wrong, and so cause all the trouble.

(*a*) The mechanism for operating the electric ignition is liable to many little derangements.

(*b*) A broken exhaust-valve stem or a broken or displaced spring will often be difficult to observe; a valve may have stuck open through stiffness or through something getting under its seat. The exhaust-valve gear should be carefully watched to see that all the valves work regularly and to their full extent.

(*c*) Stiffness in the accelerator or governing gear, or a dislodged key, pin, or feather may also hinder the lifting of the exhaust-valves, or on some engines prevent the throttle from opening itself fully.

(*d*) The simple mechanism adopted on some cars to engage the starting handle with the motor will sometimes give out, so that the handle will not turn the motor. In cars of the Panhard type the handle is made to engage with the engine by pushing a small bevel-ended tongue in against a pin put through the end of the crank-shaft; a bad 'back fire' may cause this pin to sheer off or bend and jam the tongue. The novice should be shown the way to get at this mechanism so as to know how to renew the pin or tongue. If the starting gear fails at an awkward moment, the car may be started by putting in the third or fourth speed and pushing the car with the friendly aid of a few lookers-on.

PART II

ROAD TROUBLES

We will now pass on to Part II, dealing with possible troubles encountered on the road, dividing this section into:

1. Motor stops.
2. Motor nearly stops and then goes on again.
3. Motor will not 'pull' well.
4. Motor will not govern or 'cut out' properly.
5. Unusual noises.

Motor Stops Completely

This may be divided into:

A. Overheating.
B. Starvation of carburettor.
C. Carburettor flooded.
D. Burners going out.
E. Mechanical reasons.

A. *Overheating*. The most serious cause of a stoppage on the road is undoubtedly overheating, which causes the lubrication to burn up and the piston to expand and grip or 'seize' in the cylinder. This matter of overheating should now be divided into its various causes, viz.:

Cause 1. Water circulation stopped.
2. Water all lost.
3. Faulty lubrication.
4. Water entering cylinder.
5. Too powerful a charge.   } Very unusual.
6. Incrustation of jackets.

Cause 1. Of these the cessation of water circulation for cooling is the most important. It must be the result of (*a*) the pump ceasing to act through

27

bad adjustment of its driving-gear, or through its valves or cogs jamming; its spindle being seized or bent; the interior fan worn or unkeyed; the friction wheel unkeyed, or its tyre worn out or come off.

As regards the adjustment of the driving-gear of a centrifugal pump driven by friction, the friction wheel and spindle should revolve freely when the pump is pulled away from the fly-wheel. It should be adjusted so that the spring presses it lightly but firmly against the fly-wheel; care should also be taken in packing the glands of these pumps, for they run at a very high velocity; a very slight leak of water, however, is advantageous for lubrication.

(*b*) The blockage of a water-pipe or passage will also impede the circulation, or:

(*c*) There may be an air or steam lock in the pipes. The best way of getting rid of an air lock is to open all cocks and plugs in the water system and run the engine, filling up the tank and water jackets to make up what is running out. This will eventually expel any air, and the water will circulate freely.

Cause 2. If all the water has been lost on the road through the breakage of a pipe or the opening of a plug or tap, or loosening of a joint, and no water is near, you can continue your journey spasmodically by allowing the engine to cool down, then run on a mile or two with the bonnet off or open until it shows symptoms of overheating again, when stop, paraffin your cylinders, and wait another half-hour. The pump of a car has several times been known to have been carried away by contact with a dog: on one case there was no trace of pump or dog except a tooth which the unfortunate animal left in the back tyre.

Note. Always carry rubber tubing to repair ruptured pipes.

Cause 3. If the overheating has been caused by *faulty lubrication*, it is probable that this is due to inattention to the lubricators.

Remarks as to lubrication. It should be ascertained from the makers how many drops a minute are required for the proper lubrication of the engine, and it must be remembered also that in cold weather when the oil is thick a different adjustment will be necessary from that found suitable in warm weather. It is most important that the lubrication should be regular, and with good oil but not too much; for too much oil will spoil the sparking plugs, clog the valves, and interfere with the explosive mixture. For this reason the lubricators should always be carefully closed when stopping. If a Dubrulle mechanical lubricator is used, examine the ball valves sometimes, and do not trust entirely to the sight feed. If a pressure type lubricator is used, see that the stopper is tight, for if the pressure from the exhaust leaks the lubrication will stop and in some cars the supply of petrol too.

It sometimes happens that an oil pipe or hole is stopped up and wants cleaning, or perhaps the plug at the bottom of the crank chamber has come unscrewed with the vibration and dropped off, losing all the oil, in which the cranks should always dip. The proper amount of oil for each crank case is

generally at least half a pint; an extra lubricator to the cylinders or base chamber should always be fitted, so that a little extra oil can be fed in by hand, if there is any doubt about the engine getting enough.

The following are additional causes of overheating. They are, however, of very rare occurrence:

Cause 4. The head joint may leak and admit water into the cylinders.

Cause 5. In some small engines if the throttle is kept full open, so as to admit too powerful a charge of gas, overheating will result.

Cause 6. Finally, a thick incrustation on the walls of the water-jacket, due to the use of bad water, will prevent the cooling water from taking up the excess of heat from the cylinder.

Remarks on overheating. How to tell when a motor is overheating. The symptoms are:

1. The driver can generally detect a slight smoke rising from the engine and a smell of burnt paint and burnt oil.

2. A peculiar tapping sound becomes audible.

3. The engine will continue firing for a few revolutions after the current has been switched off or the burners extinguished.

4. Steam issues from the cooling water or the water blows out of the over-flow pipe.

What to do when the motor heats. As soon as any of the above symptoms are noticed:

(1) The motor should be stopped at once.

(2) Paraffin should be copiously injected into the cylinders and the

29

engine turned by hand to free the piston-rings.

(3) The parts should then be allowed to cool.

(4) Change the exhaust springs.

N.B. Do not pour cold water into the cylinder jackets, for fear of cracking them, but rather pour into the tank so as to warm the water before it reaches the cylinders.

Dangers of a 'seize'. Overheating of the engine to this extent should be guarded against, for it is liable to cause scoring of the cylinder walls, and may warp the cylinder-head joint (if there is one), which will necessitate remaking the faces—a tedious and difficult task. The exhaust-valve lifters may become bound, the excess of heat will also cause the valve-springs, piston-rings (and possibly the occupants of the car) to lose their temper; apart from the above no damaging effects are usual.

Precautions. To enable the driver to verify the water circulation a 'manometer' should be placed on the dashboard to indicate the pressure of water, or a tap or float arrangement may be connected with the piping, so as to show whether the circulation is alright. During hard frost this is especially important, for should the circulation cease, the radiator, a pipe, or even the water-jacket itself, may be easily burst by the frost.

B. *Starvation of Carburettor.* A motor may stop from other causes besides overheating—for instance, no petrol may reach the carburettor. One of the following will probably account for this:

Cause 1. Petrol supply tap has turned itself off by vibration against tools, etc.

Cause 2. No pressure to feed petrol.

Cause 3. Supply pipe, filter or jet in carburettor blocked with a piece of waste, asbestos, dirt, or deposit.

Cause 4. If the tank is nearly empty, and a very steep hill is encountered, the carburettor may be too high for the petrol to run into it; the remedy is to pump air pressure into the tank.

Cause 5. A union may be disconnected, pipe broken or plug under carburettor dropped off, and you have lost all your petrol, or perhaps the tank has simply run dry. Remedy: leave your friend to sleep on the car, take list of petrol depots, and make your way to the nearest town; if you cannot get any proper spirit, bring out some common benzoline of about ·700 gravity and take a spare tin of petrol on the car next time.

C. *Carburettor Flooded.* If, on the other hand, there appears to be too much petrol about, and it is running out of the carburettor, the float needle is stuck or bent, or the float has punctured and petrol got inside it. In the latter case, take out the float, make a hole large enough to let out the petrol, and carefully solder up air-tight again.

D. *Burners Going Out.* If your burners go out when you start the car, as is sometimes the case, it is due to the jerk of the car sending the petrol from the burners back towards the tank. To obviate this, the tap should be opened as little as possible.

E. *Mechanical Reasons*. If the car stops from some mechanical cause, the reason may probably be found in the former section 'Motor will not Start', or in the chapters dealing with Transmission or Ignition. Most probably it will be due to:

(i) A broken valve.

(ii) Broken or misplaced spring.

(iii) Valve-gear not operating properly, or

(iv) Something has lodged on the face of the valve, holding it open. I have known the cotter of an inlet valve and parts of sparking plugs sucked under the inlet valve, where they have stuck or gone into the cylinder and even through into the exhaust box at the back of the car.

Fits and Starts

If a motor nearly stops and then goes on again, it is generally due to temporary starvation of the carburettor. There is probably some water, oil, waste, dust, asbestos, dirt or deposit of some sort at the ingress of the spirit, which, however, sometimes frees itself. To avoid these troubles petrol should never be poured into the tank except through a funnel fitted with a very fine gauze strainer or a piece of muslin. I have known a little particle of matter dance about in the mixing chamber, and once in a way it would lodge on top of the spray-nipple for a time.

It should be remembered that air must always find an inlet to the tank in order that the petrol may flow out freely, and considerable difficulty has been caused by the tiny vent-hole which is generally in the stopper of the main tank becoming blocked up by some dirt or an overcoat lying on it under the cushion. It may happen that air can get to it when you are starting up; then when you sit down on the cushion the hole becomes air-tight and the engine gradually stops.

Motor Will Not 'Pull' Well or Misses Fire

We will treat this malady under the following headings:

A. Ignition.
B. Compression.
C. Carburation.
D. Lubrication.
E. One cylinder will not work at all, and
F. Irregular missing.

A. *Ignition*. Nothing is so annoying as to drive a motor which is continually missing fire or has a 'fit of the slows'. The fault is usually with the ignition—the platinum tubes are not hot enough, or are dirty inside or outside, or the passages leading to them are clogged. When exhaust pressure is adopted for feeding the burners with petrol, the pressure-valve sometimes refuses to act and lets the pressure out. Remedy for this: grind the little valve or change the spring, and see that its lift is just one millimetre. Perhaps there is oil on the sparking plugs, or the battery is run down, or the timing is not correct, but we are here trespassing on to the province of 'Ignition'. If the root of the difficulty is elsewhere, perhaps:

B. *Compression.* The compression is poor (see 'Motor will not Start') or:

C. *Carburation.* The carburation is not good:

Cause 1. The proportions of air and gas are not well adjusted.

Cause 2. The petrol is stale.

Cause 3. Petrol cannot get free access to the carburettor (see 'Fits and Starts').

Cause 4. The gauze through which on some cars the air is sucked is blocked with dust, or the gauze which is sometimes fitted into the induction pipe is dirty, or that fitted between the exhaust and the pressure valve (in cases where a branch of the exhaust is utilized to maintain pressure in the petrol or lubricating tanks) is foul.

Cause 5. A pipe-joint is loose or has a hidden crack through which an excess of air enters.

See also 'Carburation'.

D. *Lubrication.* Too much lubricating oil is used, causing (i) valves to stick; (ii) a deposit on the sparking plugs; and (iii) an unhealthy charge in the cylinder. Excess of oil reveals itself in the form of smoke issuing from the exhaust.

E. *One cylinder will not work at all.* If one cylinder misses fire *regularly*, it is probable that:

(i) The exhaust or induction valve has given up the ghost, or

(ii) The nozzle for supplying that cylinder with spray is blocked.

F. *Irregular Missing.* If, however, the misfiring is *irregular*, and none of the defects afore-mentioned are found, we must look to less common sources for the difficulty.

How to find which cylinder misses. Endeavour first to ascertain which cylinder is the culprit. One method of doing this is to place your hand on each exhaust pipe while the engine is running. You will then get a bad burn from every one except that belonging to the faulty cylinder. A more convenient way—if electric ignition is fitted—is to stop the working of three out of four of the induction coils, changing about until you find the one that is at fault. It may be, however, that your engine has only one cylinder, or that all the cylinders miss occasionally.

Let us take the various possible causes of the difficulty.

Cause 1. Be sure that the governing gear is working properly, and that the governor does not cut out one cylinder when it ought not.

Cause 2. The induction valve may be worn, and opens too much.

Cause 3. Exhaust-valve lifters worn and do not lift enough.

Cause 4 (rare). They have expanded through being overheated, and open too much.

Cause 5. A spring displaced.

Cause 6. The exhaust or induction valve springs are not strong enough to close quickly, and an exhaust valve may sometimes open on the suction stroke.

Cause 7 (rare). In some engines the mushroom-shaped object called the diffuser, which is part of the small disc screwed into the top of the carburettor, may be too near or too far from the jet of petrol.

Cause 8. Or the size of the nipple through which the jet is sucked is too large or too small. It is very seldom that this should be touched, and its adjustment must be made with extreme delicacy, by the aid of a watch-maker's brooch-needle. It is always best to make any experiments on a spare nipple, and not to touch the one that is in use, so that if unsuccessful you may put back the old one, otherwise the last state of your carburation may be considerably worse than the first.

Cause 9. Freezing of the carburettor. Trouble will sometimes arise through the carburettor freezing, even in warm weather. The remedy is to fit a pipe to convey to it air heated by the exhaust or the burners.

There are still a few but extremely improbable causes for irregular firing:

Cause 10 (rare). There may be too much play worn in the cogs of the valve gear or ignition gear. The remedy is to advance one tooth.

Cause 11 (rare). The cog wheels of the 'two-to-one' gear may have been put together wrongly by a repairer.

N.B. Always make your own marks when taking these wheels apart, for the existing marks may not necessarily be correct. The makers often find a better position for the teeth to engage in after one set of marks has already been made.

Cause 12 (rare). It has also happened that the key or feather by which a gear wheel of the ignition or valve mechanism is keyed on to its shaft has sheared, and the wheel has moved round on its spindle, causing firing to take place at the wrong instant, and very erratic behaviour in consequence.

Cause 13. For reasons previously explained, if water can find its way into the cylinder, misfiring may result.

Finally, remember that if your engine is misfiring or not going well, the fault may of its own accord very likely disappear altogether after a little running.

ENGINE RACES, i.e. GOVERNOR WILL NOT WORK

Evidently something wrong with the governing gear. What?

Cause 1. The cam, which, by means of a small object which resembles a hammer, throws the exhaust-valve lifters out of action, is keyed to its shaft by a small screw; if this works out, as it sometimes does, the cam will move about where it likes, and lead to the fault in question.

Cause 2. Similarly if the 'hammer' gets loose or is worn, the same result will follow.

These remarks refer to the engines of the Daimler and Panhard type.

Cause 3. In these motors the governor is usually arranged to cut out one or two cylinders before the rest; if much wear has taken place in this mechanism the trouble in question may arise.

There are also springs whose function it is to bring back the exhaust lifters into action after they have been 'cut out' by the governor. If this mechanism has been roughly fitted or has had much wear, I have often found that the ends of these springs should be slipped off their knobs for the engine to govern properly; and that if they are in place one cylinder may refuse to cut out at all.

Cause 4. Of course if any of the delicate spindles, etc. connected with the governing mechanism be strained in any way, or are allowed to get dry for want of oil, the same trouble may be expected.

If the governor goes wrong at an awkward moment in the traffic, and the engine begins to race, it may be controlled by switching off and on, or retarding ignition, admitting an excess of air, or the exhaust-valve lifters may be thrown out by hand.

UNUSUAL NOISES

Regular. If an unusual but regular *puffing* noise (external) is heard, which keeps time with the engine without apparently affecting its running, it is clear that an exhaust joint has given out somewhere between the exhaust valve and silencer. If the rupture is near the engine, the exhaust gases may slightly interfere with the burners and the mixture, but otherwise no harm will be done to the motor, though the noise may frighten passing horses considerably.

A regular but unusual *tapping* coming from the engine indicates:
(i) Something loose or broken.
(ii) Too much advance in ignition, or
(iii) Engine about to seize through overheating.

If a *squeak* is heard anywhere instant attention should be paid to it, otherwise much harm may be done. A slight squeak is often very difficult to locate, and turns out sometimes to be perfectly harmless; a squeak has been traced to the rubbing of the bonnet against something inside it, to the shaking of the radiator, vibration of lamps, and such like causes, which, though trivial when found, are sources of anxiety to a careful motorist.

I have had a distinct whistling sound produced by the rapid suction of air through a brass tap at each revolution of the engine. This took a long time to discover. A slight leak of compression will also sometimes produce a squeak at each explosion.

Irregular. Popping noises in the carburettor or induction pipes. These are minute and harmless explosions caused by:
  (i) Induction valves opening too much, or
 (ii) Sticking, or
(iii) Their springs being too weak.
 (iv) Cold ignition tubes.
  (v) Retarding the ignition too much, or
 (vi) Bad carburation.

Bursting noises (irregular) coming from the engine.
  (i) These indicate: Burst joint at valve cover, sparking plug, or ignition tube. Spare washers specially made must always be carried to rectify these.
 (ii) A platinum tube may have burst. Spare ones should always be carried.
What to do if the ignition tube bursts and you have no spare one. If you have no spare one, the hole of the old one should be closed up as much as possible with a small hammer, then replace the tube with the hole in such a position as not to blow out the burner or its neighbour. If you can keep the burners alight progress can thus be made. Failing this, the faulty tube or the hole leading to it must be blocked up, and the car run home on the remaining cylinder or cylinders.
(iii) *Loud report in exhaust.* This is due to several unexploded charges having collected in the silencer, and being ignited by the incandescent products of the next fired charge; switching the electric ignition off and on will often produce this, so may a sudden retarding of ignition, or a semi-cold platinum tube.

There is no danger in these explosions—startling as they seem—beyond the risk of splitting the exhaust box or pipe.

RESUME

It will now be seen that troubles may arise from any of the six following sources:

Ignition	Lubrication
Carburation	Circulation, and
Compression	Moving parts

I have tried to classify all possible troubles according to their symptoms, so as to make it easy for the novice quickly to locate the root of evil and rectify the fault.

CONCLUDING ADVICE AND REMARKS

If your motor works well, leave it alone, although it may never seem fast enough. Many troubles arise from interference and undue curiosity.

Remember that petrol is a highly volatile and inflammable liquid; its vapour is equally dangerous.

Make sure that all petrol connections and unions are taut.

If you have a flare-up, immediately close the supply cocks or let off the pressure, take off bonnet to save the paint, and smother the flames, or let them burn out. Water should only be thrown to save woodwork.

Don't pour petrol near a naked light; it is prudent to extinguish the burners when filling the tanks of the car.

Don't spill the petrol over your clothes and then strike a match to light your pipe.

Don't go out even for a short run without complete equipment of tools, spare parts, petrol, and repair outfit, or you may be back late.

Don't let a willing ostler fill up your petrol tank with water.

Don't leave the water in your car on a frosty night, except with 20 per cent of glycerine in it.

Don't start away with your brake hard on and wonder why the motor is not pulling.

Don't pedal your tricycle for half an hour before remembering the plug, unless the doctor recommends it.

Don't let the starting handle fly off and hit you on the chin, and

Don't trouble to turn on the petrol tap if there is none in the tank.

From *Motors and Motor Driving* in 'The Badminton Library of Sports and Pastimes'

PART TWO

THE GIANTS

Ford: the Car that Changed the World

BY M. L. DEES

No one has ever disputed that Henry Ford was the greatest industrial figure of the twentieth century. He was also the most influential and controversial. He did, in fact, as Mr Dees indicates in his title, change the face of the world. For better or worse, humanity en masse *became independently mobile as a result of his prodigious work. Although there remain hundreds of millions of people who cannot hope to own a motor car in their lifetime, and total production will no doubt rise so that the output at Dearborn at its zenith will seem like a mere trickle, there can never be another figure to match up to this farm boy of Irish-English stock whose life was to become obsessed by the hugely complex and profitable business of providing the masses with four wheels and an engine to power them.*

HENRY FORD. In the seventy-odd years of motoring history, he is *the* man. Others designed great cars and engines; his was the principal contribution to the most successful design of them all—Model T. But Model T's success is only part of the accomplishment. As Ford drove his matchless management team to create an industrial complex which would put out more and more Model Ts at lower and lower cost, he was able to bring unit production expenses so low that he could raise the wages of his workers to unimagined levels, yet still become one of the world's richest men. This economic feat, coupled with the effect of Model T on the world's transportation, fostered a social revolution and opened the eyes of mankind to the staggering possibilities of twentieth-century technology. Ford, with more industrial power in his hands than anyone before or since, set out on a series of extraordinary economic and political adventures. They were not always flattering to his character or intelligence, but they brought the Ford Motor Company immense publicity and helped Ford to become a folk hero in the States during his own lifetime.

He was born in 1863 of Irish-English immigrant stock on his father's farm near the village of Dearborn, Michigan. Ford's tranquil boyhood, during which he often manifested a strong mechanical aptitude, inculcated in him an understanding of rural life and a respect for its virtues, along with an enduring dislike for the tedium and drudgery of farm labour. These attitudes were to shape his thinking for the rest of his life.

In 1879 he went to work as an apprentice in the machine shops of nearby Detroit. During this period he repaired steam traction machines and Otto industrial engines, read avidly of the experiments of Benz and Daimler in Germany, and dreamed of building his own self-propelled vehicle.

Soon, Ford had forsaken the farm for ever, and had become established as a good practical engineer. By 1893 he was superintendent of the electric power plant of the Detroit Edison Company, and began to experiment with a simple one-cylinder engine. Already Duryea, Haynes, Hiram P. Maxim, and Ransom Olds' had built horseless carriages, and a few road races had brought automobile transportation to the notice of the public.

Ford's first experience with an automobile was in the summer of 1895, when his friend Charles B. King tested a crude iron-tyred machine, using an engine of Otto derivation. In January 1896, Ford started to build his first car. Called 'The Quadricycle', it had a chassis built entirely of wood and used bicycle wheels. The four-cycle engine was based more or less upon drawings of a 'Kane-Pennington', which had appeared in a technical journal. Transmission was by chain final drive and a sliding-belt ratio change. The car was notably light, weighing around 500 lb. The first tests in May and June of 1896 led Ford to add metal reinforcement to the chassis and water jackets to the engine.

The success of the first car attracted some financial backing, and by June 1899 Ford had produced a larger, heavier car. The mechanical elements were enclosed and the sliding belt was replaced by gears. To some extent this was the prototype for a car to be manufactured by the Detroit Automobile Company, as Ford's backers called themselves. Ford left the Edison plant to become superintendent of the new firm.

Although it had certain good features and showed superior metallurgy, the Detroit car was not a success. It was complex and difficult to maintain. Ford pulled out of the failing company to take up something which interested him far more.

Ford took to the tracks for the same reason as many other racers—to make a name and some money for himself and to develop ideas and designs for his next commercial model. With the help of Oliver Barthel, who had worked with both King and Ford before, he built a light racing machine of 8·1 litres displacement with two horizontally-opposed cylinders measuring seven inches by seven. On October 10, 1901, over the horse track at Grosse Point, Michigan, Ford defeated the then fastest car in America, driven by its builder, Alexander Winton. Ford's average speed was 45·8 m.p.h.

This success encouraged Ford's sponsors to form the Henry Ford Company for the purpose of producing a passenger car, and to publicize it Henry constructed what was to be one of the United States' most famous racing car designs. Gathering about him young men who would later become paladins of his empire, among them the brilliant machinist C. Harold Wills, Henry produced two stark single-seaters, called '999' (after the crack New York Central express train) and the 'Arrow'. These were Ford's first four-cylinder cars. Their engines displaced over 16 litres and had open crankshafts and valve gear. The cars were vicious to handle and Ford and his associates were

Henry Ford with one of his racers
Courtesy Ford Motor Company

not too anxious to drive them in competition. 'The roar of those cylinders alone was enough to half kill a man,' recalled Ford. One of Ford's crew talked him into securing Barney Oldfield, a bicycle racer who had never driven a car of any kind before. After a week of practice, Oldfield and '999' were entered for the 1902 Grosse Point race, but just before the start Ford asked Oldfield not to risk his life with so little experience. Oldfield was determined, saying: 'This chariot may kill me, but they will say afterwards that I was going like hell when she took me over the bank.' Oldfield lapped the rest of the field to win in record time. It launched him on a career which made his name synonymous with speed.

Ford spent so much time on racing activities that the directors of the Henry Ford Company brought in Henry Leland, the most respected machine-shop superintendent in the country. Leland, who had done more than anyone to introduce precision standards into the manufacturing community, soon clashed with the empirical mechanic from Dearborn. Ford may also have had a grievance over his share of the business but, for whatever reason, he soon left the company.

In spite of Ford's two failures, coal merchant A. T. Malcomson and banker John T. Gray were sufficiently impressed by a new prototype to put up the principal capital for the Ford Motor Company which was formally incorporated on June 16, 1903. On the strength of the design and the offer of a

41

tenth part of the new firm, the Dodge brothers, proprietors of a large Detroit machine works, agreed to supply the engine and running gear. Gray's investment was $10,500. Such a Golconda was being born that his heirs sold out sixteen years later for $26,250,000.

Model A was a small car weighing about 1,250 lb. with a two-cylinder, 8 h.p. engine. Although plagued by defects at first, subsequent models were comparatively light, simple and efficient. The trickle of orders grew to a stream and within a year the Ford Motor Company was producing 350 units per month. From the outset Ford built a large part of his success on the concept of service. Factory representatives called on dealers and purchasers to set defects right, soothe tempers, and report their findings to Detroit so as to eliminate flaws from future output. This was in great contrast to the practice of most automobile manufacturers at that time and was immediately popular with the motoring public.

The Company planned to bring out their first four-cylinder car, the Model B, in the fall of 1902; and to attract attention to it, Ford rebuilt the 'Arrow' ('999' having been sold). On the frozen surface of Lake St Clair, near Detroit, Henry Ford and 'Spider' Huff bounced over the ice fissures to set a world's automobile speed record of 91·4 m.p.h. This was to be Ford's last success as a driver, although he made an abortive attempt at record-breaking on Ormond Beach in 1906. He constructed another racing car, '999 II', in 1912, which Frank Kulick drove at 108 m.p.h., but did no more driving and henceforth his company's colours were carried only by modified production models.

Ford did not approve of Model B. He felt it was too large and expensive. He was happier with the other models, C and F, both two-cylinder chain-drive cars which appeared at the same time. Malcomson was the force behind the concept of a large Ford, and by 1906 his counsel had prevailed to such an extent that the Company brought out the large six-cylinder Model K, but it never sold well. Ford wanted to standardize on Model N, an inexpensive four-cylinder shaft-drive car designed to replace Models C and F.

To resolve the divergence of opinion, Ford and others involved in active Company management persuaded Malcomson and his party to sell their interest. Malcomson was glad to do so, for he was involved in an automotive venture of his own. In the period 1906–7 Ford gained a majority stock interest and the control of the Company. It was a good thing to have. In that same period the success of Model N had resulted in the sale of 8,500 cars and a net profit of over one million dollars. The Ford Motor Company in four years had become the largest manufacturer of automobiles in the world—and Model T was yet to come.

As early as 1905 the Company had experimented with chrome-vanadium steel alloy, a European development which Ford claimed to have discovered

1911 Model T
Courtesy Montagu Motor Museum

while browsing through the wreckage of a French racing car at Ormond Beach. It had over twice the tensile strength of the nickel alloys used up to that time. After considerable difficulty, enough of the metal was produced to make extensive use of it in Model N, but Ford realized that to make maximum use of the new alloy's advantages would call for a design new from the wheels up, one around which the Company could organize the new, more efficient production methods which he and his staff had been planning.

Ford cannot be given full credit for Model T, although he is entitled to the lion's share. Drafting and layout was by the gifted Hungarian, Joseph Galamb. Harold Wills was responsible for many parts and John Wandersee handled the applied metallurgy. But the overall concept and inspiration, plus the final 'yes' or 'no' on each aspect, was Henry Ford's. All those who worked with Ford readily admit his great contribution.

What was so unusual and exciting about Model T when it burst upon the automotive world in 1908? The price of $850 was not specially low for the time, but the car was the best combination of lightness, power, and durability yet seen. It had left-hand drive, whereas most American manufacturers were still putting the driver on the right. The stout transverse leaf springs, which kept Model T high off the bad roads, were anchored to the chassis at only three points to free the frame from destructive torsion. The rear axle was of a stronger, more rugged design than any of comparable weight. The engine featured four cylinders cast *en bloc*, fully enclosed mechanism, and a

43

detachable cylinder head with obvious advantages in production and maintenance. The fly-wheel magneto, Ford's pet idea, put into practice by Ed. Huff, not only supplied ignition current but also fed the lighting system. Last but not least, the two speed planetary transmission was quite an improvement over the weak and noisy gearboxes which so many people found difficult to handle.

Model T was hard to start, hard riding, and given to strangely animate idiosyncrasies mainly attributable to the planetary transmission. Most of these quirks were so minor compared to the overall ruggedness and dependability of the car that owners viewed them only as adding spice to the grand adventure that was Model T motoring.

'Tin Lizzie' was rugged. This ubiquitous hack trundled across the prairies and over the mountains of America. It completed the opening of the Wild West, homogenized the culture of city and farm, and contributed tremendously to the increased pace of the economy. It gave the 'average man' a sense of freedom to move about on business and pleasure which contributed in great measure to the root strength of American ideals. As more and more Ts appeared, their owners demanded better roads from the authorities—and the result was the present vast United States highway system. To a lesser but still significant extent the same process spread around the globe. Assembly plants in many countries added to the flood of Ts which left their tracks from deepest Africa to farthest Asia.

Shortly after the introduction of Model T, mining tycoon Robert Guggenheim offered a prize for a cross-country road race from New York to Seattle. Rules were rigid: entries had to go through thirty checkpoints; new parts could be obtained only at Chicago and Cheyenne; travel on railway tracks was forbidden. Ford entered two stripped Model Ts to be driven by the teams of Kulich-Harper and Scott-Smith. The race scared away most competition, for west of the Missouri river much of the distance was virtually roadless. Other entries were a Stearns, an Acme, a Shawmut, and a 60 h.p. Itala.

Both Fords crossed the Mississippi at St Louis two hours ahead of their nearest rival. They crossed the Great Plains through deep mud caused by several days of continuous rain. They were stung by hailstorms and bogged in quicksand. The Scott-Smith car sailed off the road into a stream during a night run; the next day the crew removed the badly-bent front axle, carried it three miles to a railroad smithy for straightening, carried it back, reinstalled it, and pushed on. By the time the Ford entries had reached Opal, Wyoming, the 4,500 lb. Shawmut had caught up. Crossing the Rockies the contestants negotiated 35 per cent grades and narrow precipices which allowed no more than six inches of error. While the Scott-Smith car was being refuelled, some spectator struck a match on the side of the tank. The resulting conflagration burned off most of the bodywork but the Ford pressed on. The Kulick-

Model T derivative. This chassis and engine provided
the mainstay of numerous Special racers over many years
Courtesy Montagu Motor Museum

Harper car became lost in the Northwest Wilderness for a day and a half by
trusting an incompetent local guide, and was never able to make up the lost
time.

As the other Ford struggled through the snows of the dreaded Snoqualmie
Pass, the last great obstacle before the finish, they came upon a jubilant
Henry Ford who told them that they were well in the lead with a clear run
ahead to the finish. Scott and Smith arrived in Seattle 17 hours ahead of the
Shawmut, having covered 4,106 miles in 20 days and 52 minutes. The other
Ford was third; the Acme was over a week behind; the Itala had broken
down in Wyoming, and the Stearns never left New York. The Company
gave great advertising coverage to the victory, and quoted the encomium of
sponsor Guggenheim: 'Mr Ford's theory that a lightweight car, highly
powered for its weight, can go places where heavier cars cannot go . . . on the
steep hills or bad roads, has been proved.' Disqualification of the Ford later
on an allegation that its engine had been changed en route did not alter the
truth of the statement.

Ford dealers were quick to enter reliability runs, hill climbs, and races.
Ford publicists delighted in showing pictures of Model Ts climbing the
steps of public buildings or perched on the summit of a local landmark. Soon
enthusiasts were modifying their 'Lizzies' for speed and power as well as
appearance. A wonderful accessory business sprang up around Model T,
which rolled out of the factory in extremely stark form. Auxiliary trans-

45

missions (notably the Ruckstell rear axle unit), shock absorbers, fuel pumps, gauges, and ignition systems were among the many items produced to adorn and improve Model T. Most interesting were the overhead valve and over-head camshaft engine conversion which supplied the majority of the racing power plants during the late 'teens and early 'twenties. Best known were the *Roof, Gallivan' Rajo* and *Frontenac* (known nearly always as the 'Fronty', this was designed by Arthur Chevrolet). The T engine was prone to give up the struggle when stressed too far, but the transversely sprung chassis was well suited to the dirt and board tracks upon which it found itself. How the grandstands would roar when a hepped-up 'T-Bone' defeated a field of Millers and Duesenbergs!

From 1903–11 a group of American manufacturers licensed under George Selden's 1895 patent (covering a gasoline-powered vehicle) had been engaged in litigation with another group of manufacturers and importers who had refused to admit the validity of the patent and pay royalties on each machine they produced. Selden had never actually built a car and it appeared that his claim incorporated many elements known for years and long since patented, but many firms joined the licensees rather than face a long court battle. Ford vociferously refused to pay tribute and bore most of the court costs of the non-licensees. The patent group threatened to sue every buyer of a Ford car, but public sympathy lay with Ford in his fight against the 'automobile trust' and sales were not greatly affected. Nevertheless it was a vast relief when a high New York court ruled that the patent, though valid, did not apply to cars with engines operating on the Otto (four cycle) principle as used by Ford, his co-defendants, and nearly everyone else.

With the shadow of the lawsuit removed, Ford could concentrate on the move from his outmoded factory on Piquette Avenue in Detroit to the new Highland Park plant in the countryside. Operations commenced there in 1910 and by 1913 Ford and his dedicated staff had developed their own ideas and those of others into an organic production entity that can be said to be the first mass production factory. Henry Ford defined mass production as the focus-ing of accuracy, continuity, system, and speed, upon the manufacture of a standardized commodity in great quantities.

Accuracy meant the quantity production of completely interchangeable parts to eliminate hand fitting both in production and subsequent service. It called for extremely fine tolerances, improved machine tools, and high-speed cutting steels.

Continuity referred to the moving manufacture or assembly line to which moving component lines are geared. It was this feature that set the Highland Park complex apart from other plants with efficient layouts and precision machines.

System applied not only to the precise programming and control of the moving lines lest the flow of one break down and bring the entire establishment grinding to a halt, but also the supervision of employee working methods, raw material supply, parts inventory, and product shipping.

Speed was of course the basic reason behind the whole thing. It was company policy to discard machine tools ruthlessly, no matter how recently purchased, as soon as better models became available. Speed in assembly was increased by breaking down each operation into its simplest steps. Each such task was then given to a single man to be done as the work passed him on the moving line. Ford was thus able to hire unskilled workers—not because they would work for less, but because they were readily available. Furthermore, constant repetition of the same task developed a rhythm in the work that increased speed and accuracy. Needless to say, employees were rotated from task to task lest repetition led to tedium.

Economy prompted Ford engineers to substitute quality castings for costly forgings. Great Bliss presses spat out stamped pieces of hitherto unimagined size and complexity, to do away with laborious fabricating.

These principles appear elementary today, but the Highland Park plant caused a sensation at the time. Still, it was not enough for the Ford Motor Company. To maintain an increasing, incessant flow of product it assumed control of the sources of raw materials and each phase of their processing and transportation. Eventually, the company's own railroad and ships were bearing ore and coal from its own mines, lumber from its own mills, and rubber from its own plantations. On the banks of Michigan's River Rouge arose a monstrous plant to convert these raw materials into steel, engines and bodies for Highland Park and the other assembly plants. Ford manufacture of parts extended to starters, generators, tyres, batteries, artificial leather, cloth and wire.

The corollary of mass production is reduction in cost per unit. Sales of Model T could only match the Company's output if additional strata of demand were tapped by passing cost reductions on to the consumer in the form of lower prices. Between August 1913 and January 1914 the evolution of the moving assembly line slashed the labour content in chassis assembly from $12\frac{1}{2}$ man hours to one hour 33 minutes of one man's time. In 1909, a Model T roadster cost $825, and 18,257 were sold. By 1925 it cost $260 and over two million were produced. It was one of the great bargains of all time and the world knew it.

The Company's expansions resulted in tremendous profits. In 1913 its net income was 27 million dollars. Ford and his financial aide-de-camp, James Couzens (who left to enter the United States Senate), were men of simple tastes and keenly felt the pressure of these profits. Genuine concern for the welfare of Ford workers, plus the need to reduce employment turnover, and draw the fangs of labour agitators, led Ford and Couzens to take an unprecedented move. In 1914 they announced that at least ten million dollars out of 1914 profits would be shared with employees, and that henceforth a minimum wage of five dollars per day would be paid to all employees, including sweepers.

Like many another Ford accomplishment, the true impact of this new policy can only be gauged by the standards of the day. In that year the average American manufacturing wage was 11 dollars per week. Conservative circles gasped with alarm and forecast that Ford would ruin his business and the morals of his workers. Thousands of would-be employees besieged Highland Park. People who had never before heard of Henry Ford now hailed him as the new Messiah; he was propelled into the limelight, to bask there until the day he died.

In the words of William Richards, 'Utterances of Henry Ford, sacred and profane, were to rate thereafter with papal encyclicals.' Ford capitalized on this to publicize his wares, but after a time he actually tended to believe that he was some sort of seer. Reporters waited with pencils poised while he delivered opinions on every subject under the sun. Unfortunately, outside of business and applied mechanics, Ford was astonishingly ill-informed, inconsistent, and narrow-minded.

He displayed an abysmal ignorance of American history, yet spent millions at Greenfield Village to create a replica of an eighteenth-century American town. He backed the well-intentioned but naïve 'Peace Ship' fiasco, but embarked on an anti-Semitic crusade—which he later repudiated. He bought his own newspaper and radio station to air his views on temperance, education, folk dancing, politics, and sundry topics.

He ran for the Senate and was defeated only by the narrowest of margins. Through it all the people of America—who clearly grasped his vast accomplishments and richly appreciated his car, his salty sense of humour, and his independence—considered him one of themselves. They forgave him his errors and ignorance, slapped their Model Ts, and chuckled at his adventures.

After Ford left the old Henry Ford Company in 1903 it was reorganized as the Cadillac Motor Car Company. Under the leadership of Henry Leland, the Cadillac was developed into one of the country's finest cars. Leland left Cadillac in 1917 to manufacture Liberty aero engines. After the war, his firm, the Lincoln Motor Company, brought out a quality motor car which, like his later Cadillacs, was a large V-8. In spite of its technical excellence, conservative styling and the post-war depression caused sales to lag badly. In 1922 the Ford Motor Company bought the plant and assets for eight million dollars. Leland and his son remained with the firm but soon disagreement with Ford's people caused them to leave. There is little or no truth in the story that Ford wished to cheapen the Lincoln car, although he did expect the Lelands to adopt certain Ford production methods and steel alloys.

Henry's talented son Edsel took a particular interest in the Lincoln. Not only was the car improved mechanically, but Locke, Le Baron, and other coachbuilders built handsome bodies for it. In 1932 Lincoln introduced its *magnum opus*, the magnificent 'KB' V-12 considered to be the handsomest of all its products. Its 7·4 litre side-valve engine with cylinder banks spaced in a 65 degree Vee produced 150 b.h.p. at 4,300 r.p.m. For 1933 the 'KB' was offered along with a 6·3 litre V-12. The smaller engine lacked the intricately machined fork-and-blade type intersecting connecting rods and possessed only four main bearings to the 'KB's seven. Many have jumped to the conclusion that Ford's allegedly insidious influence had at last reached the Lincoln, but the fact is that the new twelve was a more lively, responsive, and efficient engine, turned out with a finish as fine as the earlier Lincolns. The 'KB' was dropped, and the smaller engine (known as the 'KA' in 1933 and later as the 'K') was increased to 6·8 litres and continued without basic change until the 'K' series was discontinued in 1950. The influence of Henry Ford may be seen in the fact that until the last the large Lincolns were equipped with mechanical and beam axle suspension.

The peak year for the Model T was 1923, with 2,201,188 cars sold and for the next two years sales exceeded two millions, but then they began to drop. It was becoming increasingly obvious that the end was near for Model T. The eccentricities of the planetary transmission had become intolerable as improved gearboxes appeared in other makes. The low tension ignition was manifestly obsolete, as was the pumpless thermosyphon cooling system. Model T did not satisfy newly prosperous and sophisticated Americans who wanted style and comfort as much as utility. Chevrolet, Dodge, Overland, Essex and other low-priced cars with better lines and modern improvements rapidly began to cut into Ford's market, while the rise of the used car business, where one could buy a car for as little as $10, effectively undersold Ford among those who wanted minimum transportation.

Ford clung to Model T in spite of the danger signals. Now well into his sixties, he was no longer so responsive to the winds of change or as attuned to the public's attitudes. Having long since bought out the last of the original investors, he was so much the dictator of the Company that no one, not even his son, was in a position to lay the cold facts out and make him take notice.

Finally, bad sales in 1926 convinced Ford that something would have to be done. In 1927, before plans for the new car were at all complete, he shut down T production. The vast Ford plants dragged to a stop for nearly a year while his dealers tried to stave off bankruptcy. The public watched breathlessly to see what marvel Henry would give them next.

Model A was designed in much the same manner as Model T—that is, by a small efficient team of practical engineers led by a surprisingly alert Ford who took responsibility for the crucial decisions on technical details. During testing of one of the final prototypes, the old man stepped forward

1929 Model A

and said, 'someone must represent the public'. He climbed into the car and
pushed down hard on the throttle. He hurtled across a rough field, bumping
over logs and stones. On his return he curtly commanded: 'Rides too rough.
Put on hydraulic shock absorbers.' Thus for the first time did a low-priced
car appear with this costly fitment.

The new car appeared early in 1928 and crowds inundated Ford show-
rooms to admire Ford's stylish and roomy body designs, the powerful
engine, and the three-speed gearbox. They noticed the great resemblance
to the Lincoln in the design of both radiator shell and drive train. Though
Model A had transverse leaf springs like T's, the hydraulic shock absorbers
gave an exceptionally smooth ride. Four and a half million Model
As were sold in four years, at prices ranging from $350 to $570 F. O. B.
Detroit.

Although 1929 sales figures showed Ford to be 400,000 units in advance
of Chevrolet the appearance of new Chevrolet and Plymouth six-cylinder
models seriously threatened Ford during subsequent depression years.
To beat the competition once and for all, Ford shut down his works in
August 1931 for the second time in less than five years. Once again the
dealers suffered and the public waited while the new car was prepared. Ford
galvanized his engineering staff into action. He had decided that the new car

would be a V-8 and that he would not let anyone tell him that its cylinder block could not be cast in one piece. It was done, and in March 1932 the immortal Ford V-8 made its début to eager crowds. It was the best looking Ford yet, though the resemblance to Model A was very strong.

The revolutionary engine was a 90-degree V-8 showing Lincoln influence. The first model produced 65 b.h.p. from 3·6 litres. Twenty-one years and 12,000,000 V-8s later, the 1953 Mercury boasted the same engine increased to 4·2 litres and 125 h.p.

The V-8 with transverse leaf suspension was continued until 1948. Certain chassis revisions were implemented in 1935, but not until 1938 did Ford let himself be persuaded to use hydraulic brakes.

Sales lagged behind Chevrolet more often than not, but the Ford was the most exciting car available to Americans during the 'thirties with the exception of the expensive Cord 810. In 1937 the V-8 was scaled down in every detail to make the 2·2 litre '60', which was installed in standard Ford chassis. It was only moderately popular and was dropped in 1940, in which year the Company brought out a slightly stretched out and face-lifted version of the V-8 known as the Mercury. This new make was very popular and it still bridges the gap between Ford and Lincoln.

This unusual car started life as a radical rear engine design by John Tjaarda for the Briggs Manufacturing Company, one of Ford's body suppliers. Edsel liked the car so much that he persuaded his father that a production version with conventional components would be successful. Perhaps to cash in on the prestige of the name, the new car was put in the Lincoln line rather than set up as a new *marque*. To maintain tradition, Ford engineers in effect added four more cylinders to the V-8 to create a small twelve. The Zephyr was introduced in 1936 and was immediately hailed for its aerodynamic lines and unit body-frame structure.

The Lincoln Continental was built by the Ford styling department to the design of Edsel Ford. It was intended to be his personal car, not a production model, but was so widely admired that manufacture started on a small scale. By the time the series dropped in 1948, 5,320 were sold, most of them the later, more bulbous model. Its Zephyr engine was much maligned by critics, but if detergent oils are used to keep hydraulic lifters functioning and a minor modification made to the oiling system, this power plant will give service at least comparable to its contemporary, the side-valve V-8. Unfortunately, many Continentals in use today have had the original units replaced by other engines.

The V-8 was Ford's last design effort. In the late years of that decade Ford began to age noticeably and the hand of authority began to slip. Many of his best men had left, and his son Edsel, to whom he had never given the trust and responsibility this able man deserved, died in 1943. Charles Sorensen left in 1944 after building up the Company's war production capacity and labour troubles increased severely in a firm that was once held up as the working man's Utopia.

Early in 1945 Ford suffered a severe decline. Authority passed to members of his family, and in the fall of that year Edsel's son Henry II was elected to the presidency in fact as well as name. Under his direction the Company fortunes rose again. The older Ford retired to his estate, Fair Lane, on the River Rouge. There, on April 7, 1947, the man who had remade the physical world died of a cerebral haemorrhage.

From *Automobile Year*, 1961–2

Renault: the Cloth Merchant's Son

BY JACQUES ICKX

Louis Renault and Henry Ford had perhaps only one thing in common: they each built up one of the greatest automobile factories in their country. Their character and manufacturing and engineering philosophy were wide apart. One threw away opportunity and lost his ambition: the American retained his drive and expertise almost to the end. But the huge plants at Dearborn and Billancourt stand today as monuments jointly to the almighty automobile and to two men who seized opportunity in the ripe years at the closing of the last century.

IN SPITE of the most drastic change of management which brought a great private undertaking under State control, the history of Renault, from the car-building point of view, has formed an unbroken chain from 1898 up till the present day. In 1945, when the factories changed over to their new status, the same technical personnel with the same standards of quality were pursuing the same tasks, thus ensuring the continuity of what might be termed the 'biological principle' of the concern.

Now that we can look far enough back in time to distinguish its basic pattern, the Renault story may be likened to a single piece of metal brought in turn by three men, each of whom fulfilled a well-defined role and who, by a peculiar trick of fate, was there to take over just when the stage of growth and development of the undertaking called for a change.

In this trilogy, Louis Renault led the creative phase, Pierre Lefaucheux built up an industrial power that was unprecedented in the French automobile world, and Pierre Dreyfus, in his turn, was to use this potential to the fullest advantage.

In 1898, the automobile was the universal topic of the day. Barely four years had passed since the competition in the *Petit Journal* had opened people's eyes to the immediate prospects of the horseless carriage; but during this time such a spate of new achievements had come to pass that there was a rush all over the world to take part in the 'boom'. Every good mechanic was trying his luck, and such a venture was bound to attract an enterprising, business-like lad of 21 who had mechanics at his finger-tips.

Louis Renault, the third son of a cloth merchant who also manufactured buttons, would not hear of going into his father's business, and between matriculating and being called up he felt a vocation to join the research department of Delaunay-Belleville who, at that time, were building boilers. When he came back from the army, the automobile craze was in full swing. He reckoned that if he were to start studying engineering there was a strong likelihood he might miss his big chance and so he made up his mind to take

53

the plunge right away. His parents at last consented to let him take over the gardener's lodge on their country estate (for Billancourt was then still in the country) and in it the boy installed a lathe, a drilling-machine, a forge and two workers to assist him. His aim was to design a light vehicle which would serve as a link between the de Dion tricycle (of which he had been a keen driver) and the automobile proper. Following current practice, he would sell the manufacturing rights to some industrialist.

The vehicle was ready within three months. And, as spoilt as we are today, we cannot help but recognize its admirable design and workmanship, with its tubular chassis, the perfect equilibrium of its parts, its directly-coupled, silent-change gearbox (a device shifted the driven shaft aside during the operation in order to engage the pinions in one go, across the whole width of the teeth). He employed the classical, single-cylinder de Dion-Bouton engine, a favourite with free-lance constructors, and used many ready-made parts borrowed from the cycle industry, both to facilitate his work and to bring down the manufacturing cost.

The 'voiturette' he designed turned out to be so attractive and reliable that instead of offering the manufacturing licence for sale, Louis Renault persuaded his two elder brothers, Fernand and Marcel, then aged 34 and 33, to join him in setting up a company, Renault Frères, and start constructing it on their own account. This Company came into being on March 21, 1899, with a capital of 60,000 francs. Apart from his model, the young designer also contributed a patent for the direct-drive top gear which he had been astute enough to take out on February 9th of the same year, having noticed that nobody had thought of doing so before him. By the end of 1899, Renault Frères had delivered sixty vehicles, adopted the new water-cooled de Dion engine, taken on a hundred workers and decided to double the area of their initial workshops. On top of this, doing his bit all along the line, Louis Renault had personally driven his machine to victory both in the Paris–Trouville and in the Paris–Ostend events.

The 'voiturette', then specified as having an unladen weight of under 800 lb., remained a winner for the next two years. But, following the eternal process, cubic capacity and power had increased considerably in the meantime and the 1901 model already possessed a cubic capacity of 1,020 c.c. and a nominal power of 8 h.p. as compared with 240 c.c. and $1\frac{3}{4}$ h.p. two years previously.

The great sporting event of the year was to be an impressive Paris–Berlin race which, incidentally, provoked lively polemics in that period of national reassertion. It was a spectacular affair with 53 time checks spread over three stages: Paris–Aix-la-Chapelle, via Rheims, Sedan, Bastogne and Montjoie; Aix-la-Chapelle—Hanover, via Cologne, Düsseldorf and Münster; and Hanover—Berlin, via Brunswick and Magdeburg, making 660 miles to be covered at full speed. One hundred and nine competitors were at the

Frank Hedges Butler's 1900 Renault with $4\frac{1}{2}$ h.p. de Dion engine

start on June 27, 1901, at the fort of Champigny, including six Renault 'voiturettes'. At Aix-la-Chapelle Renaults were not only holding the first six places in the 'voiturette' category, but Louis Renault on the fastest of them was being outstripped by only one light car (1,430 lb.) and seventeen 'big cars'. At Hanover it was the same story except that there were now only eight cars left in front of Louis Renault. And in Berlin he finished eighth in the general classification, with a clear lead over all the light cars. His average had risen to over 36 miles per hour.

This outstanding success inevitably opened out wider horizons for Renault Frères. In 1902, a certain Viet came to offer Billancourt a four-cylinder model which he had hoped to sell to de Dion-Bouton. The young constructor adopted it and undertook the manufacture of light cars, once again doubling the floor space of his workshops.

The sporting season that year was focused on Paris–Vienna, a terrifying trial for the period since, for the very first time, the contestants had to tackle mountains, crossing the Arlberg on the way. Furthermore, the Austrian roads were in a wild state. Nevertheless, there were no fewer than 219 entries and two light Renault cars of 16 h.p. (as against 24 for their direct rivals and up to 70 for the big cars) were there for the start, driven by Louis and Marcel Renault.

At Belfort, the end of the first stage, they only held the 3rd and 8th places in their category. But the next day, the Arlberg climb was a Waterloo for

1905 Renault Gordon Bennett racer
Courtesy Montagu Motor Museum

the favourites. They could be seen dismantling from their cars everything that could be left on the road, and letting themselves descend to the foot of the slopes to prepare for a fresh spurt. With bulging muscles the mechanics were pushing their cars along. And in the midst of the fray, Louis Renault, *without a hitch*, sailed by into first place! At the checkpoint in Innsbruck, unfortunately, his car was bumped into by Baron de Caters, and a number of spokes on his front left wheel were smashed. Renault had lost his big opportunity.

Marcel Renault, meanwhile, had hauled himself into fourth place in Salzburg. And on the dreadful roads of the last stage he managed to overtake his last opponents, the Farman brothers and Count Zborowski, winning the Paris–Vienna with a quarter of an hour to spare, on a light car of 24 h.p.!

This was the occasion to celebrate for the first time the efficient use of power as opposed to brute force. All the specialized publications vied with one another in applauding the new event and enquired whether the big designers might not have taken the wrong path and whether Renault had not hit on the solution for the future.

It is strange to note that in the long run the big lesson of Paris–Vienna was of benefit to nobody since, three years later, its very author switched over to the 'big car'.

In 1903, the tragic Paris–Madrid race witnessed the fatal accident to Marcel Renault. Louis, when the race was suspended, held second place on the general classification with his light car of 30 h.p.—having reached

1910 Renault, fully equipped for the Grand Tour
Courtesy Montagu Motor Museum

Bordeaux at an average speed of 62 m.p.h. But he gave up his sports career from that day and redoubled his industrial activities. He had already built some 3,000 cars in five years; in the three years that followed he constructed a further 4,000.

The amazing victory of the Hungarian Szisz, the former personal mechanic of Louis Renault, in the first Grand Prix of the Automobile Club de France held in 1906 on the Sarthe circuit (two days of epic struggle against Nazzaro and Albert Clément), was in its turn to double in one go the number of orders pouring into the factory. This rush, effectively dealt with, resulted in a constant rise in production, which overshot the 4,000 mark in 1908 and verged on 7,000 units in 1910—a really startling figure for European industry at that time and made up of various models with two, four and six cylinders.

With the Paris Motor Show of 1910, Louis Renault abandoned his popular two-cylinder 8 CV., and launched an ambitious programme which included, besides a four-cylinder 10 CV., three six-cylinders of 18·35 and 40 CV. respectively—magnificent cars which the leading body builders of the day fitted up with a sumptuous style that is still apparent in their charmingly archaic lines.

The giant 9-litre Renault 40 CV.
Courtesy Musée de l'Automobile, Rochetaille sur Saone

Then came the Great War, the taxis of the Marne (Renaults for the most part), the enlargement of the works to cope with armament needs, and the victorious offensive in which the two-seater Renault tank played an important part. In 1919, Louis Renault, then 42 years old, found himself at the head of an industrial empire that had now taken over every remaining inch of space available at Billancourt.

There was no problem in finding use for it either, since the return to peace brought about a general passion for motoring. On the contrary, new needs for expansion soon made themselves felt under the pressure of competition. Renault had no desire to strike its flag before the onrush of Citroen. To meet the challenge from the Quai de Javel, they bought up, lot by lot, the whole of the île Seguin, in the Seine opposite their works, and covered it with massive buildings typical of the period, after having joined it up to the main factory by means of a suspension bridge. And to compete with the new popular car, Louis Renault, who personally would probably have been inclined to limit production to his conservative six-cylinders, was forced, as it were, to go back to his beginnings with the small 6 CV., a particularly classical figure in the production car field.

However the 40 CV.—with its huge chassis perched on wooden wheels, retaining the leather cone clutch and the separate gearbox, and not fitted with front brakes until 1925—continued to cut a triumphant figure, not only on the Champs-Elysées but also at Montlhéry where it twice broke the world record for the 24 hours, at 87 then at 107 m.p.h., in the hands of

1935 Renault Airsport Coupé
Courtesy Montagu Motor Museum

young engineers of Herculean proportions and dauntless courage.

In 1927, the small 8 CV., six-cylinder 'Monasix'; in 1921, the series of straight eights, the 'Monastella', 'Vivastella' and 'Reinastella'; in 1930, début of the 'Nervastella'; in 1931, a return to the four-cylinder with the 'Primaquatre', 'Monaquatre' and 'Vivaquatre'. . . . Then, in 1936, the 'Celtaquatre' of 1,500 c.c. and, in 1937, the still familiar 1,003 c.c. 'Juvaquatre'.

However, Louis Renault, sole proprietor and absolute monarch in his huge factories at Billancourt, was producing only on a relatively modest scale. Just before the outbreak of the Second World War, with a daily output of only 250 cars, he was still lagging behind two of his French rivals, Citroen and Peugeot. This was because Renault, who had, as it were, a 'vertical' conception of industry, clung to out-of-date principles; multiplying the number of models and manufacturing every single car component on the spot. In point of fact, this man, now over 60, who had built up Billancourt from a gardener's lodge, had lost his creative drive. There was nothing left in him of the brilliant young pioneer, the giant of competition, the inspired designer. Nothing remained but a fighting industrialist, ailing and self-centred, who had lost interest in all save his factories, with which he identified himself. Having forgotten everything else, there was nothing to prevent him working for Germany, the occupying power, to preserve his treasure.

Within a few hours after the Liberation, Billancourt had turned into a revolutionary hotbed, where summary justice was being dispensed. The situation grew worse, threatening an industrial potential that France sorely

RENAULT

The Renault six-cyl. models, each built to an ideal, are smooth, silent, fascinating cars. Delightful to look upon, delightful to drive, they convey to their owners a subtle sense of superiority and individuality.

12·5 H.P. MONASIX RENAULT LTD.		12·5 H.P. MONASTELLA DE LUXE	
Saloon.....................£288		Models from £310	
21 H.P. VIVASIX RENAULT LTD.		21 H.P. VIVASTELLA DE LUXE	
5-str. Saloon £390		5-str. Models from............£511	
„ 7-str. Limousine £450		„ 7-str. Limousine £565	
40 H.P. 8-cyl. REINASTELLA Chassis..................£1550			

The Renault range in 1930

needed. The Government, reluctant at first, decided to send to Billancourt the former Director of the Compagnie des Fours—Pierre Lefaucheux, a giant of a man with a rugby background that had given him the physique of a dreadnought. In that Autumn of 1944, he was the man to master the situation; his authority at once brought cohesion into the factory staff and restored relative calm among the workers.

On January 16, 1945 (Louis Renault having died mysteriously in captivity), an enactment by the Provisional Government of the French Republic stipulated that the Renault Works were to be nationalized without compensation. The principle was laid down of a State undertaking (Régie) that would function along just the same lines as a private company, and whose profits would be shared between the State and the workers.

What was the production programme going to be? Pierre Lefaucheux examined everything the research department had in its files: an 11 CV. for which Louis Renault had already ordered the equipment, a new version of the 'Juvaquatre' (with separate chassis), and a very odd little vehicle that adumbrated the 4 CV. This was a personal project by Fernand Picard, the deputy director of research, who had undertaken it as early as September 1940. The first engine, which developed 19·2 h.p. and weighed 115·5 lb., was put on the test bed in February 1942. And although all the blueprints were destroyed during the bombardment of March 3rd of that year, a preliminary car, with two doors and weighing 974 lb., was ready on December 23rd, and road tests were performed—come what may, and without any permission, one suspects—on January 4, 1943. On March 17, 1944, a second car, more developed in 'shape, was put on the road. By the end of the year, these two prototypes together had run 17,000 miles.

When the time came for the new managing director to make a decision, he took care to consult again his ten most qualified colleagues. Seven of them were in favour of the 11 CV.; only two advocated the 4 CV. But on November 9, 1945, after thinking it over for a whole night, Pierre Lefaucheux announced that he had opted for the latter. Six days later, a third prototype was on the road.

To gauge the boldness of Pierre Lefaucheux's bet, one has merely to recall the cool reception given to the 4 CV. until as late as 1948. The public evinced no enthusiasm for the miniature motor cars then on the market. But, at the same time, Lefaucheux had taken on a second bet with himself which committed him a great deal further: the decision to turn out the 4 CV. at a daily rate of 300 units. The production of Fernand Picard's 4 CV. (it was his design and not, as a stubborn legend would have it, Dr Porsche's) soared later to 600 units a day.

The dominating feature of this epoch lies in the policy of decentralization. This was indeed unavoidable, since it would have been impossible to find another square yard at Billancourt. But the innovation consisted in the setting up, under the Company's expansion programme, of a model factory in the middle of the countryside. The construction of these works at Flins, in the Seine valley, took a very short time. Just one year after the bulldozers had set to work, in August 1950, three presses were already in operation, the driving power being supplied by a locomotive hired for this purpose. By January 1st, 'Juvaquatres' were being turned out. After the failure of the 'Fregate' (for which the works had been destined), Flins was given over to the construction of that brilliant derivative of the 4 CV., the 'Dauphine', the appearance of which in 1956 was a prominent landmark in the popular car market.

The rest of the story is well known: the scope of the original plans has by now been trebled, and 2,000 cars (the mechanical parts for which are brought from Billancourt) are born there each day.

One day in February 1955, Pierre Lefaucheux, alone in his car as usual, was driving towards Nancy where he was to give a lecture. As he was entering Saint-Dizier, he skidded on a sheet of ice and was killed. When the news reached Billancourt it seemed that disaster had struck. Who was now going to take over the elaborate organization, comprising over 50,000 workers and producing 200,000 vehicles per year? Who was going to carry on the work, now in full swing, at Flins, especially as the 'Dauphine', in its finishing stages, was due to come out in a short time? If politics were to dictate the Government's choice, much was to be feared. But the man appointed as successor to Pierre Lefaucheux was the very man Renault wanted.

Chairman of the Lorraine Basin Collieries (Houillères du Bassin de Lorraine), Pierre Dreyfus was already working for Renault in his capacity of vice-chairman. But he was so attached to the Houillères that he hesitated before accepting. When he gave his final answer, after studying his predecessor's files, he took it upon himself to make the personal acquaintance of each member of the administrative staff. For he too had his governing idea: the architectural organization of a community which, forming a framework for the material plant, was to constitute a living and practically autonomous body. This would set up its own momentum which he would merely have to direct. Pierre Dreyfus achieved this internal transformation patiently, smoothly, making only slight changes at one time. The Régie Nationale des Usines Renault has become a cohesive entity, independent of circumstances and even of its origins. As a means of production and distribution, it can henceforth apply its power to anything, according to the needs of the moment.

Pierre Dreyfus, aware that the motor car is still very much part and parcel of our times, has concentrated his attention on heightening Renault's impact on the world. He has been putting into use, so to say, the instrument that was forged by Lefaucheux. By setting his sights boldly and wholeheartedly on the European Common Market, turning the Régie into a meeting-point of diverse industrial efforts (over half his returns go to suppliers), and driving wedges into foreign markets, he has within five years stepped up the annual output from 200,000 to 500,000 vehicles. The Company's exports have been as high as 55 per cent of production, and the United States market until recently absorbed almost as many cars as the French.

Let us not forget that, 20 years earlier, Renault ranked third in the French car industry; today, well at the top in national production, its share of which totals 42 per cent, the Régie Nationale des Usines Renault now holds third place in Europe and sixth in the world. That is how things stand today in this undertaking initiated sixty years ago in a gardener's lodge where a lad of 21 worked with his two assistants.

As well as Billancourt, the point of departure; the Pierre Lefaucheux Works (Flins) where the 'Dauphines' are made; the brand-new factory of Cléon, further down the Seine valley, which is now turning out mainly gearboxes; Le Mans, whose chief activity is agricultural tractors (26·5 per cent of French production); Choisy-le-Roi, with its rolling stock; Orléans, where all the valves will soon be manufactured, the Renault Company controls assembly plants in Great Britain, Spain, South Africa, Brazil, Ireland, Australia, the Philippines and Mexico. Its cars are also assembled by Alfa Romeo in Italy and built under licence by Hino in Japan. They are distributed in 97 markets.

The extension of automation in the factories, as Pierre Lefaucheux predicted, is going hand in hand with an increase in personnel. By the end of 1959, the number of workers in the French establishments amounted to 65,657 persons, guaranteed a permanent job under contract, despite the seasonal character of the car market. In 1960, the share of profits handed out to the personnel amounted to one thousand million French francs. Every day the Renault Works produced 2,400 vehicles, 2,000 of which are 'Dauphines'.

Renault pays the same taxes as any other French industrial concern and the workers receive a generous proportion of the profits, but the sum of ten million New Francs allocated to the French taxpayers who own the Régie is appreciably lower than the amounts which comparable industries in private hands pay annually to their shareholders by way of dividend.

This survey of sixty-two years of history would be incomplete were we not to take a glance at the future.

It is claimed in the Régie that in the long run only five automobile powers will be able to hold their own in the European Common Market, since no more could fit in and remain viable. Renault has every intention of figuring among these five.

From *Automobile Year*, 1960–1

GC 293 — Clockwork Motors.
Models of Renault, Voisin, Delage
and Panhard. Extra superior clockwork, patented ; winds up in front
with cardan drive. Forward and
rear drive, and stop by lever. Steering of the car by the driver's hand
wheel, with electric headlight and dry
battery. In box   .. each **10/6**
Other makes from **9/6, 8/6, 7/9, 6/3,
5/6, 3/6, 2/6, 2/-, 1/6, 1/-**

PART THREE

CAUSES LOST, AND CAUSES GAINED

In this age of giant corporations, intensive competition, and profit and loss stakes beyond the conception of the early motor car manufacturers, it is difficult to realize that, say in 1920, there were listed in Britain alone some 220 indepen- dent British and foreign names (and 302 models) from which the customer could make his choice. Many of these companies operated on the smallest scale in tin shacks and with high ideals and hopes; many more were possessed of better capital and worse intentions; a few were in the hands of men of engineering genius lacking financial support and guidance; others in the hands of delightful eccentrics in love with cars; one or two found the 'tide in the affairs of men, which, taken at the flood, leads on to fortune'.

We have already seen what two of these giants accomplished. Multitudes of other men fell by the wayside, some of them deservedly, some by ill fortune. Like the railway shares seventy years earlier most had perforce to wither. The demise of some, the flourishing in some specialist field of others, makes fascinating recent history; none more so than Lord Montagu's small masterpiece on the bizarre activities at Maidenhead in the 1920s and 1930s. The steam car, a saga in itself, is as strange a lost cause as any. The L29 Cord was as romantic and melancholy a failure as was Sir William Lyons's first Jaguar, the S.S.I. of 1931, a shrewd and splendid triumph. And 'W.O.'s 3-litre Bentley attracted from its earliest days a prestigious mystique *that by some delightful paradox continues to intensify nearly forty years after the last chassis left Cricklewood.*

Here, then, in this Part are some causes lost, causes of wonderment, and causes triumphant: a brief account of the first Jaguar, and the first Cord, with ironic hindsight overtones; a piece of reminiscence by 'W.O.' on the birth pains of his 3 litre; an essay on steam written when its high pressure boilers might still have blown away internal combustion; and Lord Montagu again on 'The Jam Factory'.

Lyons's First Jaguar

BY LORD MONTAGU OF BEAULIEU

In a stereotyped age, the S.S. stands alone—boldly individualistic—daring to be different. At a time when mere cheapness is frequently of greater account than worth, the S.S. note of quality is insistent. While affinity between appearance and performance tends to become less, the S.S. proffers both—in full measure.

S.S. catalogue, October 1934

Excruciatingly rakish little sedans, they appealed largely to the same types that went for yellow Auburns in this country.

Ralph Stein, *Sports Cars of the World*, 1952

———

THE NEW S.S. appeared at the Olympia Show in October 1931, and sparked off a flood of controversy. From the earliest days, Sir William Lyons blazoned his ideals in the forewords to his catalogues and in press advertising, but even now the world is not quite sure what it thinks of the first complete cars from Foleshill. *The Motor* praised 'a radiator of outstanding design', but *The Scribe*, writing in *The Autocar*, preferred to sit on the fence, with the observation that:

'Anyone who was not ultra-smart in appearance, clean cut, and well groomed, would look as absurd in a S.S. Sixteen as would a costermonger in a choker, sitting in a Rolls-Royce *coupe de ville*.'

Ralph Stein's comments on yellow Auburns were typical of a more critical and Vintage-club-ridden era, and even so whimsical a writer as the late W. H. Charnock summed the S.S. up as 'a real cad's car' in *Motor Sport* in 1953. Some people even cast aspersions on the originality of the design, hinting that the car derived from the L29 Cord of 1929, by which view they showed a remarkable ignorance of the past trend of Lyons's policy and concept of body design.

Be that as it may, the S.S. was a *fait accompli*, and carried the ridiculously low price-tag of £310, for which the customer could have a car conforming to what Americans of the 1960s would term the 'Classic formula'—i.e. a bonnet at least half as long as the whole vehicle.

Not that the S.S. represented a new idea—it was rather the logical development of what Lyons and Walmsley had been doing first at Cocker Street, and then at Foleshill, over the past four years. It did not mark the transformation of the Swallow Coachbuilding Company from body-builders to manufacturers, for chassis were still purchased complete, and were only offered up to their bodies in the Swallow factory. But it did establish their product as a marque in its own right, even if it had to languish for three

SWALLOW

S.S.1 three-quarter view

SPECIFICATION

COACHWORK. Coachbuilt, with leather grained head and large travelling trunk, the body represents the finest example of craftsmanship.

THE DOORS. Flush fitting, and exceptionally wide, ensuring ease of access, are hinged on two chromium plated heavy barrel joint hinges. The locks are of the heavy tapered striking plate type with private lock incorporated in the off-side handle, the near-side lock is fitted with interior safety catch.

THE HEAD. Leather grained, with chromium dummy head joints. Chromium weather mould protecting door, and chromium bead down hinge pillar and waistline.

TRUNK. Leather grained with futuristic heavily chromium plated hinged security catches and key lock. Provides spacious accommodation for travelling cases.

SLIDING ROOF. Entirely new design. Perfectly flush fitting and invisible in the closed position. Large opening, quickly operated.

WINDOW LIGHTS. Protectoglass winding windows.

WINDSCREEN. 12 ip. Protectoglass single panel, opening to any desired position, closing on to rubber inset, fitted Lucas duo blade electric wiper.

BONNET. Stainless steel hinge and heavily louvred side panels with quick action security fasteners.

WINGS. Deeply domed 9 in. section, with swaged centres. Deep side valances ensuring adequate protection.

UPHOLSTERY. Finest quality "Vaumol" furniture hide, heavily pleated in artistic design, and thickly carpeted floor in colours to harmonise with the exterior finish.

CABINET WORK. The instrument panel, door cappings, and fillets are finished with centre panels of highly polished "Fiddle Back" Sycamore, in colours to tone with the upholstery, the moulded edges being polished black in relief.

INSTRUMENTS. The illuminated panel is mounted with electric clock, trip speedometer, ammeter, oil pressure gauge, electric petrol gauge.

SEATS. The front seat with deeply sprung 9 in. cushion and back squab the latter adjustable provides maximum comfort for two, or occasionally three adult passengers. The rear seats are designed for juvenile passengers, although suitable for the occasional use of an adult.

HEAD ROOM. Ample head room for the tallest passenger is a feature made possible by the special dropped chassis frame.

ACCESSORIES. The complete suite of interior fittings in polished chromium and matt finish, incorporating interior mirror, roof lamp and switch, rear blind with driver's hand control, ash tray, companion set, and ladies' vanity set the latter mounted with mirror and Houbigant compacts.

Jaguar genesis: a page from the first S.S.1 catalogue

seasons among the special carosserie in Olympia's National Hall before being promoted to a place among the manufacturers in the Grand Hall. (*The Autocar*, to its credit, adopted a more realistic attitude, listing the S.S. as a separate make as early as February 1932.) But whatever officialdom might think, the S.S. was designed as an entity, even if it did use a large proportion of stock components; and the work was not undertaken by Lyons and Walmsley for Standards. The Standard Motor Company's co-operation was vital to the success of the project, but they were suppliers, and not sponsors.

Previous Swallow-bodied cars had been family saloons packaged in such a way that they not only looked bigger, faster, and costlier, but actually performed better. It became obvious that there was a future in a specialist car at a low price, and that two litres was a good size—big enough to give a satisfying performance without elaborate tuning, yet small enough to dodge the burden of the horsepower tax. This followed the lead of Cecil Kimber, who had introduced his 18/80 M.G. in 1929—but the 18/80, though it retailed for a third of the price of a Bentley, and was only some 10 m.p.h. slower, was not particularly cheap at £545, or nearly £200 more than was asked for its prototype, the Morris Six. Swallows had to find a chassis which was compact, inexpensive, and in large-scale production. Lyons liked six-cylinder engines, but while his liking was tempered by a healthy distrust of the 'light sixes' of $1\frac{1}{2}$ litre capacity which the slump had bred, he was anxious to combine the 'long, low look' with a higher degree of forward vision than had been possible with the unmodified Standards, Swifts and Fiats of 1928–30. An underslung frame was therefore desirable, and this would mean a special chassis.

Standards were the obvious suppliers. Not only were they returning to prosperity in the teeth of the depression, but excellent relations had been established with Captain J. P. Black through the agency of the Standard Swallow already in production. Further, the company had introduced a compact and simple two-litre 'six', the 16 h.p. 'Ensign', which was infinitely preferable for the Swallow concern's purposes than such machines as were made by their other chassis suppliers. Austin's 'Sixteen' was elephantine and indestructible, while Wolseley's overhead-camshaft 2 litre 'Viper' was ruled out, since it had been designed to take identical coachwork to that used on the big 21/60 h.p. 'County' model. And, the firm reasoned, if the 16 h.p. Swallow Standard saloon could be sold economically at only £275, a completely new car utilizing Standard components should be possible at a retail price of little over £300.

The recipe, as it turned out, was simple enough. The Standard's $65 \cdot 5 \times 101 \cdot 6$ mm. (2,054 c.c.) side-valve engine was adopted in untuned form, the stiff seven-bearing crankshaft lending itself to further development as required. The price paid for this was, of course, the high cost of a major overhaul when it was needed, hence the presence of later S.S. and Jaguar engines, and even Chevrolet Sixes, in some surviving S.S. Is. This was not, of course, a significant factor with later units, which were noted for their longevity. Standard's four-speed gearbox was blessed with reasonably close ratios and was likewise retained, though in the interests of fast cruising and durability the higher of the two optional top-gear ratios (4·66:1) was used in all the first S.S.s, whereas most Standard Sixteens were supplied with a 5·11:1 top gear. The Marles-Weller cam and lever steering gear and the front and rear axles were likewise stock Standard components.

Nonetheless, the Swallow Coachbuilding Company's claim that the chassis was 'specially manufactured by the Standard Motor Company', exclusively for them, held water, as more conventional packagers found to their cost. The double-drop frame was underslung and the wheelbase, at 9 ft. 4 in., was three inches longer than the Standard's. The front semi-elliptic springs were mounted outside the chassis frame. The engine was set back seven inches to give a 'sports car' look. Lyons and Walmsley might adhere to Standard's Bendix-Perrot cable-operated brakes (they were not to adopt hydraulics of any kind till 1949), but they used Rudge-Whitworth 'racing-type' wire wheels in place of the plainer Magna type. Like all cars of the period in the 'sporty' class, the S.S. had a central remote-control gear lever. The centrally-mounted handbrake was oddly cranked to allow three-abreast seating, though, as *The Autocar* commented at the time, 'the passenger sitting in the middle must dispose his feet to miss the gear lever'.

On this inexpensive, robust and simple chassis Lyons designed a rakish coupé, with a very long bonnet, helmet-type cycle wings and a relatively deep windscreen, in spite of which the complete car stood a mere 4 ft. 7 in. off the ground, as compared to the Standard's 5 ft. 8 in. A new V-radiator with vertical chromium bars, crowned by a Swallow motif, completed the *ensemble*. The famous S.S. hexagon, incidentally, did not appear on this grille, and the instruments were likewise oval, as they were to remain till the 1934 season. This attractive monogram did, however, figure prominently in the first S.S. catalogue, which gave customers a choice of six basic colour schemes.

Though the S.S. I was the principal offering, and was to remain so until the advent of the Jaguar name in 1936, a pretty little coupé on similar lines, the S.S. II, was also listed. This used a modified 1,052 c.c. Standard 'Little Nine' chassis, and sold for £210. The major styling difference between the S.S. I and S.S. II was the use of a painted radiator shell on the 9 h.p. model.

The S.S. monogram not only served to differentiate the new cars from their predecessors; it furnished a convenient mystery. Opinions differed as to the significance of the initials; some said they stood for 'Standard Swallow', others opted for 'Swallow Special' or 'Swallow Sports', and the diehards translated them into picturesquely alliterative abuse. The fact is that no definition was intended, let alone published—translation was left to each individual's taste. Standards might, and probably did, assert that the machines were Standard Swallows, but all cars built up to March 1945 are correctly referred to as S.S.s, whether of the Jaguar series or not, and nobody would ever dream of regarding even an early Jaguar as a 'Standard Swallow'!

The new models took the motoring public by storm. The bright colour schemes, the elongated bonnets, the '£1,000 look', and the actual price asked astonished trade and public alike. The influence even spread to the doors of the nursery, almost the first 'Dinky Toy' produced by Meccano being a realistic scale model of the S.S. I coupé. Henlys, Swallow's distributors, cheerfully contracted to buy half the output, and, provided at least 1,000 a year could be made, the new car was a safe bet. In fact, 1932 deliveries amounted to 776 cars, but by 1932 standards this was excellent, and only a foretaste of what was to come. The use of well-tried components successfully circumvented the teething troubles that often accompany an entirely new model. Thus it mattered little that the S.S. had done hardly any motoring when it appeared at Olympia for the first time.

In January 1932, *The Autocar* published the first road test of the S.S. I. By the sports car criteria of the day it could hardly be described as 'very fast', but it should be remembered that the average 2 litre family saloon of the period was distinctly breathless at 60 m.p.h., and the Standard Sixteen could only just better this figure. The Lea-Francis 'Ace of Spades' could carry four people at over 70 m.p.h., but it required an o.h.c. engine to do this, and at £495 it was not exactly cheap. In the circumstances a speed of 71 m.p.h., with 60 m.p.h. available on the close-ratio third, was a performance of which no one had any need to be ashamed. The Bendix brakes were evidently behaving themselves, for a stop from 30 m.p.h. was accomplished in twenty-nine feet, while the excellence of the forward vision was commented upon. 'Obviously,' *The Autocar* observed, 'the S.S. I makes its primary appeal on the question of smart appearance, but while that alone might satisfy a few, it would not be sufficient for those who desire a performance above the average.'

The road-holding likewise came in for praise, which is interesting in the light of later critics' views on the S.S.'s tendency to 'run out of road'.

'It holds the road admirably, being very steady on bends and corners and giving the driver a feeling of complete confidence in its stability. Coupled with this is steering which is light and positive, the driver knowing his course to a fraction of an inch.'

Fifty-five m.p.h. was deemed a comfortable cruising speed, but evidently Swallows were already questing more urge. Though they did not publicize the fact overmuch till the following year, they were already offering an optional power unit in the shape of the 2,552 c.c. Standard Twenty.

From *Jaguar: a Biography*, 1961

Front-Drive to the Fore

INTRODUCTION BY Auburn of the Cord front-drive automobile marks a new era in the automotive industry, in which America leads the world. While Europe took the first lead in the front-drive principle of automotive propulsion, limited production facilities and the smaller markets kept these cars from making great headway.

The history of the front-drive car in America is mostly a racing history, but it is replete with progress and accomplishment. Barney Oldfield as early as 1912 introduced the front-drive car to the American speedway, piling up many records with his car known as the 'Christie', but it was left to Jimmy Murphy and Harry Miller to introduce the all-American front-drive car in 1924. Murphy died in that year, and the car was finished by Miller who entered it in the Indianapolis Speedway races Decoration Day, 1925. The car was driven by Dave Lewis and won second place (100·82 m.p.h.) in the fastest race ever held on the speedway.

Since that time the front-drive car has been a formidable contender in every major race in the country with such drivers at the wheels as Pete DePaola, Harry Hartz, Leon Duray, Cliff Woodbury, Pete Kreis, and Hepburn.

It is interesting to note the comment of Harry S. Miller on the reasons for his going over to the front-drive type racing car. He says:

'I do not believe that the front-drive car is any faster than the rear-drive type. The reason why it can make better time on the speedways is that it is unnecessary for the drivers to slow down around corners, the skidding of the front-drive type being reduced to a minimum. The success of the front-drive car has been in the safety factors which it provides. It is a monumental record that in the five years front-drive cars have been used on the speedways there has never been a death due to one of these cars getting out of control.'

While racing has its interest to the public, most car owners want to know what the front-drive has to offer them. The consensus of automotive engineers is that the chief contribution of the front-drive type automobile is, like that of the racing car, safety, with a second consideration of comfort, and possibly a third in economy. Three factors make possible the added safety of the front-drive car: its unusual lowness of design (it fairly hugs the ground), its lack of unsprung weight, and its 'pulling' traction.

Some two years ago Harry Miller became associated with E. L. Cord, President of Auburn, in the production of a front-drive car. After eighteen months of experiments, with experimental cars on the roads day and night,

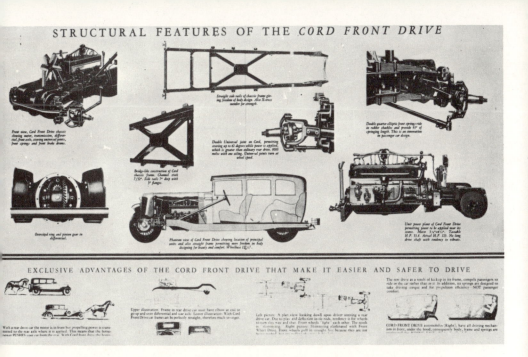

Brave lost cause: a page from the L29 Cord catalogue

the Cord front-drive car, built around the Miller patents, was announced.

Probably the most noticeable feature of the new car is the closeness with which it hugs the ground, and yet it has a road clearance equal to most rear-drive cars. An ordinary size man standing beside it can look over the top. The phaeton-sedan, for instance, is only 61 inches high at the peak point, but even with this low construction head room is a full 38 inches. The average rear-drive sedan stands 70 to 73 inches with the same amount of head room.

Striking in appearance also is the long hood which is 46 inches in length, giving the car an unusually fleet and powerful appearance. The front fenders have an overall length of 80 inches, and are the longest used on any production car. They are of the one-piece type and their long, sweeping lines add again to the fleet appearance. The radiator is of the 'V' type similar to the design used on Miller racing cars, although much larger, with the top line of the hood practically parallel with the ground. The body itself is streamlined throughout, with the rear seat on the same level as the front.

From a mechanical and engineering standpoint the front axle and method of drive are of chief interest. With the new Cord front-drive the engine, the transmission, the drive shaft, the differential, and the driving axle become a single power unit, thus adding to the efficiency.

The front axle is three-quarter floating, and consists of a latitudinally bowed tubular member joining the steering knuckles. The propeller shafts are entirely separate from this, entering only at the ends where the steering knuckles are attached. The transmission and differential are all located directly back of the front axle and are mounted on the frame of the car, becoming sprung weight.

Universal joints are provided in the propeller shafts, the two inner ones being of the Universal Products type, and the two outer ones of a special constant velocity type patented and used for the first time by Auburn in the front-drive car. It is this special universal joint that has made the Cord car possible. Heretofore, designers of front-drive cars have been hampered by their inability to obtain a universal joint which would give constant velocity to the front wheels when making a turn. Race drivers who have used the front-drive cars were under the handicap of having to make wide turns. Through the use of this new type universal joint the turning radius of the car has been reduced to 21 feet, or less than that of any rear-drive car of the same wheelbase.

Another outstanding feature of this front axle is that the kingpin is perpendicular and that no transverse inclination has been necessary. This permits the use of a longer king pin and greater bearing surface, resulting in easier steering.

In detail, the car is powered by a straight-eight, 125 horsepower, Lycoming motor, which has been developed especially for this model. This engine is reversed from the usual type, the fly-wheel being in front, next to the transmission. The rear axle is of the L-beam type, and is approximately of the same weight as the front axle of the ordinary rear-drive car.

Brakes are Lockheed, 4-wheel internal expanding hydraulic, with a division of braking 60 in front and 40 in the rear. The emergency brake is operated by a hand lever well forward in the front compartment, and brakes on the rear wheels. The gear-shift lever extends through the instrument board and operates by a thrust turn.

The chassis frame has been made unusually strong, the channel stock being 7x3x7/32, and is unusually heavily reinforced by an X-cross bracing. Front springs are of the double quarter elliptic type, with the spring ends set in rubber. The rear spring is of the semi-elliptic type, and is built unusually rugged.

Through the elimination, at the rear, of the differential, transmission, and long drive shaft, it has been possible to design straight body sills, the elbow type of the rear-drive being unnecessary for the clearance of rear axle housings, which enables the rear of the body to be set much lower, the rear seat being on the same level as that of the front seat. The body of the car rides unusually low, and while the overall height is considerably less than that of the rear-drive car, the head and leg room are greater. Average front head room is 38 inches and the rear 38 inches. The front seat is adjustable.

Four models are available, a Sedan, Phaeton-Sedan, Cabriolet, and a Brougham, all on a chassis of 137·5/8 inch wheelbase.

A Noisy Birth

BY W. O. BENTLEY

THE HOSPITAL matron was standing in the loft doorway, hands on hips, a formidable and displeased figure. 'Go and see what she wants,' I asked Gallop when I caught sight of her.

He came back in a few moments, a wry smile on his lips. Heaven knows how he had heard the indignant message he passed on to me through cupped hands: 'She says we're to stop this row at once. There's a man ill next door.'

'Tell her to go away,' I shouted back. What was the illness of one man? In here the birth of a new engine was taking place. 'A happy sound to die to —the exhaust roar of the first 3-litre Bentley engine!' someone remarked with awful irreverence later.

We gave it twenty minutes on the bench; then I told Nobby Clarke to switch off, and the gentle hum of traffic in Baker Street seemed a thousand miles away. Perhaps the poor man was really ill, though I fear my conscience wasn't struck till later. On that exciting morning in October 1919, I had too many things on my mind.

On January 20, 1919, Harry Varley, Burgess and I had sat down with nothing but a few bits of paper and some ideas in a small office on the top floor of a building in Conduit Street, London. There, to my instructions and to the accompaniment of endless technical talk, they had worked for nine months with hardly a break on the drawings of the design.

The seeds of it all had, of course, been sown during the war when I had decided that it just wasn't going to be enough for me to return to the agency business, profitable though it had been, and would be again. The creative instinct is strong in most engineers, and, just as I hadn't been satisfied for long to work on someone else's rotary engine, so I had to produce my own car.

Briefly, and without getting too technical, what I had in mind was a bigger engine than the D.F.P.s, which was a good and sound little unit, but there was a limit to how much you could push it; it was not, in fact, a natural power-giver. An engine with overhead valves, and enough of them, a capacity of 3 litres, would be about right, so that we should not have to force it too much to start with; a reliable unit which would require the minimum of maintenance and would stand up to long distances at high speed.

75

3-litre Bentley engine

I had for a long time admired both the racing 3 litre Peugeot—one of the classic designs of all time—and the 1914 Grand Prix Mercedes engines. Both were natural power-givers; the Peugeot had two camshafts directly over each line of valves, with the plug in the centre, while the Mercedes had one camshaft running along the centre and the valves working through rockers and multiple plugs at the side of the head. The head was very well cooled, with water all round the valve seats and also round the plug bosses.

We approved of both these principles, except that we thought that the chain of gears driving the twin camshafts on the Peugeot would be a tricky proposition for the quiet running I thought was essential. I finally decided to go for a centre camshaft working the valves through rockers, with a bevel drive to the camshaft, and cast-iron cylinders, very open at the sides so that we could clear the sand away from beneath the exhaust valves.

People have asked me from time to time why we only had two-wheel brakes on the early 3 litres. The answer is that we didn't know enough about four-wheel brakes. Apart from racing, they had, I think, been used only on the Argyll, and until we had done some research on them we were afraid that the slightest unevenness in their application would affect the steering. But almost as soon as the car was in production we made enquiries of Perrot, who held the patents for what we considered a satisfactory front-wheel braking system, and it was his formula that we eventually used, a double differential looking after the compensation problem.

The market I had in mind for this car, which seemed likely to be as neglected as it had been before the war, was the fast sporting one. If the capital could be found, I thought we could meet it as successfully as we had between 1912 and 1914 with the D.F.P. The policy was a simple one. We were going to make a fast car, a good car, the best in its class; and when we had begun to show a profit and had obtained our own machine shop, then we would make a smaller, cheaper car—a bread-and-butter car in fact—as well.

Burgess, of course, I had known and worked with for years, and I have already told of his deftness and accuracy as a draughtsman. As hard a worker, as useful and with an even better theoretical knowledge, Harry Varley had been with Vauxhall and had done much good work there. These two worked on the drawing-board together, always efficiently, though later on perhaps rather less happily at times when their artistic temperaments got the better of them.

For several months Bentley Motors consisted of the three of us, while my brother H.M. continued to look after D.F.P., making the money we were going to need. And he made a lot of it, about £20,000 in the first roaring boom twelve months after the armistice. Conditions were the same as they were in the late 1940s, with everybody wanting cars, everybody with money, and anybody who could turn out something with four wheels and an engine making it at a feverish rate. H.M. even had a relay of drivers working from the French factory, racing chassis as fast as they could go to the Channel ports.

This boom was all very nice, while it lasted, but it had an unsettling effect on us. It obviously couldn't last, and we wanted to be on at least the tail end of it—which inevitably led to haste and frayed nerves. As we completed drawings for one part, so we had it made, a risky procedure we had to follow to save time. Anyone who has tried to make motor cars—or anything else for that matter—in boom times will know all about the frustrations and head-aches involved in getting materials and in having anything made. With a four-year backlog to make up everyone had full order books, and there was hardly a factory in Britain seeking or even ready to welcome new customers. Here was our first difficulty. The second was not only much greater but almost inconceivable to anyone in the motor car business today. We had to have *everything* made: gearbox, clutch, differential, bearings, stub axles— everything. There were no proprietary makes we could draw on, no ready-made back axles, no gearboxes, no universal joints complete with cardan shaft and so on. To design and build a new motor car in 1919 without sub-stantial capital was like being cast on to a desert island with a penknife and orders to build a house.

The only people we could get to help us were at a works in Bristol. A man there called Peter Purves was wonderful at getting our stuff through, whipping the bits out by a compound of zeal, determination and bullying so efficiently that we decided we must have him for ourselves. 'Come and bustle for us,' I asked him one day. 'As a sort of liaison officer.' And he agreed. Purves had all the right qualifications—diplomacy, the ability to mix well, and intelligence. He became the company buyer later and stayed with us to the end.

As things progressed we had to get in more help, and next came Clive Gallop on the design side. Gallop had fought in France with the R.F.C. as a pilot. He had driven at Brooklands and—even more attractive to me—had worked for Peugeots. We had talked engines for hours in the past, in the same language and with identical enthusiasm, the first time on a train to the Midlands, and I think he had been half expecting the invitation I sent him in the summer of 1919. It was Gallop who helped to evolve the camshaft of the first 3-litre.

Jimmy Enstone was next, ex-Camel pilot, as Company Secretary, and then, with all the blueprints complete and most of the parts made, along came Nobby Clarke, late of No. 4 R.N.A.S. Squadron. Number 4 Squadron, the first to get Bentley-Rotary-engined Camel fighters, was my favourite, and I had had frequent contact with Petty Officer Clarke, the chief mechanic. It was as future head mechanic of Bentley Motors that I had kept my eye on him, and by a piece of happy telepathy or something, he wrote to me from his home in Kent. 'Why don't you call to see us?' I answered his letter of enquiry. 'We need someone to put this engine together.' By September he was doing just that in the loft above D.F.P. service station in New Street Mews which we had then taken over, and doing it with all the skill and dexterity I had expected from him.

Thanks to high-pressure work and co-operation all round, that engine took shape with remarkable rapidity. There it sat on its roughly knocked-together bench, with its single magneto and large pre-war Claudel racing carburettor, all glinting aluminium and copper, and around it we all assembled, like the members of some sect drawn together to witness an ancient rite.

'Let's try to start it now,' I said to Gallop—and the manner in which it didn't has been told by others so I won't linger over the awful anxiety while Clarke tested the valve timing and fiddled with the carburettor. Benzole did the trick—and at once the three-inch exhaust was bellowing and the straight-tooth gears screaming with enough noise to awaken the dead. . . .

From *W. O.: the Autobiography of W. O. Bentley*, 1958

The Progress of Steam

BY ANTHONY G. NEW

TIME FLIES so quickly in the motoring world, and so phenomenal has been the rapid development of the petrol-engine, that many people are apt to forget the important role played by light steam-cars of the American runabout type only a few years ago. So much has happened since then, and there has been such a vast amount of progress made during the intervening period, that this feeling is perhaps only natural. It is, nevertheless, one which should in fairness to the modern steam-car be laid aside when considering the position of our old friend 'steam' today. Because there are comparatively few firms engaged in the manufacture of such pleasure vehicles, it does not by any means follow that 'petrol' has killed 'steam', and it should, rather, be borne in mind that this very fact may to a great extent be actually accountable for the present predominance of the internal combustion engine, for, if anything like the same amount of collective energy had been bestowed upon steam problems as has been brought to bear on questions relating to petrol-engines, some equally startling results might have been obtained.

Looking at the matter impartially, it may fairly be said that four or five years ago the two great rival systems were almost on a par with one another as regards their successful application to pleasure vehicles. In both cases, comparatively little more had been done than to design and build miniature models of the stationary steam plants and gas-engines then in common use. It is true that a considerable amount of ingenuity had to be brought to bear on them in many ways, but so much thought was needed in overcoming other difficulties connected with the transmission of the power to the wheels, and with matters relating to the carriage itself, as distinct from the propelling agent, that comparatively little time could be devoted to the development of special motors for the work. Each system was naturally found to have its own special drawbacks, and it is just these drawbacks that have had to be gradually overcome. As it happened, there was a much greater inclination to devote time and money to internal combustion engines than to steam, for it was felt that they were relatively undeveloped, and that their prospects of improvement were therefore much more rosy than those of the older system —steam. Then the full force of engineering and inventive skill came to bear on change-speed gears, on ignition devices and upon carburettors; while, on the other hand, a *coup de grace* was temporarily given to steam-cars, in the estimation of the public, owing chiefly to the fatal mistake made in America of attempting to supply the demand at too low a price. The once popular

79

1909 White Steamer
Courtesy Montagu Motor Museum

little steam vehicle was, in fact, much too shoddily built, and this fact, combined with the inherent drawbacks of fire-tube boilers for pleasure-cars, caused steam-cars as a class to fall into general disrepute.

It is interesting, however—and some such retrospective review is almost necessary as a preface to a consideration of the improvements of the past year—to speculate on what might have happened, had events taken a slightly different course at that time. Just in the same way that Daimler, and then de Dion, were showing the world how to build a petrol-motor as distinct from an ordinary gas-engine, so Serpollet in France, and then the White Co. in America, were constructing steam-cars on a totally different principle from those in ordinary use. Who is bold enough to say that petrol-cars would today have acquired their remarkable preponderance over steam vehicles if the work of Serpollet and of the White Co. had received the same amount of general recognition as did that of Daimler and de Dion, or if the original Daimler firm and the firm of Messrs de Dion-Bouton had had to carry the whole development of petrol-engines upon their own shoulders? One is apt to think that the two cases—that of modernizing *internal* combustion engines and *external* combustion engines—are not on a par with one another; but there is, in fact, a very close analogy between them. The modern petrol-engine is the old gas-engine, rendered flexible, constructed in a light high-speed form, and rendered essentially hand-to-mouth in its action—by taking the fuel in the required doses as it actually needs it, and converting that fuel immediately into power. Do not these things also constitute the precise difference between the modern 'flash'-steam system and ordinary steam plants?

The very fact that there are so few firms engaged in the manufacture of steam-cars renders it also extremely difficult to deal with the progress of the year in the general way that can be adopted when speaking of petrol-cars. No two makers work on precisely similar lines, and the absence of keen competition renders it comparatively easy for those who have established a reputation to maintain an easy lead. Such rapid all-round development is, moreover, hardly to be expected as with petrol-cars; and, however good any type of car may be, it is bound to take time to gain public confidence. So far, the real history of steam as applied to pleasure vehicles is the history of the 'White', which, by the persistent and practically unaided efforts of a single firm of makers, continues year by year to secure more and more adherents, against all odds. During the past year they have again improved their car immensely, so that it is even better able than ever to hold its own in competition with the other cars of the day. In 1904 it was the free-engine, combined with improved efficiency and with greater length of chassis to suit more roomy bodies, that constituted the main advance, while this last year it has been even greater efficiency, together with a new burner, and 'down' flues instead of side flues, that represent the progress of that period. Each year, too, the construction has been rendered more substantial throughout, and a much more handsome, easy-running, and powerful model has been produced.

The system itself, with its automatic control of the water and of the fuel, has undergone no radical change from the first; but what is most striking about the cars now on the market is a direct outcome of the abolition of the side flues. Thus it is that any form of body, including those with side-entrance doors to the main portion, can now be used, whereas formerly the flues rendered any side entrances impossible.

All other makers of 'flash' steam-cars have still had to contend with the risk of burnt tubes in the generator, and, *per contra*, with the inconveniences arising from running at times with the steam insufficiently superheated. On the 'Miesse' car, for instance, no attempt whatever is made to render either the fuel-feed or the water-feed automatic, both being controlled independently by the driver. Such an arrangement has at least the merits of simplicity, and the cars undoubtedly have remarkable capabilities when handled by those who have taken the trouble to understand them. Much is to be said, moreover, for the contention that new tubes for the generator are inexpensive, and that one can therefore afford to keep them always hot, without troubling much if they do at times become somewhat overheated.

The 'Serpollet' cars should, no doubt, have been mentioned before the

'Miesse', in view of their earlier origin and their wider reputation, but the models now being built by this pioneer firm differ so much from those which have hitherto been sold that their present system may almost be regarded as an entirely new development. In this country, too, very few Serpollet cars have been seen during the last year or two. Originally, the Serpollet system for feeding the generator with water and with fuel consisted of an arrangement by which the main engine operated the two pumps simultaneously, and the two pumps were so connected up together that a fixed ratio always existed between the quantity of water that had to be vaporized and the quantity of fuel that was available for doing so. Further than this, there was nothing really automatic about the system, for the throw of the pumps was regulated by hand, but the feed was at least partly automatic, since it depended upon the speed of the engine.

Now, however, M. Serpollet has adopted what he calls a 'petit cheval' for operating the two feed-pumps. It is a small donkey-engine, having reciprocating parts only—no crank-shaft and no fly-wheel—and it is fed with steam through a pressure-reducing valve, instead of by a direct connection with the generator. The reducing-valve prevents the pressure of the steam, when it reaches the donkey-pump, from exceeding a certain comparatively low value, however high the pressure may be for the main engine. It is thus brought about that even if the driver leaves the valve fall open to the donkey-engine, that small engine cannot continue to run when the pressure in the generator attains a certain maximum, for then the back-pressure, against which the water-pump is called upon to work, exceeds that of the steam in the donkey-engine. Quite a different kind of automatic action results from this arrangement, even though the entire system is still only semi-automatic.

How far this new system is an improvement over the earlier Serpollet system is a matter on which it is impossible for anyone who has not actually tried it to express any definite opinion, and the writer has, so far, had no personal experience with it. From what one hears, however, it is said to be a distinct advance in the right direction, and this view, at any rate, appears to be confirmed by the fact that two or three other manufacturers on the Continent are already copying it more or less closely. At the recent Paris Salon, by the way, it was rendered evident that more interest has now been aroused in steam-cars over there, for amongst the exhibitors were no less than three new firms showing new models.

Apart from 'flash' systems, very little has been done during the year with steam-cars, only one make being in evidence upon the market. Even for the heavier classes of vehicle, 'flash' generators appear likely to replace ordinary boilers, and already the large 'Clarkson' omnibuses that are running in London and other places operate upon this more up-to-date system. It has, in fact, become generally recognized that ordinary boilers, with their large mass of metal and great volume of water, take too long to heat up, and continue to generate steam too quickly after the demand for it has decreased, to render satisfactory any automatic control, while, in addition to this, they are both heavy and bulky. In automobile work, the power required varies so much and so continually that some 'hand-to-mouth' system of generation— direct from the fuel—is almost essential, while, on the subject of weight and space, everyone knows how great is the extent to which both have an important bearing. Another very serious drawback is, moreover, that ordinary steam—even when moderately superheated—requires a much larger condenser than the comparatively small radiator which is found to be sufficient for condensing the exhaust steam with a 'flash' system. Again, size and weight tell against ordinary stationary practice, since, even if *in*adequate provision is made for condensation, the extra quantity of water which has in consequence to be carried involves weight and storage capacity.

Advocates of steam-cars have, on the whole, every reason to be satisfied with the way in which their prospects have improved during 1905, and with the extent to which renewed interest has been taken in them by the buying public. The White Co., who have practically been alone in keeping alive the steam-car business ever since such cars as a class lost the public confidence, have naturally had a very uphill fight while so doing, and could only have succeeded in building up the remarkable connection that they have in this country by having an exceptionally good model to offer. This fact has evidently become more and more fully recognized by everyone, and is not only bringing a well-deserved return to that enterprising firm, but is benefiting every maker of satisfactory steam-cars.

The Motor Yearbook, 1906

The Jam Factory

BY LORD MONTAGU OF BEAULIEU

ONE OF the hazards of the run up A.4 from the West to London is the crowded and narrow High Street of Maidenhead. There was talk of a by-pass in my father's day: gargantuan earthworks started in 1937, only to be interrupted by the war, and as I write the earthworks are rearing up again around the fringes of the town. Yet still Maidenhead remains a traffic hazard, as it was when one wore 'whites' on the river, and the town was the alleged home of some one hundred and fifty night clubs of all types and denominations.

If you turn sharp left at the traffic lights by the Town Hall and proceed up the Cookham Road, past the garage which fathered the prototype Heybourn cyclecar, you will find yourself in a medley of administrative offices, modern housing and a few red-brick survivals of Victorian days.

There is little evidence of industrialization, for the industrial emphasis of the town has shifted south across the railway to the Boyn Valley and Cox Green, but if you persevere you will come upon a wide gateway, flanked with red-brick pillars, on the left-hand side of the road. Large notices will advise you that this is the home of St Martin's Chunky Marmalade, but will remain silent on the subject of cars. Tread respectfully, for you are in the presence of the jam factory, most legendary of all the homes of the lost causes.

Unlike the manufacturers of Birmingham and Coventry, who succumbed to cut-throat competition rather than to the snares of heterodoxy, the jam factory tried everything: friction drive, rear engines, straight-eights, slide valves, electrics, and petrol-electrics all emerged from this dreary conglomeration of sheds. Between the end of 1914 and the summer of 1936 well over a thousand cars, from 7 h.p. miniatures to formidable luxury vehicles, drove out of the gates and nosed their way into the streets of Maidenhead, on their way up the Bath Road to London and the markets.

The intriguing aspect of the Maidenhead saga is that Cordwallis Works seemed to exercise a hoodoo on the manufacture of cars. Firms either saw the Cookham Road and died, or saw the red light and went elsewhere... Both Marendaz and G.W.K. attained their successes in other works before translating themselves to Maidenhead and the Official Receiver. The Imperia, which had sold quite briskly for an imported car before the First World War, languished and died a slow death there. Auto Electrics moved to Guildford and abandoned all their interest in car manufacture; while Sir Dennis Burney, recognizing the limitations of Cordwallis Works as anything more than an experimental workshop, arranged for the limited series production of his designs elsewhere. You can still spot exciting cars outside Maidenhead's hotels, expecially in the summer, but the odds are heavily against their being the products of Maidonian labour. Only in the little pubs of North Town, Summerleaze and Cox Green will you hear nostalgic talk of the old G.W.K. days.

It is unlikely, however, that these sombre thoughts crossed the minds of Arthur Grice, J. Talfourd Wood and C. M. Keiller as they planned a new light car together in their experimental workshops at Beckenham in 1910. Grice had conceived the idea that a friction gear he had seen used for grinding optical lenses could be applied to a light car. He had succeeded in interesting Wood in this project, and on the strength of a rough sketch on the back of an envelope they had gone to work, joined by Keiller, who had met Wood while they had been training together in the Great Western Railway workshops at Swindon.

Both their plans and the facilities at their disposal were limited in the extreme. They rented a small stable at Beckenham, while Grice, who at that time handled the London end of Messrs George Anderson, crane manufacturers of Carnoustie, had an office in Victoria Street through which he was able to conduct the business of the partnership. Plans to use Chater-Lea frames—then proprietary components with a wide currency—were frustrated, since the Chater-Lea concern was not interested in such a small contract, but eventually two Coventry-Simplex twin-cylinder marine engines, a pair of old de Dion-type tubular radiators, a set of Chater-Lea wire wheels of non-detachable type and a Chater-Lea front axle were procured; the rest they made themselves.

The principles of the friction transmission were simple. The fly-wheel of the engine served as a driving disc, which engaged with a driven disc shod with a 'tyre' in the form of a ring faced with fibre or cork. The second disc was mounted at right angles to the fly-wheel so that it could be slid across it, engaging at four different points. This action was controlled by notches selected by a thumb-operated plunger on the 'gear lever'. The clutch mechanism engaged one end of the driven-disc shaft. At the other end the shaft was universally-jointed, the drive thereafter being by shaft to a differential. De-clutching moved the driven disc out of contact with the driving disc, while full depression of the clutch pedal actuated a transmission brake. In other respects the car was conventional, though the engine lived below and behind the seats and the radiator was mounted in front. The rear-mounted engine, incidentally, contributed very largely to the success of the early cars, as unquestionably the whip encountered in the long drive shafts of the later four-cylinder machines rendered the transmissions less reliable.

By 1911, a company had been formed and operations had been transferred from the stables at Beckenham to Home Works, Datchet, not far from Windsor. Their landlord here, be it said, was my father, for Datchet was part of the family estates until 1917, and I am still Lord of the Manor of Datchet. Here series production was undertaken, using the 86×90 mm. vertical-twin Coventry-Simplex engine. Apart from the provision of detachable wheels in 1912, no major alterations were carried out to the basic specification, and 1,069 cars, mainly the very similar Models A and B, were turned out between the establishment of the Datchet works and the discontinuation of private car manufacture in favour of Admiralty contracts in 1915.

Grice, Wood and Keiller were early in the light-car field. Captain Wood is still most insistent that the G.W.K. was never a cyclecar, which name he associates with the belt-drive and plywood brigade such as the Tamplin and Carden, while the presence of conventional driving controls helped to allay any misgivings the public might entertain on the subject of friction drive. Both Wood and Keiller realized the importance of competition work, the former having been one of only nine finishers in the 1910 Scottish Six Days Motor-cycle Trial, and G.W.K.s were entered in every possible event. The two partners were awarded Gold Medals in the 1912 London–Edinburgh run. Keiller collected another 'Gold' in the 'Six Days', and a stripped touring model won a five-lap race at Brooklands that May, beating an A.C. and a Morgan. Hill-climbs also saw the partners in action, Wood winning the Cyclecar Class at the Streatham and District Club's event at Titsey in September. In October, the indefatigable Wood was again out after records at Brooklands.

The year 1913 saw Wood and Keiller out again, reinforced by Cyril Wilberforce, the company's Caterham agent and, on occasions, Rex Mundy, later to be associated with K.L.G. sparking plugs. Competition was fiercer now, for H. F. S. Morgan—also a former Swindon apprentice—was pitting his three-wheelers against the more substantial G.W.K.s, and the name of G.N. was making itself felt. A Morgan won the Cyclecar Race at Brooklands that March, though only after the opposition from Datchet had been defeated by tyre trouble, and two months later, in the Herefordshire Cyclecar Trial, the honours again went to Morgan. Nevertheless, both Wood and Keiller won Gold Medals in a 'Scottish Six Days' that included that memorable nastiness, the Pass of the Cattle—and anyone who laughs at the crudities of friction drive should recall the raised eyebrows which accompanied the inclusion of this formidable section in the 1936 Scottish Rally.

With Haywood's tuned Singer Ten entering the lists, the G.W.K.s were now strongly challenged in speed events, but they went on winning. By the end of 1913, *The Motor Cycle* was observing that 'the G.W.K. has won its spurs and can be purchased without fear of future reprisals', and for 1914 no improvements were deemed necessary beyond the adoption of a stronger timing gear and bevel pinion, and some improvements to a body which was already adequate for most purchasers in the G.W.K. class. The little cars bridged the gap between true cyclecars like the G.N., which demanded a degree of mechanical skill and a spartan attitude to life, and big cars in miniature like the Morris-Oxford, already making its mark and keeping its competitors up to scratch. The Datchet product weighed 6½ cwt. in chassis form, as against 4¾ cwt. for the G.N. and a resounding 8½ cwt. for the Morris. Not that racing cars were neglected, for Wood was now using a slender streamlined single-seater at Brooklands, and getting round very briskly.

In the New Buyer's Number of *The Light Car and Cyclecar* in March 1914, G.W.K. Ltd. took two full pages in the advertisement columns to plug their successes during the past seasons, giving the lie to dark hints on the advent of an American 'cyclecar armada' said to be on its way. Far more useful to the company, however, was a contribution by Captain Wood in the same issue, entitled 'The Case for Friction Drive'. This combined some sound advice with propaganda, the writer arguing that, on grounds of simplicity and ease of servicing, the system took a lot of beating. Facings for the fibre wheel cost only ten shillings apiece, and could be replaced without undoing anything save twenty bolts which held it to the wheel, while the question of facing material itself (G.W.K. tried all manner of linings, including millboard, Ferodo, and cork) was laughed off with the observation that during a record attempt at Brooklands he had 'found some linoleum lying about, and used it'. Slip could be eliminated by keeping the discs free of grease, while flats in the fibre facing, the great bugbear of friction drive and the cause of transmission slip, resulted from letting the clutch in too slowly, or driving with the handbrake on. 'I do not say,' Captain Wood continued, 'that it must be let in with a bang, though little harm will be done if it is, but it must be let in far more quickly than an ordinary clutch of the cone or plate type.' These instructions may seem elementary to the modern motorist, but it must be remembered that the Edwardians looked upon the gearbox as a means of starting from rest and coping with near-vertical gradients, and that the habit of slipping the clutch to propel oneself over the crest of a hill was almost universal among lay motorists. 'Flats do not prevent the car being driven,' Wood continues consolingly, 'but of course they will set up a disagreeable knocking noise.' No skilled driver, however, need go in fear of 'flats', and fibres were good for 7,000 to 10,000 miles by 1914.

When war broke out, the wind had apparently set fair for G.W.K. Ltd. Their £150 light car had the merits of simplicity and reliability. The standard article was capable of 55 m.p.h.—indeed, the owner of one of the few surviving 'twins' still claims mile-a-minute speeds—while fuel consumptions of the order of 45 m.p.g. were readily obtainable. Captain Wood remembers driving one of the Scottish Six Days cars from Edinburgh to Byfleet in less than thirteen hours. A small but brisk export trade was being built up, cars being shipped to East Africa and Ceylon. The prejudice against friction drive had been overcome, and people were beginning to take it seriously. General Motors in America hurriedly bought up the makers of the Cartercar, a transatlantic apostle of the system: its sales were uninspiring, but the patents had considerable potential value.

Unfortunately, his partners had reckoned without the personality of Arthur Grice. Grice was congenitally incapable of pursuing an idea beyond the prototype stage—no sooner had a system been made to work than he was off chasing some new pipe-dream. He seems to have divided his time between the exploration of other people's ideas for possible patent infringement, and the acquisition of an interest in them with a view to their exploitation by his own companies. Self-destruction by an ultra-keen interest in the patent laws was a characteristic of other lost causes, notably Argyll. Grice could not resist experimentation, and he had already all but dropped out of G.W.K. Ltd. to pursue his lifelong diversion of forming companies. In 1912, he had floated Rotary Units Ltd. to develop a pumping engine said to have 'five eccentric cylinders'. The G.W.K. company was asked to make this engine, but it never worked, and the newly-founded firm was left in abeyance for another eight years until its progenitor found a new use for it, having in the meanwhile repurchased all the shares at cut rates. A year or so later he joined forces with a Belgian marble merchant, M. A. Van Roggen, to whom he had sold diamond bandsaws while still with George Anderson's. They formed G. & V. R. Ltd., for which concern premises on the Cordwallis Works site at Maidenhead were acquired. A car of sorts was certainly built (or, more probably, imported), but by the outbreak of war nothing concrete had emerged from this project.

Whatever mysterious contrivances were being evolved at Maidenhead, Grice suggested to his partners that the body-shops of the expanding G.W.K. business be shifted from Datchet to Cordwallis Works, and, shortly after the outbreak of war, the rest of the factory followed suit. Wood had joined up, leaving the wartime management of G.W.K. to Grice.

The move to Maidenhead was the turning-point. Neither the finances nor the standard of work were ever the same, and many of the old G.W.K. employees I have met say that the 'family' atmosphere of Datchet was never recaptured. However, Grice's fertile brain had not been idle in the war years, and there was no shortage of ideas for a new car by Armistice time. Unfortunately, they were the wrong ones.

After the unqualified success of Models 'A' and 'B', it might have been expected that production of these types would be resumed by the reorganized company, G.W.K. (1919) Ltd. So it was, for a short time in 1919, when a hold-up in the supply of four-cylinder engines forced the company to run off about a hundred cars of pre-war type, using units left over from pre-war stocks. Grice, however, had set his heart on a four-cylinder car.

G.W.K. 1920 10·8 h.p.
Courtesy Montagu Motor Museum

Already a prototype had been made, and had been running since 1915, but this was simply a twin-cylinder chassis fitted with a side-valve M.A.G. engine mounted at the rear and retaining the original Model A layout. Wood held the view that the company's only hope was to produce a redesigned twin-cylinder machine with conventional transmission, but Grice had a *fait accompli* in the shape of Model F by the summer of 1918. This looked just like a conventional car, and had a front-mounted 66 × 100 mm. (1,368 c.c.) Coventry-Simplex side-valve engine, quarter-elliptic suspension and electric lighting. It was an altogether bigger and heavier vehicle, chassis weight being 10½ cwt. and the wheelbase 9 ft. 8 in.

From the start, this vehicle proved a headache. Wood and Keiller laboured hard to overcome its numerous failings, which included wheel-shedding, transmission whip and unpleasant ringing noises from the driven disc, which last aroused adverse comment in the contemporary motoring press. By the end of 1921, they had transformed it into a reliable motor car, Wood winning 'Golds' in the 'Edinburgh' and the 'Scottish Six Days' in 1920, while in the 1921 'Land's End' G.W.K. again featured extensively in the awards list. Unfortunately they had to contend not only with labour troubles, but with Grice's brilliant plan for collecting a Post Office contract for light vans based on the new Model F chassis. But, with the new car still suffering teething troubles, the result can be imagined. The vans were unreliable, the Post Office drivers found friction drive beyond them, and the trial contract merely served to dislocate private car production further. The protracted moulders' strike of 1920–21 held up deliveries of parts, and even the departure of Grice to resuscitate Rotary Units Ltd. in 1920 could not save the company.

In 1922, G.W.K. (1919) Ltd. went into liquidation, Wood and Keiller resigned, and the story of a gallant little car really came to an end. Unfortunately for the firm's reputation, though, the projects continued, and for the next eight or nine years floods of directors came and went. The Academy of Projectors were given full rein and they had a wonderful time.

Grice, meanwhile, was operating at the foot of Holtspur Hill, Wooburn Green, under the style of Rotary Units Ltd. This impressive title covered no more than a pair of large Army huts which had once formed part of the wartime hospital on Lord Astor's nearby estate of Cliveden, and had been transported to Wooburn by Grice. Here he reverted to a twin-cylinder rear-engined machine resembling the original G.W.K. very closely in appearance. The engine was said to be a product of Rotary Units Ltd., but was actually a side-valve 998 c.c. V-twin Bovier. The drive from the fly-wheel to the driven disc was taken by a Hardy universal joint, and a central chain took the drive to the back axle. The finished article sold for £275—the same price as the four-cylinder G.W.K.—complete with oil sidelamps, but *sans* starter. Such deviations as there were from the specification of the Maidenhead cars were undoubtedly due to the need to avoid litigation.

Rotary Units struggled on until 1923, during which period about fifty cars of various types were made. In the company's short life, it produced the original rear-engined car, a front-engined 'twin' (£280, or £297 with water-cooling), a four-cylinder s.v. car with a 63×100 mm. (1,247 c.c.) engine (£268), a similar type with conventional three-speed box and shaft drive (£297), a third variation on the same theme retaining the friction transmission without the chain, and, finally, a 'Service Model' with unitary construction of chassis and body, which was displayed at the 1922 Show. The standard colour was khaki, with electric lighting, and it cost a mere £186. There seems to have been no standard form of Unit No. 1, and the make featured little in contemporary competitions, though one F. Salter won a Silver Medal in the 1921 Land's End Trial. Mr Leonard P. Lee, the present head of Coventry Climax Engines Ltd., served part of his apprenticeship at the Wooburn works.

In the meantime the G.W.K. directors, who had a saleable car on their hands, set about getting advice as to how to market it. Their chosen vessel was Percy Richardson, late of Daimler and Sheffield-Simplex, who was appointed managing director in February 1922. But despite the successes of the *marque* in trials, especially in the hands of Pope and Jackson, little headway was made. However, 1922 saw a reversion to a rear-engined layout with Model J. This retained the frontal radiator, and, owing to the use of a fairly long bonnet, was not readily distinguishable from Model H, the 'conventional' car which had been evolved by Wood from the unreliable

Model F. It was unsuccessful, though it will crop up again in the G.W.K. story.

In 1923, Jackson and Pope pulled off their accustomed Gold Medals in the 'London–Edinburgh', while the standard Model H two-seater was reduced in price from £285 to £210 in an attempt to attract customers. More important, however, A. G. Grice tired of Rotary Units Ltd. and returned to the fold, while his associate M. A. Van Roggen also joined the Board.

The picture of the last few years of G.W.K. is a sad one. There were stocks of parts on hand sufficient to asemble as many cars as the market would take, and it was the company's practice to keep a few chassis in readiness for any orders that might come in. There was little production as such, and certainly the company's past policy of over-buying enabled it to keep ticking over feebly in fits and starts until 1931. But the writing was on the wall. Serious competition work stopped after 1924, and activities were confined to the assembly of the odd G.W.K., to sundry Grice experiments including the Grice three-wheeler of 1925–6, which had friction drive and a single wheel in front, and to research work on two other oddities, the French Lafitte and the London-built Waverley.

The former had a three-cylinder radial engine, friction-and-chain drive and a dashboard gear lever after the manner of the f.w.d. Citroen, and suffered the indignity of conversion into a service van after Grice lost interest. The latter had a 75×102 mm. rear-mounted flat-twin engine, and actually appeared at the 1926 Show as a £100 car. Its arrival at Cordwallis Works was variously ascribed to Grice's ambition to produce it there, and to his determination to prevent Waverley Cars from infringing his patents by producing it anywhere. The latter is almost certainly the truth.

Half-hearted evolution of the G.W.K. design continued. For 1924, a 1½ litre (69×100 mm.) engine was offered as an alternative power unit, while *de luxe* models were at last given a starter as standard equipment. Front-wheel brakes of Stevenson design were available at £10 10s extra. In 1925, the firm offered an all hand-controlled car, aimed at disabled drivers. This had no pedals at all, clutch and footbrake being operated by downward movement of the steering column into a slot below. Full depression gave the effect of a clutch. One or two of these hand-controlled G.W.K.s were sold, though R. G. Jackson, the then sales mananger, says they were horrible to drive. In 1926, the firm tried to cash in on the low-priced market with a fabric-bodied 'Chummy', intended to sell at £100. The list price was actually £159. At the 1926 Show, the G.W.K. appeared for the last time, a fabric-bodied drophead saloon being priced at £335.

Meanwhile, a new development had arisen. Van Roggen persuaded Grice to interest himself and the ailing G.W.K. concern in a Belgian car, the Imperia.

The Imperia was a ready-made lost cause. In pre-1914 days, this Belgian

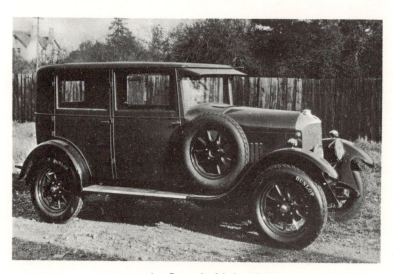

1927 11/27 Imperia fabric saloon
Courtesy Montagu Motor Museum

marque had enjoyed quite a fair success on the British market; indeed, a Miss Edith Paterson had leapt to fame by putting fifty-three miles into the hour at Brooklands on a 16 h.p. Imperia in 1908, at a time when women were not permitted to compete in ordinary races. But in Edwardian days the Imperia had possessed no markedly eccentric features. Nor, outwardly, did it possess them in 1924, being a solidly-built small car resembling nothing so much as a slightly down-at-heel Panhard–Levassor in miniature. It boasted a conventional four-speed and reverse gearbox and four-wheel brakes, but under the bonnet there was one of those weird and wonderful power units devised by those determined people who sought to give the poppet valve premature burial. The Imperia engine was, in fact, a slide valve, in which the slides were located on either side of the cylinder wall, moving vertically and covering and uncovering double ports.

Not that the Imperia was a bad car. Van Roggen won the small-car class in the 1926 Monte Carlo Rally on one of the 11 h.p. (66×80 mm.) models, and a tourer tested by *The Autocar* in 1924 was quite good value at £375, giving a top speed of 46 m.p.h. and a fuel consumption of 32 m.p.g., this in spite of the fact that the weight was something of the order of seventeen cwt. The whole vehicle was solidly built for an '1100', necessitating a depressing 5·1:1 top gear. A saloon was submitted for road test in 1926, and was found to be undergeared as well as much noisier than a conventional sleeve-valve. At the same time it was announced that 'the car is to be manufactured in this country at the G.W.K. works'.

In the event, it never was. The G.W.K. company underwent one of its periodic reconstructions at the beginning of 1927, and emerged as Imperia Motors Ltd. But the new company did not make or even assemble Imperias, and it made precious few G.W.K.s either, having recourse to general repair work in order to keep going. A few experiments were carried out with a 'plastic' form of body construction, the principal ingredients of which seem to have been hair and plaster of Paris but the sum total of the Imperia operations amounted to perhaps four dozen cars imported in four years. These were sold initially through the London firm of W. G. Nicholl Ltd., Mr Nicholl being a director of the Maidenhead concern. A 66×80 mm. 'six' of similar design arrived on the scene in 1929, but very few were sold in England. The main interest of the Imperia venture was the advent of Mr Alfred Dougill.

A. W. Dougill dominated the company's later years. His main concern was the development of Cordwallis Works into a Trading Estate, and by the time of his death in 1941 he had achieved this. None the less, it is likely that Grice was attracted not so much by Dougill's business acumen as by his connections with his pet hobby-horse, friction drive.

Mr Dougill's father had built a series of experimental cars in Leeds between 1896 and 1898, and in 1899 acquired the British sales agency for the friction-drive cars designed by Ludwig Maurer of Nuremberg. He was also, incidentally, responsible for the assembly in 1899 of that curiosity, the Lawson motor-wheel, a true 'mechanical horse' which was mounted between the shafts of a trap. From 1902 to 1906 the younger Dougill assisted his father in the manufacture of a small number of cars and trucks, using a double-disc system of friction drive, under the trade-name 'Frick', and the elder Dougill patented these designs in the latter year. In 1907 the son joined Wolseley, remaining with them until the company was wound up at the end of 1926, by which time he was their works manager. In the course of his career at Adderley Park, he had been closely connected both with Count Schilowsky's famous gyro-car and with the Brennan gyroscopic mono-railcar, which had a Wolseley petrol engine and was made at the company's Crayford works. Such a man would surely appeal to Grice.

By 1930, the G.W.K. was no more than an entry in the *Buyer's Guide*, while Imperia operations were only on a token scale. They exhibited at the 1930 Show, but that was all. No G.W.K.s were displayed on this occasion. Nevertheless, Grice was having his final fling, in the form of yet another rear-engined four-cylinder car. The old Coventry-Climax engine was retained—there were still quite a few lying around at Cordwallis Works— but this time it was mounted well over the axle, driving forward. A punt-type chassis reminiscent of the early Trojan was used, and indeed the finished article looked uncommonly like a punt on wheels, this effect being heightened by the use of a convertible 'roll-top' with rigid sides, styled on the lines of the camping punts so popular on the Thames. The price was £165; a simplified version, to be priced 'in the neighbourhood of £100', was hinted at, but never materialized.

In the meanwhile a Mr Murphy had started a firm by the name of Auto Electric on the Cordwallis Estate. This concern made two experimental vehicles in the 1928–30 period, the first a little battery-electric car with a motor 'at each corner', four-wheel drive and four-wheel independent suspension, and the second a petrol-electric device, using yet another unwanted Coventry-Climax engine—presumably because it was there! This latter was never completed, and both ventures were abandoned when the firm moved to Guildford.

However, 1930 saw a far more interesting arrival in the form of Sir Dennis Burney, the designer of the airship R.100. Burney aimed to produce a car with optimum weight distribution, efficient suspension and a true aerodynamic form. Streamline Cars Ltd. never interested themselves in series production: Sir Dennis told me that Cordwallis Works were totally unsuited for anything other than prototype work, which is hardly surprising in view of the fact that in 1930 one large shed housed the remnants of the G.W.K. project, Imperia Motors Ltd. and the Burney experimental shop. The partitions between each section were of beaverboard, and one shudders to think what might have happened had they collapsed.

Burney started with a clean sheet of paper. His car had its engine mounted over the rear axle, and had independent suspension to all four wheels, transverse cantilever springs being used at the rear. His first experimental car was produced at the airship station at Howden in 1928, and consisted of a 12/75 f.w.d. Alvis chassis turned back to front, with the steering locked and the dead rear axle of the original Alvis design replaced by a conventional steering axle. Unlike Grice, Burney did not feel himself bound by any aesthetic conventions, and the original design had a short nose falling away immediately in front of the driver, the radiators being mounted in the logical position at the rear, one each side of the engine. The 'aeroplane-fuselage' effect of the body was rather spoilt by the use of conventional cycle-type front mudguards, turning with the wheels. The gearbox was of four-speed 'crash' type, with central remote control. One small concession was made to the diehards in that buyers had the choice of an alternative body style, with a vestigial bonnet housing a petrol tank in front of the driver. All cars had exhaust gas heaters to front and rear compartments.

Sir Dennis, however, conformed to the fashions of the later Vintage years in fitting his cars with a straight-eight engine, a true lost cause in the form of a 3-litre (66 × 108 mm.) Beverley-Barnes. This unit had twin overhead camshafts and bore a superficial resemblance to an Alfa-Romeo, the employment of Marelli coil ignition heightening the similarity. It is hard to know why this obscure power plant was chosen, but it was fairly potent, giving 80 b.h.p., sufficient to propel the heavy Burney at a sustained 70 m.p.h. In any case, the depression had hit Beverleys hard, and their very small sales were dwindling away to nothing, so it is scarcely surprising that they were seeking to invade the proprietary engine market. In standard form the Burney listed at £1,500, which was a high price even for seekers after the bizarre.

The Burney created a sensation, especially when it was announced at the end of 1930 that H.R.H. The Prince of Wales had ordered one. The 1932 models boasted a dummy V-radiator, and the designer took one of these to America on a lecture tour, where it was favourably received. Despite the fact that on this occasion a Lycoming 'six' engine, as used in the contemporary Auburn, was installed, nothing happened, and the American public had to wait another twenty-seven years for a rear-engined car at a popular price.

Altogether twelve cars were made between 1930 and 1933, nine of them with the twin-cam Beverleys, which proved unreliable. Apart from the Lycoming unit in the car which went to America, the last two had o.h.v. Armstrong-Siddeley Twenty engines. Streamline Cars Ltd. remained in existence for some time after the closure of the Maidenhead factory in the spring of 1933, but only design work was undertaken, and the 2-litre Crossleys built under Burney patents in 1934 were made entirely at Manchester. At one stage the presence of a Crossley-Burney prototype at Cordwallis Works brought forth a wild rumour that the whole Trading Estate was to be turned over to the mass-production of rear-engined cars, but this, I am assured, was baseless.

By 1932, Grice had retired to an island in the Thames, where he was selling replacement facings for friction discs, while Dougill kept the Imperia business ticking over. Into this void came the colourful personality of Captain D. M. K. Marendaz. Marendaz had spent most of his life in the motor industry, having served his apprenticeship at Siddeley-Deasy before fighting in the R.F.C. during the war. Upon demobilization, he went to work with T. G. John at the Holley Bros. factory in Coventry, and was thus connected with the early days of Alvis. A former brother-officer of his, Mr Hulbert, was at this time in partnership with G. P. H. de Freville, a well-known Ford agent. De Freville had bought the design rights to a 1,500 c.c. side-valve four-cylinder engine of sporting potentialities.

It was Marendaz who suggested that a batch of fifty of these de Freville engines should be laid down at Coventry, and the result was the 10/30 Alvis. He then contracted to build 500 gearboxes for the Emscote cyclecar, an ephemeral of the immediate post war years sponsored by Marlowe, a former works manager at Standard, and Seelhaft, who had been Marendaz's senior in his apprentice days at Siddeley-Deasy.

Marendaz, having made 260 gearboxes for cars which never materialized, decided to go into partnership with Seelhaft, the result being a little 10·8 h.p. car with Coventry-Simplex side-valve engine known as the Marseel. Apart from the adoption of worm final drive it had no very unusual features, but between the summer of 1920 and the closing of the factory in 1925, it won over 250 trials awards, many of them in the hands of its designer, who raced a blue and white example, nicknamed 'Blancmange', at Brooklands.

The Marseal range (the spelling was changed after Seelhaft's retirement in 1923) embraced the usual diversity of models, ranging from a 1,247 c.c. 9/20 to an o.h.v. small 'six'. The 12/40 h.p. car had a polished aluminium body in the manner of those times, and was said to be good for 75 m.p.h., while in 1922 some experiments were carried out with a four-cylinder in-line oil-cooled engine of 1,018 c.c., rather reminiscent of the Bradshaw-designed units used in a number of contemporary motor cycles and in the Belsize-Bradshaw light car. Despite 6,000 miles of successful road tests, this model never reached the production stage. Altogether, the Marseal made quite an impression, and about 1,200 were built, with bodies by Lawson or Hancock and Warman (the latter subsequently doing much of Riley's bodywork), before the firm went into liquidation. Characteristically enough, the demise of Marseal Motors Ltd. followed closely upon the introduction of the six-cylinder car.

After a brief period on the Stock Exchange, Captain Marendaz took premises in 1926 in the London General Cab Co.'s garage at the Camberwell end of the Brixton Road, which building also housed, in addition to the freshly reconstituted cab concern, Ettore Bugatti's London depot and, from 1928 onwards, the British concessionaires for the Graham-Paige. The main activities of D. M. K. Marendaz Ltd. were a garage and tuning establishment. The firm also sold second-hand sports cars, contributing some of the more exciting items, such as Alfa-Romeo or Lea-Francis, to *The Autocar's* series of Used Car Road Tests. More or less as a sideline, he also constructed—or rather assembled—about twenty Marendaz Specials. Most of these used four-cylinder s.v. Anzani engines, separate gearboxes and cone clutches. The 1½ litre (69 × 100 mm.) car retailed at £495 as the 11/55, or in supercharged chassis form at £750 as the 11/120. A smaller version in the same chassis was the 9/20, with 59 × 100 mm. (1,093 c.c.) o.h.v. engine. The four-wheel brakes were so arranged that the pedal acted on the front wheels and the lever on the rear. With their V-screens, Bentley-shaped radiators and flared wings they were exciting-looking little cars, and though limited capital prevented Marendaz from supporting a big racing programme, he was a tireless performer at Montlhéry, cleaning up record after record. The World's Class 'G' 24-hour record fell to a stripped 1,100 c.c. two-seater in February 1928, driven by its designer and Douglas Hawkes; this in spite of the fact that a mechanic backed the car into a petrol pump during the proceedings and damaged the rear axle. Marendaz, Forrest and Hanks also collected the 1,500 c.c. 24-hour record at 59 m.p.h. under impossible conditions of fog, while Marendaz also set up a number of long-distance records with the big straight-eight Graham-Paiges, even putting up the fastest lap as yet made at Brooklands in a saloon, at 90·06 m.p.h. Incidentally, his open Graham-Paige was the car which won the very last race ever run at Brooklands, in August 1939.

At the same time, he was experimenting with a small straight-eight of his own, with exhaust-over-inlet valves. This had cylinder dimensions of 52×88 mm. (1,495 c.c.), and was catalogued in chassis form at £600, or £750 with supercharger. A special Anzani crankshaft was used, and the block was made specially in Birminghan to Marendaz designs, but this project came to naught, though certainly the engine was completed. This may have been the car which cropped up in 1931 as a 'Miller-Marendaz Special'.

Late in 1931 came a small side-valve 'six', the 13/70, which was of fairly conventional design apart from one or two intriguing features, including the employment of a 2:1 reduction gear for both brake and clutch pedals. Brakes were Lockheed hydraulic. The engine's appearance was enhanced by an aluminium cover plate which concealed the plugs; 70 b.h.p. at 4,700 r.p.m. was claimed from the 1,869 c.c. (59×112 mm.) unit, which was creditable, though much unkind nonsense was published about the alleged origin of these engines. They were in actual fact assembled by Marendaz, the camshafts and crankshafts being made by Continental Motors Corporation—hence the rumour, no doubt, that they were surplus Erskine engines bought when Studebaker got into financial difficulties. The blocks were produced by Birmid in Birmingham. Dual coil ignition was used, and fuel was fed from the rear tank by an Autopulse electric pump. The car was cloaked with a very pretty four-seater 'International' body which owed its inspiration to Max Millar, *The Autocar*'s artist, and, apart from the stub exhausts which rather spoilt the general effect, the resemblance to a miniature Bentley was very pronounced—so much so, in fact, that in 1933 *The Autocar* found it necessary to deny rumours that Rolls-Royce were bringing out a new small Bentley. The rumour mongers had clearly spotted a 13/70 Marendaz, and had drawn the obvious conclusions. This model was listed at £375.

Clearly a factory less cramped than the Brixton Road workshops was indicated; so Marendaz took on the lease of one of the buildings at Cordwallis Works. When I met him, incidentally, he was rather hurt at the suggestion that the works of Marendaz Special Cars Ltd. occupied yet another section of the congested shed in which the G.W.K., Burney and Imperia enterprises were eking out a precarious existence. In actual fact, they were located in a completely separate building, and remained there until the company went into liquidation in the late summer of 1936.

In May 1932, Marendaz Special Cars Ltd. was formed 'to carry on the business of manufacturers of, and dealers in, cars, motor cycles, engines, airships, aeroplanes, etc.'—not so illogical in the light of subsequent events.

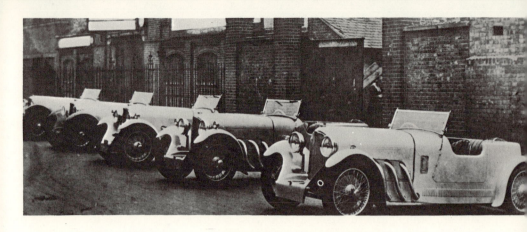

13/70 Marendaz sports tourers
Courtesy Montagu Motor Museum

Capital was only £5,000, but this did not deter Marendaz from making quite an impression during his tenancy of Cordwallis Works. In September of that year, Mrs E. B. Norris, Mayoress of Maidenhead, christened the first 13/70 to leave the newly-commissioned works, though it is to be regretted that by this time the locals were becoming cynical on the subject of the native motor industry, and *The Maidenhead Advertiser* gave far more publicity to the launching, two years later, of the first *traction avant* Citroen to roll off the lines at Slough.

Three basic models of Marendaz were offered: the 13/70, the bigger 2·6-litre 17/97 at £475, both with Marendaz engines, and the 15/90 with a 65×100 mm. i.o.e. Coventry-Climax six-cylinder engine, which was introduced for the 1935 season and had become the staple product by 1936. Supercharged variants were also marketed, and the cars competed regularly in the National rallies of their day, mainly in the hands of Captain Marendaz and Mr and Mrs A. E. Moss, the parents of Stirling Moss. In 1936, Mrs Moss even had built for her a special short-chassis version of the Coventry-Climax-engined car with an ultra-light two-seater body made of fabric on a light steel frame, which she ran in the R.A.C. and Scottish Rallies that year, gaining a first-class award in the former. An even more noteworthy success was scored by Miss D. Summers, who was the first woman to win a race at Brooklands (in 1936) after the fair sex had been admitted on equal terms with the men. What is more, she did it at the first meeting of the season, and on a standard 15/90 Marendaz tourer! The Coventry-Climax-engined Marendaz proved very successful, and it is only regrettable that it appeared on the scene when the company's fortunes were already at a low ebb. At £425, it represented remarkable value for the enthusiast, and when road-tested by *The Autocar* it recorded nearly 82 m.p.h. on top and 73 m.p.h. on the very close-ratio third.

'Great Britain's fastest and safest 2-litre' was soon to succumb to the

Maidenhead hoodoo. All the same, the 2-litre car did quite well in the 1935 T.T. in the hands of W. T. McCalla, while a supercharged 17/100 h.p. tourer had the distinction of featuring in the production of 'Man and Superman' at the Cambridge Theatre in August of that year. Bernard Shaw, however, stuck to his Lanchester Ten.

But Marendaz was looking to other fields to redress the adverse balance of the car business. He had shown a marine engine at the 1933 Olympia Show—his only London show appearance since the Marseal days, though a 17/90 (as the 17/97 had been renamed) was displayed at the Kelvin Hall in 1934—and now he prepared designs for a two-seater light aeroplane. All to no avail: the company was wound up in July 1936, the remains being taken over by Colliers of Birmingham, who already owned the remnants of Clyno, Swift and A.J.S., among others.

Thus perished Maidenhead's motor industry. Cordwallis Works passed into the hands of the manufacturers of preserves. As late as 1935, Imperias were still theoretically being imported into Great Britain, while Mr Dougill advertised Imperia Motors Ltd. as a source of spares for the Derby, having taken over the stocks held by Ortons of Cookham, the erstwhile concession-aires. But the Imperia was doomed to lose its identity, and when the make reappeared at Earls Court in 1937, under the aegis of Minerva Automobiles Ltd., the cars were found to be no more than restyled f.w.d. Adlers. Later on, Imperia took a further step away from individuality by manufacturing Standard 'Vanguards' under licence.

Captain Marendaz's aircraft business in Bedfordshire was just getting under way, and the Cirrus-powered Marendaz Trainer was undergoing trials, when the war intervened. Afterwards he emigrated to South Africa, and when I met him in 1959 he had started a factory in Meyerton, Transvaal, for the manufacture of the first stationary diesel engines to be made anywhere in Africa.

The Maidenhead area also harboured other short-lived ventures, in addition to the products of the jam factory and the Heybourn cyclecar. There was the Payze, a conventional light car assembled at Cookham in 1921, but far more interesting was the 1½-litre Squire, which burst upon a startled world in September 1934.

Adrian Squire was a brilliant young draughtsman who had worked for M.G. at Abingdon, and is remembered there as a man who never turned out a crude job, even simple brackets being rendered with delightful precision on his drawing-board. Late in 1934 he formed the Squire Car Manufacturing Co. Ltd. at Henley to market a 1½-litre sports machine built to the highest possible standards and regardless of cost, as might be understood from the fact that a two-seater was listed at £1,195.

The engines were specially-built twin overhead-camshaft 69×100 mm. Anzanis, a Roots-type supercharger driven from the forward end of the crankshaft being used. This potent engine was mated with an E.N.V. pre-selector gearbox, and the standard top-gear ratio of 3·6:1. It gave 100 m.p.h. at only 4,300 r.p.m.; hence the startling performance. Ignition was by coil, and a large S.U. carburettor was used. A massive and low-built frame with extra-wide side-members was combined with long underslung semi-elliptic springs, and the powerful hydraulic brakes had fifteen-inch drums. The bodywork was not skimped, either, being undertaken mainly by Ranalah and Vanden Plas, though the lightweight two-seaters were built by Markhams of Reading.

As the firm had its headquarters in a small garage at the top of Remenham Hill, on the London road, space demanded that a certain amount of machining should be 'bought out', and Stuart Turner, the marine engine firm, undertook some of the work for Squire. Every car was supplied with a guarantee that it had lapped Brooklands at over 100 m.p.h.

Unfortunately, there were snags. The production of such a design needed more resources than the company possessed, and even the ranks of the connoisseurs included few purchasers in 1935 who were prepared to expend four figures on a 1½-litre car, however superb the workmanship. Even a steady reduction of prices could not save the day, though by mid-1936 a Squire two-seater could be bought for a mere £795. Also, the brakes were almost too powerful, and at least one car had to have a flitch-plate welded on to the frame. Luis Fontes' racing model retired from the 1935 B.R.D.C. 500-Mile Race with a cracked rear dumb-iron. The lighter cars also suffered from axle patter.

Nonetheless, the Squire deserved a better fate. Apart from Fontes' abortive Brooklands appearance, the late Duke of Grafton raced a stripped lightweight two-seater once or twice at Donington.

A production batch of twelve chassis was laid down, and when the company was wound up in July 1936 eight cars had been made—five short-chassis, two long-chassis, and one special racing car for Fontes. Also on the stocks was a 1,500 c.c. o.h.c. six-cylinder racing car, which Squire had designed with the intention of beating Frank Lockhart's 1½-litre Flying Mile record of 164 m.p.h. Only a few engine parts had been made at the time of liquidation, and it was allowed to die with the company. Adrian Squire went to work for the Bristol Aeroplane Co. Ltd., and was killed in an air raid in 1941.

Yet this was not the end of the story. Mr Val Zethrin of Chislehurst had bought a Squire in 1935, and was so impressed with its potential that he purchased the name, goodwill and spares a year later. He went further than that, and between 1937 and the outbreak of war completed two further Squires, a short-chassis Corsica drophead coupé and an open car which he bodied himself. After the war, the late Robert Arbuthnot planned to finance limited production of the *marque*, but this scheme fell through.

Undeterred, Mr Zethrin made up yet another short-chassis Squire, and as I write he is working on the twelfth car, 'but as I am designer, draughtsman, welder, turner and fitter, it takes time, and it goes so quickly,' he comments ruefully. There seems little doubt, though, that there will be a market ready across the Atlantic for as many Squires as Mr Zethrin can make, for in 1959 I heard of one of these fantastic thoroughbreds—one of three, incidentally, in America—changing hands for $8,000. I had a run in the ex-Duke of Grafton car in Cape Town in the winter of 1959, incidentally. Squire's departure from Henley coincided with the end of Marendaz Special Cars Ltd. But the last word, curiously enough, was left to Reichsmarschall Göring. Maidenhead, despite its proximity to London and the wartime importance of Air Transport Auxiliary's airfield at White Waltham, survived the war unscathed—save for one minor incident. On July 1, 1944, the peace of the riverside town was disturbed by one flying-bomb, which descended upon a converted Victorian mansion backing on to Cordwallis Works. Four families were rendered homeless, but Britain's jam ration remained intact. While we all know that no great measure of control over the V.1 was ever possible, it is hard to dismiss this as a coincidence. Had some boffin in the Wilhelmstrasse fallen behind hand with his intelligence, and conceived a violent fear of the design potential of the jam factory?

From *Lost Causes of Motoring*, 1960

PART FOUR

THE ROAD

The Last Miles into Brighton

BY C. G. HARPER

Landowners, farmers, and every lover of the natural beauty of the countryside all expressed dismay, indignation and even violence at the depredations caused by the coming of the railways, with their great incisions driving through hillside and woodland. Today, expedience has won overwhelmingly, and there is not a vocal Ruskin or Wordsworth in the land: only individual plaintive protests and demands for compensation. King Car has conquered more overwhelmingly than ever did the Regal Railroad. In America, Britain and the Continent of Europe the cry for greater highways—three-lane, four-lane, six-lane—rings without cessation.

But while the bulldozers and earth-removers carve out greater-than-ever motorways, thruways, autoroutes, autobahnen and autostrada, let us catch a passing glimpse of what one of the busiest roads in Britain must have been like nearly seventy years ago.

THIS ROUTE to Brighton is singularly rural and lovely, and particularly beautiful in the way of copses and wooded hollows, whence streamlets trickle away to join the river Adur. Villages lie shyly just off its course, and must be sought, only an occasional inn or smithy, or the lodge-gates of modern estates called into existence since the making of the road in 1813, breaking the solitude. The existence of Bolney itself is only hinted at by the pinnacles of its church tower peering over the topmost branches of distant trees. 'Bowlney', as the countryfolk pronounce the name, is worth a little detour for it is a compact, picturesque spot that might almost have been designed by an artist with a single thought for pictorial composition, so well do its trees, the houses, old and new, the church, and the 'Eight Bells' inn group for effect.

Down the road, rather over a mile distant from Bolney, and looking so remarkably picturesque from the highway that even the least preoccupied with antiquities must needs stop and admire, is Hickstead Place, a small but beautiful residence, the seat of Miss Davidson, dating from the time of Henry the Seventh, with a curious detached building in two floors, of the same or even somewhat earlier period, on the lawn; remarkable for the large vitrified bricks in its gables, worked into rough crosses and supposed to indicate a former use as a chapel. History, however, is silent on this point; but, as the inquirer may discover for himself, it now fulfils the twin offices of a studio and a lumber room. The parish church of Twineham, little more than a mile away, is of the same period, and built of similar materials. Hickstead Place has been in the same family for close upon four hundred years, and as an old house without much in the way of a history, and with its ancient features largely retained and adapted to modern domestic needs, is a striking example both of the continuity and the placidity of English life. The staircase walls are frescoed in a blue monochrome with sixteenth-century representations of field-sports and hunting scenes, very curious and interesting. The roof is covered with slabs of Horsham stone, and the oak entrance is original. Ancient yews, among them one clipped to resemble a bear sitting on his rump, give an air of distinction to the lawn, completed by a pair of eighteenth-century wrought-iron gates between red brick pillars.

Sayers Common is a modern hamlet, of a few scattered houses. Albourne lies away to the right. From here the Vale of Newtimber opens out and the South Downs rise grandly ahead. Noble trees, singly and in groups, grow plentiful; and where they are at their thickest, in the sheltered hollow of the hills, stands Newtimber Place, a noble mansion with Queen Anne front of red brick and flint, and an Elizabethan back, surrounded by a broad moat of clear water, formed by embanking the beginnings of a little stream that comes welling out of the chalky bosom of the hills. It is a rarely complete and beautiful scene.

Beyond it, above the woods where in spring the fluting blackbird sings of love and the delights of a mossy nest in the sheltered vale, rises Dale Hill, with its old toll-house. It was in the neighbouring Dale Vale that Tom Sayers, afterwards the unconquered champion of England, fought his first fight.

He was not, as often stated, an Irishman, but the son of a man descended from a thoroughly Sussexian stock. The name of Sayers is well known throughout Sussex, and in particular at Hand Cross, Burgess Hill, and Hurstpierpoint. There is even, as we have already seen, a Sayers Common on the road. Tom Sayers, however, was born at Brighton. He worked as a bricklayer at building the Preston Viaduct of the Brighton and Lewes Railway: that great viaduct which spans the Brighton Road as you enter the town. He retired in 1860, after his fight with Heenan, and when he died, in 1865, the reputation of prize-fighting died with him.

At the summit of Dale Hill stands Pyecombe, above the junction of roads, on the rounded shoulder of the downs. The little rubbly and flinty churches of Pyecombe, Patcham, Preston, and Clayton are very similar in appearance exteriorly and all are provided with identical towers finished off with a shingled spirelet of insignificant proportions. This little Norman Church, consisting of a tiny nave and chancel only, is chiefly interesting as possessing a triple chancel arch and an ancient font.

Over the chancel arch hangs a painting of the Royal Arms, painted in the

PYECOMBE: JUNCTION OF THE ROADS.

The last miles into Brighton—1906 and 1964

time of George the Third, faded and tawdry, with dandified unicorn and a gamboge lion, all teeth and mane, regarding the congregation on Sundays, and empty benches at other times, with the most amiable of grins. It is quite typical of Pyecombe that those old Royal Arms should still remain; for the place is what it was then, and then it doubtless was what it had been in the days of good Queen Anne, or even of Elizabeth, to go no further back. The grey tower tops the hill as it has done since the Middle Ages, the few cottages cluster about it as of yore, and only those who lived in those humble homes, or reared that church, are gone. Making the circuit of the church, I look upon the stone quoins and the bedded flints of those walls; and as I think how they remain, scarce grizzled by the weathering of countless storms, and how those builders are not merely gone, but are as forgotten as though they had never existed, I could have it in my heart to hate the insensate handiwork of man, to which he has given an existence: the unfeeling walls of stone and flint and mortar that can outlast him and the memory of him by, it may well be, a thousand years.

From Pyecombe we come through a cleft in the great chalk ridge of the South Downs into the country of the 'deans'. North and South of the Downs are two different countries—so different that if they were inhabited by two peoples and governed by two rulers and a frontier ran along the ridge, it would seem no strange thing. But both are England, and not merely England, but the same county of Sussex. It is a wooded, Wealden district of deep clay we have left, and a hungry, barren land of chalk we enter. But it is a sunny land, where the grassy shoulders of the mighty downs, looking southward, catch and retain the heat, and almost make you believe Brighton to be named from its bright and lively skies, and not from that very shadowy Anglo-Saxon saint, Brighthelm.

From *The Brighton Road* by C. G. Harper, 1906

The 'End-to-End' in '97

BY HENRY STURMEY

Some ten years before C. G. Harper wrote of the Brighton Road, one of the pioneers of motoring in Britain fulfilled his ambition by driving his new autocar from one end of the land to the other—from John o' Groat's to Land's End, in 1897. This epic journey, fraught with anxieties and troubles of every kind, from 'fired brake drums' on Kirkstone Pass to 'wild animals' in Carlisle, also included a number of other 'firsts' and records; including, claimed Sturmey, the longest distance traversed without replacement of radiator water.

It is possible to criticize the prose style. But this account of Sturmey's undertaking constitutes a unique record and impression of the pioneering loneliness experienced on the roads, and the self-reliance demanded of the crew when only an ostler or passing shepherd might be in the vicinity to give help. It is extracted from a series of articles Henry Sturmey wrote for The Autocar. *He does not specifically mention the make and model of his car, but evidence suggests it was a very early Coventry-Daimler with a 4 h.p. German engine.*

I HAD often thought I should like to go over the celebrated cyclists' record-breaking course, the longest straightaway journey possible in this country, viz., the route from Land's End to John o' Groat's, but, as years wore on, lack of condition mainly, as well as lack of time, prevented the accomplishment of the tour upon that popular means of progression—the bicycle. When, however, I became possessed of an autocar, the desire was still within me, and at the time of placing my order for my machine (now considerably over a year ago), I held some hazy notion that, if all went well, I might get a very original, enjoyable, and eventful journey out of a tour by autocar over the celebrated roadway.

When my car was promised for delivery early in May, I projected the pleasurable trip for some time in June, when, with lengthy days, the journey could be loitered over, and the camera dallied with *en route*, but, when time after time I was asked by the company to give up my turn for a motor to some other pressing customers (and being a director I could not do otherwise than comply), the prospect of making the trip last year appeared but an uncertain one. However, the car at last arrived, with my annual holiday yet untaken, and the prospect of a fine autumn, and, having by a few hundred miles' running satisfied myself that the car was all right, although the prospects of the tour did not strike me as being so enjoyable, I decided to

Nineteenth-century motoring: 1899 Canstatt-Daimler
Courtesy Montagu Motor Museum

make it forthwith, largely to prove the capability of my own vehicle, and through it the practical utility of autocars in general, and so, if possible, to remove in some degree the opinion which I felt to be largely held by the British public, that autocars were utterly unreliable things, which broke down, or exploded, or ran away, or did some other unexpected and undesirable thing about every five miles.

So I made my preparations forthwith. My original intention had been to tour down along the South Coast, and visit several relatives on the way, and to finish up the tour by running north from Land's End to John o' Groat's, this being the direction usually taken by the cyclist record breakers, and one which it struck me would be preferable, as I should then get the sun and most probably the greater part of the wind behind instead of in my face all the time, but, as the year had now drawn on, and I could not start before October 1st, had I adhered to my original plan, it would have been the commencement of November ere I reached the northernmost point. As I was not too desirous of striking snowstorms (which have been known to occur in the North quite as early as this), I decided to alter my plans, and start from the North. Naturally, as the journey would be one of some importance, and, as its success or failure would be likely materially to affect the prospects of the movement, I desired to take every precaution against failure. My usual driver knowing but little more about the machine than I did myself, I asked the loan of a man from the Daimler Co., and it was decided that my companion for the journey should be Richard Ashley, a young engineer, who, although not a driver, had been for some months engaged in the motor-testing shop of the company, and was consequently thoroughly competent to effect any repairs to either the motor or the machinery, should they become necessary. Just to get his hand in, he took a few lessons in driving a day or two before the start, so as to be competent to take a turn at the helm, should I so desire it, though I intended to drive and manage the car entirely myself. In order to prevent the possibility of delay should any parts give way, he got together and packed into the car duplicates of most of the attached pieces, such as a spare circulating pump, governor hammer, thrust pins, piston rings, band brake, floats and spindles, induction valves, burners, wicks, exhaust valves, and chain couplings, with a full supply of nuts, bolts, screws, washers, etc., and he spent the best part of the day previous to starting in getting together a collection of tools for his own use, should they be required, likewise taking a supply of asbestos grease, flour emery, oil, blacklead, lubricating grease, etc.

I also had, at Mr Ellis's suggestion, a 'devil' fitted beneath the car, said 'devil' being a long heavy rod, like a crowbar, pointed at the rear end, and hinged to underframe, which, whilst held up by a cord when not in use, could be let down on a steep incline, so that, should the car stop, it would dig into the ground, and prevent the vehicle running back. This was the only special alteration I had made to the car to fit it for the journey, but I also had four tanks made, each holding four gallons of petrol, and built so as to fit into the body of the carriage, two fitting under the back seat, and the other two, one on each side, immediately behind the two front seats. With these tanks full, as well as the running tank of the car, I filled up with twenty-one gallons of benzoline, and Ashley was sent forward on September 29th with the car by passenger train to Wick, which, some twenty miles from John o' Groat's, is the nearest point to that objective which could be reached by train. I arranged to go North myself from London, and join the car there on the 30th, giving Ashley instructions to overhaul the vehicle upon arrival, and inspect all the nuts, in case they should have been jarred loose by the vibration of the long train journey. For our personal comfort I carried three heavy waterproof rugs, three great coats, thick mufflers, fingerless gloves and an umbrella. In order that I might have a ready guide, I took the four volumes of the new Road Books of the Cyclists' Touring Club, although Mr G. P. Mills, the greatest of the cycle record breakers, had very kindly furnished me with his itinerary, hotel list, and notes on the road. As I should be traversing much country where an autocar had never been seen before, and I anticipated questions innumerable at every stop, I got what I called some 'save trouble cards' printed as follows:

111

What is it?

It is an autocar.
Some people call it a motor car.
It is worked by a petroleum motor.
The motor is of four horse-power.
It will run sixty miles with one charge of oil.
No! it can't explode—there is no boiler.
It can travel at fourteen miles an hour.
Ten to eleven is its average pace.
It can be started in two minutes.
There are eight ways of stopping it, so it can't run away.
It is steered with one hand.
Speed is mainly controlled by the foot.
It can be stopped in ten feet when travelling at full speed.
It carries four gallons of oil and sixteen gallons of water.
The water is to keep the engine cool.
It costs less than $\frac{3}{4}$d a mile to run.
The car can carry five people.
It can get up any ordinary hill.
It was built by the Daimler Motor Co. of Coventry,
And cost £370.
We have come from John o' Groat's House.
We are going to Land's End.
We are not record breaking, but touring for pleasure.

I arrived at Wick at 5.30 p.m., to find Ashley awaiting me, accompanied by the proprietor of the Station Hotel. I found the car had only reached Wick by the previous train. Everyone was very attentive, and the car had found accommodation in some stables near the hotel. I was required to clear the car at the station, and was somewhat horrified to be asked to pay £17 0s 6d, as carriage upon it, somewhere about £10 too much, in my estimation. By the time I had cleared up this matter, and ascertained that my baggage might arrive by the next train, due at 11 p.m., darkness was rapidly setting in, and the rain was descending. From the height of the station, Wick, with its few scattered lights and houses peering through the gathering mist, looked quite picturesque and interesting as I wended my way down to the Station Hotel, where I learnt that the one subject of conversation in the town was the arrival of the motor car. Ashley informed me that it was as much as he could do to get along, or to get at the car at all when he drove it down to the stables. My baggage did not arrive by the train expected, and Saturday morning (October 2nd), although dull, was fairly fine, with the sun trying hard to struggle through the clouds. Taking a stroll round the harbour before breakfast, I was much interested in the immense fishing fleet laid up, the fishing being over, and in the large trade done in dried fish. Ships and shipping and the fishing industry always have a great charm for me. As my baggage had not arrived, and there was no definite prospect of its appearance, I decided upon running out to John o' Groat's, and returning in the morning, and deciding my subsequent movements by the news as to the baggage, so bidding Ashley bring the car up at nine o'clock, we got away at 9.10, with a big crowd all across the street surrounding the car, and giving us a cheer as we moved off.

Leaving the town by a long steady rise, we had to halt a few minutes whilst a restive horse was taken up a side road for us to pass, and then away over a good broad road of an undulating character, but somewhat heavy with wet. The country was wild, bare, and comparatively uninteresting, but the most appeared to be made of it, for crofters' cottages and small farms were continuous almost the whole of the way, and one or two good-sized villages were passed through. The people appeared to have had some notification of our coming, for they were waiting, and gathered in knots at intervals throughout the route, giving a hearty cheer, and waving hats and handker-chiefs as we went by. We followed the telegraph wires, and had no difficulty in finding our way. After we had been running about ten miles the car began to steam, and Ashley (who was not used to car work) was very nervous about our water supply, although I assured him that he need not worry. So to satisfy him we halted and filled up with a couple of gallons from a roadside tap.

Shortly after, we sighted the new road making a short cut to John o' Groat's, but as my guide book described it as very steep and soft, I thought I would try the old road, and, following the road which ran round the hill, entailing a long steady ascent, we made good progress, though here I noticed some signs of the clutch slipping on the gradients. There are no hedges in these parts, and the cattle and horses in the fields were tethered with long ropes. As we passed, these mostly set off at a run, and found themselves pulled sharply up, but one or two horses snapped the rotten cords by which they were tied, and trotted off into the valleys below. Having got round the hill, we took an abrupt turn to the right, and, running mostly downhill, found ourselves heading straight to a large isolated house, which we took for John o' Groat's, but it turned out to be a farm, and another sharp turn to the right had to be taken. Just here a horse in a field close by broke its lariat, and went off at a great pace, and when we last saw it it was, like 'Charley's Aunt', still running. Then climbing up a steady incline, we caught sight of the pointed roof of the John o' Groat's Hotel, the road taking us nearly all round it. Finally striking a straight run in we rattled at a good pace down the somewhat steep incline towards it, our approach being greeted by some seven or eight persons standing around the flag-post waving their handkerchiefs in welcome, and, as we drew up to the doorway, the buxom landlady stepped forward and gave us a hearty 'Welcome to John o' Groat's'.

John o' Groat's is situated at a slight elevation from a low shelving shore, just beneath the hotel, a small jetty, providing a little harbour for boats, being carried out. In the distance the bare bleak-looking islands known as the Orkneys may be seen, and at the time of our visit several boats from the islands were lying at the jetty, and the islanders busily engaged in loading peat from the mainland. When I stepped out from the car, the sun came out from behind the clouds, and during our brief stay at the northernmost point in Great Britain favoured us by shining gently. My camera was quickly unlimbered, and several shots taken of the house and its surroundings.

The news of our intended arrival had spread, and, in addition to a few fisherman who strolled up, we found the local doctor and gamekeeper, and the inhabitants of the hotel, looking out for us. They were all much interested in the car, and after I took a shot of the car and the house, and getting the landlord to hold the camera for a photograph at the start with myself on board, which photograph, however, as I expected, was hopelessly blurred (few people but an expert can hold a hand camera properly), we got ready to make the actual commencement of our journey, having first, of course, duly entered our names in the visitors' book. As the gamekeeper was going our way, we gave him a lift, his dog likewise, so that we left John o' Groat's with four aboard. Our start was made exactly at noon after a stoppage of nearly an hour, and we sailed off in great style amidst the handkerchief-waving and plaudits of the little assemblage that had gathered round. We had not proceeded far, however, before in mounting the somewhat steep rise from the hotel we found the clutch slipping badly, so the car was stopped at once to enable us to readjust, an operation occupying some five or ten minutes. Then, taking the new road which rose considerably for over a mile, and took us over a high heather-covered hill, we enjoyed our compensating run down on the other side, and considerably edified our friend the game-keeper as to the pace an autocar can travel, leaving several cyclists who had at first essayed to follow far in the rear.

Ere long, we arrived at the domicile of our passenger, who, of course, insisted upon 'opening a bottle' of 'real Scotch'. Shortly after this we made another halt to change a lamp, as the car was travelling poorly. By this time it was raining, and, as we were facing the wind, extremely cold, and as Ashley had come away in a hurry without his overcoat, I wrapped him up in our third rug. The new lamp made a wonderful difference, and, travelling in fine style, we ran into Wick at 1.50. My luggage had not arrived, so there was nothing else to do but to wait in Wick till arrival of the evening train, by which it was expected. At John o' Groat's we had heard of a coaching party who had been there in the morning, though we had not encountered them on the road. This said coaching party turned up at dinner, and I was much amused by the remark of one of them, who enquired what the presence of the motor car at John o' Groat's meant, to which another promptly replied that he 'supposed it was an advertisement—Sunlight Soap, or something else of that kind,' which, whilst not flattering, showed that some people, at any rate, thought no one would use an autocar except for advertising purposes.

The next day was Sunday, and the morning opened gloriously, but by nine o'clock it was raining heavily. My luggage had not yet arrived, but I heard of its possible presence at Helmsdale. It could not, however, reach Wick until the evening, and I had either to wait in Wick all day for it, or start early and intercept it at Helmsdale. I decided to adopt the latter course, although I had intended leaving any travelling until the afternoon, so when, shortly after 10.30, the rain ceased, and the sun again made its appearance, we got everything on board, and, strapping the large Willesden canvas waterproof sheet, with which it had been covered up on its railway journey, over the back of the car, so as to cover in all the baggage, we started. The car ran splendidly, but the rain soon again made its appearance, and, as we ran, on a continuous rise, southwards skirting the sea, we could observe the gathering clouds, black and angry, collecting in great force around the hilltops towards which we were trending. It was a bleak open country through which we travelled, with very few houses, the road continuously rising until we were running upon the tops of the cliffs, with the sea far away below, just visible through the rain and mist.

Up here it was blowing a full gale, though the wind being west we were protected by the high hills under the lee of which we were running, until the road took a sudden turn to the right, crossed a bridge over a ravine, and took us clear of the protecting headland. We rounded the bend sharply, and ran into the wind. The rain cut like hail on our hands and faces, and the force of the blast nearly brought the car to a standstill. I only just dropped in the slow speed in time to pull through, and it was as much as I could do to see to steer. Then, down a sharp declivity from the summit of the bridge, and along a level exposed road we drove, the wind and rain beating with full force upon us. We had traversed about a mile when Ashley looked back and suddenly exclaimed, with dismay in every tone, 'We have lost the sheet!' Sure enough, our waterproof canvas covering, heavy as it was, had apparently been carried clean away, and as the rain had been descending in torrents all the time, our back cushion and baggage were soaked through.

'What shall we do?' said Ashley, and just as I was thinking of turning back to look for it, it occurred to me that it might not, after all, be left behind, so, said I, 'Look over the back of the car,' and there it was trailing from its rear fastenings in the mud.

Having made things fast and fairly snug once more, we trundled on to Latheron, long before reaching which place, however, even my boxcloth driving coat and our heavy waterproof knee wraps were soaked through. We were wet to the skin, and the cushions of our seats nothing more than pools of water. As the inn at Latheron did not appear to offer much accommodation for travellers, and none for the car, and as there was nothing to be gained by stopping, we thought we might as well go through with it, and take things as they came.

Latheron Hill, which the traveller enters upon after passing the inn, is an exceedingly dangerous one. The C.T.C. Route Book rightly advises caution in descending it, and Ashley had been warned of it at Wick, with the comforting assurance that several bicyclists had been killed upon it, so I kept the car well in hand from the commencement, and it is certain that any vehicle getting out of control would be doomed to destruction, for, after running very steeply down, the bottom of the hill finishes at a bridge, which crosses a ravine at nearly right angles to the road. As the bridge is narrow, and the parapets but a couple of feet or so in height, to topple over into the gully below would be the easiest thing possible. From the bridge the road turns equally sharply in the opposite direction, and a steep climb is encountered on the other side, which, however, gave us no trouble, and we soon ran down the long winding hill into Dunbeath. Out of this place there is a very steep climb for about half a mile, the little village itself lying at the head of a creek, and the road climbing up the side of the valley to the top of the cliffs again. However, we got up without any difficulty and, the car driving splendidly, we made good pace up the long continuous rise which followed, at the summit of which, however, the motor got a fit of the glows, and at the same time our clutch commenced to slip, probably through the wet getting in, owing to the sodden roads and the soaking rain we were experiencing. As it slipped so badly that progress became very tedious, we sought what little shelter a low hedge afforded and readjusted it, and at the same time applied a good coating of resin, with satisfactory results. Shortly after, the rain ceased, and as we descended the steep and winding hill into Berriedale the sun once more favoured us with his attentions.

Berriedale Hill is an extremely awkward one. It is very long, and in places very steep and winding. At the very worst bit of all, however, the road takes a turn sharper than a right angle, with a precipice of one hundred feet or so to drop over if one overshoots the mark. Needless to say, both brakes were requisitioned, but we got down without difficulty, though I 'had my doubts' all the way till we were there, and then commenced to ascend the other side, getting beautiful peeps of the Berriedale valley, with its magnificent autumn-tinted foliage, from time to time through the trees which line the road. As the sun was now shining gloriously, and everything looking beautiful and fresh after the rain, it was most enjoyable.

This hill out of Berriedale was the steepest I had yet encountered, the gradient being given as one in nine. It leads up from the Berriedale valley, which is very little above the level of the sea, to the top of the Ord of Caithness. We had not proceeded far when the motor stopped, and I dropped the 'devil' and got speed up again. Then was made another start, to be followed almost immediately by another stoppage. The cause of the stoppages, however, was, by the failure of the lamps, discovered to be lack of oil, Ashley (not being used to car work) having been afraid to fill the tank too full, and I may here say that the gauze protector to the opening of the running tank, which cannot be removed, makes it very difficult to know when the tank is full, save by intuition.

After replenishing the oil supplies from our reserve store, we made another start, and then went gaily up without a hitch, the motor 'cutting out' all the way. The road over the Ord of Caithness is bare and bleak, and, as the machinery was grinding and making a lot of trouble over it although the road was level, we called another halt, dosed the chains with heavy lubricant, and gave a general oil-up all round, after which things greatly improved, and then we commenced a descent of something like seven miles from the top of the Ord into Helmsdale. This is long and winding, with several very sharp and awkward turns, so that the car had to be kept well in hand at all points. At one place I nearly made a hash of it. Running down one side of a gulch, we crossed a little bridge, at what appeared to be the bottom of the hill, and, as the road looked like rising on the other side, when we got round the bend I took off the brakes, but, in an instant, the car was shooting away at twenty to the hour. Ashley quickly slipped the rug off his legs, ready to jump, if occasion required, but I as quickly had the brakes on again, and the car well in hand in the next fifty yards; and the Commercial Hotel, Helmsdale, was reached at 4.10, the distance for the day being thirty-eight miles.

Our friends of the coaching party who had travelled to Berriedale the previous day turned up an hour later. As we were both wet through, Ashley went off to get into dry clothes, but, as I was not expecting my baggage to arrive till six o'clock, I lined myself with newspapers, and, as that hour approached, strolled up to the station to make enquiries, and found my bag had been quietly awaiting me there all the time. However, as I had already got outside a good meal, and the little hotel was the reverse of exciting, I went to bed and stayed there, after seeing that all our things were given as much drying as it was possible for them to get. . . .

. . . I may here remark that there is nothing in the world that I know of so effective for inducing sleep as a good day's ride at speed through the mountain air on an autocar. It was not that I was tired, but I was just sleepy, and I found throughout the tour that, by the time I had had dinner, and written up my notes and an odd letter or two, I was pretty well in the land of nod without any further trouble.

Thursday morning was very fresh and beautifully fine, and, as the morning mists cleared away, the run out of Pitlochry was greatly enjoyed. We soon found ourselves climbing steadily long rilling hills, through magnificent scenery of distant valleys and thick beech woods, with pheasants, partridges, rabbits, squirrels, and any amount of small life, frequently presenting themselves as the hum of our motor awoke the silent echoes. Edinburgh was to be our destination for the day, and overnight I had looked up the timetable of the ferry-boats, and found that there was no boat between 3.20 and 6.30, so I decided to make a dash through to catch the earlier one. The fine scenery continued to Dunkeld, which was beautifully situated on the banks of the Tay, and here I stopped the car in the centre of the bridge, and took a couple of hurried snap shots at the scenery on either side. Shortly we were climbing another long gradient, the road winding through Birnam Wood and Pass, the splendid trees beneath which we travelled being brilliant in all their autumn colouring, but the roads, though fine in surface, were somewhat sticky with wet under them.

After running over some considerably high ground, we ran down over a well-graded road for some miles into Perth, the entrance to the city being along a fine broad road, upon which we encountered numerous flocks of sheep and cattle, for which we had to be continually slowing down. As we had no intention of stopping anywhere for lunch, but wished to go right through, we stopped a couple of miles out of the city, and filled up our oil-tank, and then, driving straight through, we commenced a long steady climb on the other side over a broad road with a finely-graded smooth surface, the view of 'the fair city', as we looked down upon it from the gradually increasing heights, being very striking, and fully justifying the name which has been accorded it.

From this the country considerably altered in its aspect, being of a very ordinary character to Kinross, and then for some miles the road (taking us through the small mining village of Cowdenbeath) was simply vile. I had to keep the speed gear down a point to save our springs in many places, and at two or three spots railway lines crossed the road at right angles, and in very bad condition, so that the utmost care had to be taken in driving. We were now running through a much more populated country, and it was amusing to see the people in the villages as we passed through rushing into their houses to fetch out their friends, who usually made their appearance at the door just as we vanished round the corner. Half the population turned out at Cowdenbeath to watch us climb the steep little hill through the village, and when we got fairly clear of this place after another climb, we had a big double drop down into Burntisland, having run the fifty-nine and a half miles without a stop (save to replenish our oil supply) in five and a half hours. I found we were twenty minutes ahead of our time, so I was able comfortably to look round and get my ticket for the boat. The clerk in the ticket office was very quick to sum up the situation. 'A motor car,' said he,

'Yes.' 'That will be a four-wheeled carriage without a horse,' and he charged accordingly.

The ferryboat soon drew up, and then I had rather a novel experience, for, after taking the car down a steep and very rough incline to the ship, I waited for them to put out gangways, but they simply said: 'Come along; it's all right,' so I had to drive straight off the quay on to the deck, which was done without any trouble. Coming off again, however, on the other side was not quite so easy, the car having to make a drop of about six inches, which gave the springs, metaphorically speaking, 'beans', and then the run into Edinburgh, all uphill, was made in half an hour. The last half-mile was exceedingly steep—in fact, one of the steepest roads of the journey, the ascent finishing with Pitt Street, which is granite-setted throughout. However, the car went steadily at it, and took us straight up without any trouble at all, though I confess to having had my doubts as to how we should get on when I saw the gradient we were tackling.

Running down from the top of Pitt Street, I was soon in Princes Street, and promptly made my way to the General Post Office. Through the traffic the surrounding noise entirely drowned the sound of the motor, which was quite disconcerting, as, not being able to hear the motor, I kept thinking it was not working properly. At the Post Office the crowd that assembled was one of the largest I have seen, and when I came out I found the car the centre of a seething mass of population, stretching right across the broad pavement to the Post Office itself, and three parts of the way across the road. I think the policeman in charge of the traffic at that point was very glad when I turned round and rolled off in the opposite direction. Right down Princes Street we ran through the traffic, the horses taking very little notice of us indeed, and, after dropping my luggage at the Palace Hotel, I ran up to the North British Rubber Co.'s factory, where, owing to the kindness of my friends there, I found a fresh supply of petrol awaiting me. The sound of the motor quickly attracted the hands in the rubber mill, and when I took Mr Stuart, the manager, for a run up and down the extensive yard between the mills, some hundreds of the hands had left their work and come to look on, so that I fancy those in charge were not sorry when I took my departure. Mr Stuart was much struck with the almost new condition of my tyres, after the work they had done, and, needless to say, was pleased thereat, they having been supplied by his firm.

Ashley all this time was getting very nervous as to the amount of oil in our tank, for we had emptied the last drop in our cans into the running tank, and he was very fearful lest we should run out of oil before we got the car stored for the night, 'For, of course,' he said, 'everyone would say at once it was a "breakdown", if we had to stop to refill in the middle of the town.' However, by my own calculations of quantity, I thought we should just about do it, and so we did, but when Ashley came to empty the tank, which

I told him to do before refilling, he found barely half a pint left, and half of that was water, so we had run it very close. We had used just twenty-six gallons of petrol from Wick and John o' Groat's to Edinburgh. Another point worthy of note is that the whole day's run from Pitlochrie, sixty-five and a half miles, had been done with one supply of cooling water. This is, I believe, the longest distance which has yet been done without a fresh supply, and the knowledge of what we could do upon occasion kept our minds easy for the rest of the tour. I considered I was mighty lucky to get such a lengthy run in Scotland without rain, and, as I had had quite enough of getting a soaking, I ran up the next morning to the depot of the North British Rubber Co. in Princes Street, and bought a couple of heavy mackintosh capes deep enough to hang well down over the backs of the seats, behind, and to fall well over the knee rugs in front. Then, taking up the manager, in company with a reader of *The Autocar*, who had signified his desire for a ride, I ran up Princes Street again to the Post Office, and there received a light mackintosh cover, which I had had made, but which was not ready in time for me to take with me. This was D-shaped, and so arranged as to strap over the entire back part of the car, the front edge strapping to and overlapping the backs of the front seats, thus converting the entire back of the car into a covered receptacle, beneath which all our baggage, coats, and other impedimenta could rest, free from both rain and dust. With this and the capes I felt ready for anything, even another passage over the Ord in a storm.

As on the previous day, enormous crowds gathered around the car at the Post Office. Amongst them one of our passengers espied one of the city fathers, and Mr Councillor —— was given a seat, the car with the luggage being by this time pretty well full. We rattled down Princes Street in fine style, and then, putting down two of our three passengers, we followed the tramlines over the roughly-paved Morningside Road, and had a three miles climb up a hill which required the first speed the greater part of the way, and which gave us a magnificent view of the country when we arrived at the top. A fine run down on the other side was spoiled by the presence of a lot of new metal, and then we put down our remaining passenger, and, as it looked threatening, fitted on the waterproof cover to the back of the car, and donned our capes, and had scarcely done so and got under way again ere the rain came down in torrents, and we quickly found the benefit of them. For several miles the road continued to climb with undulations, and the roads soon became exceedingly heavy with the wet. We had not travelled far before the car slowed down, and an investigation showed that one of the lamps required attention. It was quickly changed, and a few miles further on, finding our speed again diminishing, we saw that the other lamp had given out, and this also was replaced by the remaining spare one, Ashley remarking that, if we had any trouble at all, it seemed to come with the wet weather. However, although these incidents delayed us in all some twenty minutes, including the slow travelling before we made the changes, when they had been attended to, the motor ran beautifully, and we arrived at Biggar rather late for dinner, the twenty-nine miles having taken three and a half hours.

After filling up with oil and water, and refreshing the inner man (which we did without delay), we got away in glorious sunshine, the storms of the morning having entirely cleared off, and we enjoyed a fine run downhill to Abington. Through this village the road was exceedingly bad and heavy, so much so indeed that, for the greater part of the distance, the second speed had to be resorted to. Once through the village, however, things considerably improved, and we soon found the road steadily rising, but not to such an extent as to necessitate either of the slow speeds. This continued for five or six miles, the country gradually getting wilder and bleaker, until in the middle of a wild expanse, with a steep hill rising on each side, we came to a stop for want of oil, and, whilst we were replenishing our tank, a shepherd found his way across the fields, and informed me that we had stopped at Beattock Summit, seven hundred feet above the sea, and almost exactly opposite the source of the Clyde. This proved to be the top of the hill, and we were soon bowling down the gradients of the other side at top speed in fine style— indeed, for the next twenty-five miles I only had to shift the speed lever four or five times. The road for the most part, and for about ten miles, was all downhill, following closely the course of a tumbling rocky mountain stream.

At first I thought I would make for Moffat, which lay a little to the left off the main road, and where I knew I could get good accommodation, but, as the car was running in such fine style, and everything being so much in our favour, I decided to go on and endeavour to get diggings at Beattock Bridge. However, when I arrived here, it was to discover that Beattock Bridge meant Beattock Bridge, and nothing else, so far, at any rate, as I could discover in the gathering gloom, so there was nothing for it but to go on another eight or ten miles to Lockerbie. As it was not quite dark, we lit the lamps, and sped on. Shortly the moon rose, and, under the light of the orb of night, and over a road for the most part broad and slightly undulating, mile after mile we flew in fine style. Scarcely anything in the way of vehicles or foot passengers was encountered, though I had a narrow shave of a collision with a two-wheeled trap, the driver coming along without lights in the gloom. As I could only see the horse with the figure of the man immediately above, it looked for all the world like a man riding, so that, keeping my course in the middle of the road, I was within an ace of taking his wheel off, only just perceiving its existence in time to get clear with a mighty swerve. However, a miss is as good as a mile, and nothing beyond a momentary scare resulted. Needless to say, I 'said things' as he vanished into the darkness in our rear. We ran into Lockerbie shortly before seven amidst a yelling crowd of juveniles and hobbledehoys, who, with their shrieks and gesticulations, reminded us more of a pack of savages than civilized beings.

The sound of the horn seemed particularly to strike their fancy, and for an hour after all was stowed away for the night, I could hear them outside yelling 'Ach-ach, ach-ach-ach' to each other in imitation thereof. The forty-seven miles from Biggar were accomplished in under four hours, and the day's run brought up to seventy-six miles.

Saturday opened gloriously fine, and it was splendid travelling in the clear crisp air of the early morning. Once clear of the town the roads proved a continuation of the excellent running of the previous day—broad, undulating and in fine condition, through a rolling agricultural country. No hills were met with to necessitate first speed, and we were not long in running through Gretna Green, and, crossing the little bridge which marks the border line between Scotland and England, we were soon heading for Carlisle in splendid style. Soon, far below on the right, was seen the broad expanse of sunlit waters of the Solway Firth, the road taking us round the head of it. When we got within a couple of miles of Carlisle we ran into a small village with an exceedingly wide street—indeed, it could not have been far short of fifty yards in width. As we drew out of the main road into the more open ground, Ashley caught sight of a two-wheeled brewer's dray loaded up with beer barrels, the horse in which showed signs of uneasiness, and I promptly stopped whilst yet some sixty yards away from it. The vehicle was standing outside a public house, and, as frequently happened, there was no one in charge. The stoppage of the car, however, made no difference to the horse, which very quietly and deliberately turned right round, and then, having once got straight with its back in our direction, started off down the road as hard as it could go. As there were a number of children playing about in the street we were fearful of a mishap, but, luckily, the horse took a course which cleared them all. Soon the driver appeared in a state of considerable excitement, and started running up the road after his horse, we following slowly after, and rating him soundly for 'leaving wild animals unattended on the highway', his reply being that he 'could not get his book signed' for delivery without leaving it, to which we retorted that if the company *must* use wild animals they should send someone to look after them. A quarter of a mile farther on we came up with the runaway, which had been stopped by some men in charge of some brick carts, and we were soon going full speed ahead again for Carlisle.

As we entered this town facing a good stiff breeze, a young fellow of the dude order, whilst yet ten yards in front of us, lifted his nose with a lordly sniff of affected disgust, whereat I felt inclined to get out and kick him, as it was an absolute impossibility for a sniff of the petrol to reach him where he stood. Beyond a short visit to the G.P.O. to wire the news of my arrival in England, we made no stay in Carlisle, but pushed on for Penrith, encountering fine broad roads the whole way, with, however, a few fairly steep gradients following each other in quick succession. As we progressed, the full panorama of the Westmorland Hills opened out on our right, the mountain peaks standing up in a group for all the world like the points of a ducal coronet, whilst the effect of the heavy clouds massing around their tops was grand in the extreme. Penrith and the George Hotel were reached in good time for lunch, the forty-two miles having been accomplished in three hours forty minutes. Of course, there was the usual crowd, and the stable yard of the hotel was soon besieged. The sight of the Westmorland Hills on the way down attracted me, and finding by the road book that I should only be making another ten miles of it, I thought it would not be at all a bad idea to take a peep at the Lake District and spend Sunday there. So, instead of crossing Shap Fell and going straight to Kendal, I turned off to the right and made for Ullswater.

The run was a fine one and with numerous ups and downs, but I met with nothing of a difficult nature, which made me for the nonce somewhat sceptical of the steepness of the Lake District inclines of which I had heard so much. Arrived at Ullswater I took a photograph or two, and then found an excellent and perfectly level, though very narrow, road skirting the lake, giving magnificent peeps of water, wood, and mountain at every turn, the dark cloud-topped purple hills overhanging the lake being particularly fine and the effect of the varied colouring with reflections in the still waters below exquisite. After running a couple of miles or so we suddenly met a young woman with a cartload of youngsters—some seven or eight wee children in a small pony cart drawn by a diminutive specimen of the equine race, but, for all his diminutive size, he proved a stiff nut to crack, and although I stopped he absolutely refused to be comforted. Whilst the young woman hauled the youngsters out and placed them in safety on the bank, Ashley endeavoured to coax the animal by, but it was no use, and I had to stop the motor before he could be induced to proceed. A mile or so farther on another short stop was made to oil the pump, which was not throwing water so rapidly as could be wished, and then running round the head of the lake we had a very steep climb over a sharp projecting spur of rock, which came near stopping the car, but did not. Then, bearing away to the right over a narrow and exceedingly winding roadway, I suddenly perceived in front the long zigzag ascent of the Kirkstone Pass, which, judging by the road book, I had thought I was missing by the route taken.

However, there was nothing for it but to go straight ahead and see what the car could do, so at it we went, and soon found ourselves on the first speed. For a quarter of a mile the motor cut out at every few revolutions, but the road gradually became steeper, and the laborious beating of the motor slower and more irregular. Just then a carriage descending necessitated a halt, as the horse was restive, and the occupants afeared, and we had to stop the motor before the beast was pacified. When we got under way again the road continued to increase in steepness, and also at this point became very loose, several patches of newly-laid metal being encountered. I negotiated these by running the wheels on one side of the car upon the narrow strip of hard road at the side, but after a few more turns of the road had been passed, both Ashley and myself found it advisable to dismount, and I walked by the side of the car, steering from the ground. Then upon another patch of loose metal she stopped, and the devil sank in until it was nearly vertical. We got the engine going again, and made another start, I steered as before and Ashley behind keeping his eye on the devil. A slow, tortuous progress was thus made, dodging the newly-laid metal, and keeping one wheel in the gutter all the time to do so. Twice we had to stop to let the motor get up speed again, and then on the very steepest bend of the hill on a patch of recently laid stones, completely covering the entire surface, without a single inch of hard ground anywhere, we came to a stoppage again. Just then a shepherd, coming down from the hills above, was met, so as the patch was not above thirty yards in length, I got the engine going again, and with Ashley and the shepherd shoving up behind, made another start. I had just pulled through the loose stuff, after which, for another hundred yards the car took herself along, and then first myself and then Ashley climbed in, and we found ourselves safely at the top of the pass, 1,050 feet above the sea.

The gradient is given as one in eight, and I think *with a hard surface* the car would just have done it without any stoppages, or without the necessity of dismounting, but the soft and loose road surface made all the difference. Then we ran on until the 'highest inhabited house in England' was encountered a quarter of a mile farther on, and, enquiring the way to Ambleside, I was told I could go either straight ahead or by the shorter road turning to the right down the hill. So far as I could see, both roads looked much on a par for steepness, and certainly the short cut looked awkward enough for anything. We could see it going straight down the hillside, zigzagging between stone walls for over a mile, and with a gradient which has been given as one in eight, but which certainly looked much more like one in six, and I fancy must exceed the gradient given.

Ashley was doubtful about negotiating it, but as we had to get down somehow, I thought I might just as well try this road as any other, so I brought the car to a standstill on the edge, and then, with both brakes half on, allowed her just to drop over, bringing my cycling experience into play, and keeping her in hand from the start. We descended very cautiously for a hundred yards, and then Ashley asked if I had both brakes hard on, to which I replied, 'No! Only half on, and I can stop any minute.' To prove the correctness of my assertion I did so, and again proceeded, much reassured by the incident. Steadily and slowly we crawled down the hill until seven-eighths of the journey had been completed. Just as we turned the last zig-zag, and there only remained a couple of hundred yards of perfectly straight road in front of us, I suddenly felt the car moving on. Both brakes were promptly clapped on full, but in an instant we were bounding away at thirty to the hour, and I grasped the fact that the car had run away. I took the situation in at a glance, and seeing that the foot of the hill was followed by a short stiff ascent, I felt that all I had to do (as there was nothing in the road) was to steer a straight course, so, jamming both brakes on with all my force (though they appeared to have about as much effect as water on a duck's back), I set my teeth and, gripping the steering handle, steered a dead course in as near a bee line as possible with the result anticipated, and the car pulled up on the opposite slope.

Then came a mile of undulating road, to be followed, as I remembered from the road book description of the route, by another descent as long and as bad as the first. It was this that began to worry me—'How should we get down it?' However, when we reached it I drew the car up and just allowed it to drop over the top, clapping both brakes on at the same time. Directly I did so, however, and the car commenced to feel the incline, I felt it begin to 'slide', and, knowing that there was not a moment to be lost, and there happening to be at this particular spot, instead of the stone wall which lined the rest of the road, a steep sloping bank, I sang out to Ashley, 'Look out. I am going to run her up the bank,' and promptly did so, and, as we had no great speed at the time, without mishap.

Then came the puzzle, 'What's to be done now?' and we set to work to investigate the cause of the runaway. At first I thought the brake-band had broken, but when Ashley got at it he found the brake-drum had fired, and was nearly red hot. By means of some spare nuts he tightened up the brake-band as far as it was possible to do, but I was not by any means satisfied with that, for I knew perfectly well that on a really steep gradient the tyre brakes were of but little use. It also occurred to me that if the firing of the drum was the cause of the runaway, the tightening of the band might have but little effect, so, as we happened to have a packet of powdered resin with us, which we had brought in case of any slipping of the clutch, I put about a tablespoonful of it on. It ran at once like water, and formed a paste around the drum, Ashley opining that it would be of little use, as in that condition it would only last a few minutes. 'Anyway,' said I, 'if it lasts to the bottom of the hill it is all I want,' and we made another start, carefully manoeuvring the machine down off the bank. I told Ashley to walk, so as not to have any more weight on the car than was necessary, and proceeded slowly with the hand brake on. Directly the car commenced to gather speed and got beyond a two-mile pace I applied the foot brake, with the result that the car was brought up standing with a jerk, and refused to budge an inch. Then I had to fairly kick the brake off while Ashley shoved for all he was worth to start the car down the hill—he having screwed up the brake-band so tight as to throw the clutch out of gear altogether, we could not use the motor for starting. However, the shoving was effective when the brake shook free, and we started again, only to be pulled up with a jump directly I applied the brake, and repeating this operation at intervals we found our selves at last safely at the bottom, or nearly so.

It was now quite dark, and we could see a few lights below, so we stopped to light our lamps and release the brake-band a little, so as to allow the driving clutch to work, the while three or four pedestrians made their appearance out of the darkness. 'How far am I from Ambleside?' said I, thinking I must now be pretty close, to which I got the somewhat disconcerting response of 'About eleven miles.' I had no desire to travel eleven miles over unknown roads in the dark in the Lake District after the foregoing experience of them, so as I was informed there was such a thing as an hotel 'below', as soon as we got going again I made for it, to find that I was in Ambleside after all, and in a very few minutes we ran into the extensive covered coachyard at the rear of the Salutation Hotel. Here we were immediately surrounded by a host of men of a 'hossy' character, but no one came forward as in charge of the place, while the noise of the motor and the people around—who appeared anything but friendly disposed—beneath the covered roof, coupled with the surrounding inky darkness, made things somewhat confusing, so as soon as I stopped the motor I enquired, 'Now where's the ostler?'

At first, no one spoke, but then a man came forward. 'Will the car be all right here?' I asked, but his reply was not very reassuring, and I heard around me muttered expression of dissent at my 'bringing a thing like that *without horses* here for,' so that altogether things did not look very promising for the safety of the car and my belongings. However, I was too pleased to be once again in something approaching safe quarters to trouble much about that, though Ashley was considerably perturbed at his surroundings, and didn't at all like leaving the car to their tender mercies. Upon enquiry I found that the Salutation Hotel was closed for the winter, so I had to make my way to the Queen's, an adjacent one in the same proprietary. I was assured that the car would be all right, so, taking the Boots with me, I packed him and Ashley off with our movable belongings, and left the car where it was for the night.

The twenty-four miles from Penrith had occupied three hours and twenty minutes, bringing the day's journey up to sixty-six miles. This day proved, without a doubt, by far the most eventful of the tour. When I got fairly into the hotel I breathed freely once more, for the descent of the last gradient had certainly been considerably trying to the nerves. I never before thoroughly appreciated what 'breathing free' meant. When next morning I found a leaden sky, a full gale bending the trees on the hillsides and rushing between their tops, and the rain descending in blinding sheets, I was by no means averse to staying where I was, attending service in the picturesquely-situated church, where the Archbishop of Cape Town was officiating for the day. The season was practically over, but there were one or two visitors staying at the hotel, and with one of these I chummed up, and when evening came, with a clearing away of the clouds and a brilliant moon, accompanied him on a walk to Rydal Water, very beautiful in the moonlight, taking also a peep at Wordsworth's seat and house *en route*.

Ashley occupied the best part of the morning in putting the adjustments of the car to rights, and cleaning off the resin which we had put upon the brake-drum. It took him over two hours to get this clean, and for some days after, it made its presence felt by the suddenness of our stoppage when the brake was applied at all quickly. I had thought that the wooden lining of the brake-band would have been destroyed, and that we should have required to have fitted our spare band, but this was not so, the wood being only hardened and slightly blackened by the heat, so that a readjustment only was necessary. The metal brake blocks of the tyre brakes, however, had suffered considerably in the lightning spin downhill, both being worn quite through at the thinnest part of their sides. The incident impressed me with the fact that for perfect safety a third brake is decidedly a necessity in really hilly country, and I may note that both driving wheels of my cars were provided with brake rings, but I had not had them fitted, as I thought they would not be wanted. Had I done so, I should have sailed comfortably down without any trouble, as I should have had the third and most powerful brake to fall back on.

Monday morning opened dull and showery, though, as luck would have it, we missed most of the showers during the day. Not knowing what I had before me in the way of hills, and being desirous of reaching Preston early enough to take fresh petrol supplies on board in daylight, I started early over wet, heavy, and in places somewhat slippery, roads. Running down through the streets of Ambleside, we were soon travelling by Windermere, the lake looking dull and gloomy with a cold wind sweeping over its surface, accompanied by banks of misty rain. We did not, however, run along far by the side of the water, but were soon climbing up through Windermere, passing the station *en route*. This is a steep climb towards the top, and the motor had to 'do her prettiest' to get there, but she did it, and then we had an undulating road with several fairly steep climbs to Kendal, upon entering which place another adventure befell us. A horse attached to a light four-wheeled railway lorry, left unattended outside a shop, started up the hill into the town for all it was worth, and, as this said hill was crowded with traffic of various kinds, I feared an accident. I had not gone far before I saw a dark object dash at the horse's head and roll under the wheels, and I thought for the moment that someone had tried to stop it and been thrown, but it turned out to be a coal sack thrown at the animal, which only had the effect of frightening it the more, and causing it to swerve, when off came one of the fore-wheels. Still, this did not check its career, for it vanished into the crowded and very narrow centre street of the town at the top. When I came up to this spot, I saw the office of the local journal on the right, so pulled up, and went in and had a chat with the editor to explain the incident. Ashley, in the meantime, became the centre of a crowd which just about filled up the little street. I was pleased to find that the runaway met with proper appreciation, the policeman at the central point informing Ashley that 'it was his own fault'. When we moved off, another hundred yards farther on, we passed the wreck of the lorry minus both its front wheels.

With the motor running at its best, and the weather improving as we got away from the hills, though traversing country possessing but little interest, we ran into Lancaster in time for lunch, just entering the town as all the operatives were leaving the factories, and finding ourselves again the centre of attraction as we dropped into line with the traffic, and crawled through the narrow tortuous streets. Leaving the main road, we struck away to the right, and made for the railway station, adjoining which is the County Hotel, the accommodation provided at which, both for car and man, was excellent.

From Lancaster onwards the roads deteriorated considerably, the method of repair adopted in the district being about the most unscientific that could be imagined. I frequently had to slow down the car to prevent being bumped quite to little pieces. Through Garstang and on to Preston the country remained uninteresting, the constant evidence of manufactories, and the extremely monotonous nature of the country being rather depressing than otherwise. However, we made good time into Preston, and got in about four o'clock, making a run of fifty-seven miles for the day.

After securing rooms, and leaving our belongings at the Castle Hotel, we motored down to Messrs Coulthards, who had very kindly consented to secure a supply of petrol for me, and here, whilst Ashley filled up all our reserve drums, as well as the running tank of the car, I had a very interesting run round their works, and saw the new oil-fired steam goods waggon put through its paces, as well as some of the machinery and parts of vehicles which the firm were building for Pennington-motored carriages for use in Western Australia.

Tuesday was a glorious morning, and, being desirous of getting as far on the road as I could, I started early. I may here say that I had arranged to attend an important meeting in London on Thursday, and this fixture had throughout the tour hung upon me like a nightmare, and I missed lingering upon many bits of beautiful scenery in Scotland and elsewhere, for fear of landing myself by Wednesday night at a point too far away from town to be comfortably or conveniently reached, so we started from Preston at 8.45, going slowly over the rough sets through the town, and making many stops for objecting horses, for I always make it a rule to drive with the utmost caution, and to slow up as every horse is approached, so as to be ready to stop completely if any nervousness or fear is shown. Fair running was encountered to Wigan, the bad sets through which town necessitated slow progress with much bumping, and similarly unpleasant travelling carried us through Warrington, after which the road improved considerably.

I was making for Tarporley for lunch, the motor running splendidly the whole of the time, until on the last hill before the drop down into the town we came to a stop, and found ourselves out of oil just half a mile from our destination. This was soon remedied, and we filled up the running tank here, instead of at the hotel, and then dropped gently down to the Swan, losing as little time as possible over lunch, and getting away again within half an hour of our arrival.

On leaving the town, Ashley noticed something flying round with the wheel, and I stopped the car, to find that one of the worn brake blocks had sliced a long, thin shaving of rubber off the tyre. This was promptly removed, and I wired to the makers to send on a pair of new blocks to meet me at Gloucester, and took care not to use the tyre brakes more than was absolutely necessary until I got there.

Throughout Cheshire I found the roads excellent in surface, well engineered, and possessing the best signposts encountered in the whole of my journey, whilst the milestones, too, were looked after in first-class fashion, although these might be coloured differently to advantage, it being difficult to read the lettering with the present colouring. Perhaps the Cheshire County Council, who I know are taking a very practical interest in doing their work thoroughly, will make a note of this. We were not long in running beneath the towering heights of Beeston Castle, and then enjoyed a fine run towards Whitchurch, making splendid progress all the time over very good country until we were pulled up by the stoppage of the pump. Ashley made no mistake this time, but, after we had backed the car into the ditch, so as to throw the front higher than the back, and thus bring the pump above the water level, got straight to work, and the clearing of the valves and lubrication was soon done. We then ran the car in a circle, and reversed its position, so that the back was higher than the front, and the pump was soon working the circulation in the best possible style.

A little after this we took a wrong turn (the first of the tour), going to the left, instead of the right at a V-road on a common, and ran through fine pine woods over splendid roads, passing a racecourse on our right before we discovered our error. However, I preferred not to return the way I had come, but took the first turn to the right that I encountered, and, as I expected, at the expense of a couple of miles extra running, found myself once again on the main road for the very pretty and quaintly-rustic little town of Hodnet. After one small adventure with a startled pony, which went off at full speed in front of us until its driver was able to turn it into a side road, we ran with our lamps alight over good and winding roads, giving top-speed running most of the way to Wellington, the tall Wrekin, frowning over the town, just making its appearance through the darkness. We ran into the Wrekin Hotel at 7 p.m., having accomplished the run of eighty-six miles (the longest day's trip of the tour) in a shade under eight hours' travelling time. Of course, there was a crowd, and everyone was talking about the motor car, which was the first that had been seen in the district. In the evening, after dinner, I went for a short stroll through the quaint old streets, and suddenly became aware of the fact that I was an object of particular interest to two small boys, who I discovered to be following me with open awe-struck eyes, they evidently having witnessed my arrival, and looking upon me as a sort of *rara-avis*, or wild beast show. The incident was at least amusing.

The next morning was fine and bright, with the sun shining gently through a misty haze. We got away at 9.15, and found the roads in the immediate vicinity of Wellington none of the best, encountering to commence with a series of successive rises, over which we made slow travelling, more especially as freshly-laid stones were about, and towards the top of the last incline the steam roller was at work. As we passed this long-legalized autocar, I overheard one of the men say to his mate, and referring to us, 'Here comes *one of the fliers*,' evidently recognizing a generic similarity between the two.

From this point for the next four or five miles the road was exceedingly bad, being loose in places with many patches of stones, the road itself winding and turning with dangerous sharpness at several points, and as we ran through a colliery district some parts of the surface were of the bumpiest description. Once clear of this, however, things greatly improved, and a very enjoyable run was made to Bridgnorth, the approach to which was exceedingly pretty, a high red sandstone bank covered with trees flanking the road on the left, whilst on the right lay the river with meditative cattle on the brink, and the town itself, softened in the haze, forming a suitable background to the picture. Unfortunately, I was rather hurrying to make Gloucester early, so did not stop for a photograph, which I have since regretted, as the scene was one of the most truly picturesque of the whole journey. The town itself is very prettily situated on the right bank of the river, although I saw but little of it, as the road turns sharply to the left after following the outskirts of the town, and then we traversed a road through a very pretty wooded country to near the top of Shatterford Hill, where a thirty minutes' halt was necessitated by our refractory circulation pump again requiring lubrication.

Then followed the descent of Shatterford Hill, which is steep and winding, with two separate divisions, and we met several cyclists walking up. From this point the road was excellent, and we ran into Kidderminster in good time. Whilst passing through the town I noticed that the float feed was overflowing, showing that the float was most probably leaking, so I pulled up at the Post Office, and wired to the works for a new float to be sent to Gloucester, and kept my eye on the float for the rest of the day, though I found it did not overflow so long as the motor was working hard. Shortly after leaving the town several halts had to be made for restive horses, the farmers hereabouts seem to be very fond of sending great strong horses of the Clydesdale order out in charge either of young boys or decrepit old men, who had very little power over them. However, the Bell at Worcester was reached in fine style at 1.50, and after a moderate halt for lunch we were once more under way, again having considerable trouble with horses, and on one occasion having to stop the motor before a horse drawing a wagon in charge of a doddering old man could be induced to pass us. A game-keeper coming along at the time rendered some assistance, and, as he seemed considerably interested in our vehicle, I gave him a lift on his way for the next mile and a half, and made one more convert to the benefits of auto-caring.

A prettily-wooded country followed, and all went well until just before reaching the village of Kempsey. As we rounded a curve on the top of the hill, I saw a light trap coming up, and, viewing the possibility of objection, slowed down the car to nearly walking pace, and, seeing that the pony as it approached closer was pricking up its ears, I stopped, but I had no sooner done so than up it went on its hind legs, and, after performing sundry aerial tricks with its forefeet, the driver turned it round, and trotted it down the hill in the direction from whence he had come. I thought he was making for a cross road a few yards to the rear, but, instead of doing this, he continued his course down the hill until he came into the village itself, when I saw him stop at a house from which a man in his shirt-sleeves came out. Thinking that he had called out the man to hold the horse, and not seeing any valid reason why I should remain at the top of the hill any longer, I came slowly on until I was nearly level with him, when the pony again showed consider-able uneasiness, and would not allow us to pass. At the same time the occupant of the trap grew choleric, and used 'langwidge', talking vaguely about 'name and address'. As the pony still objected, and I chafed at further delay—having wasted already some ten minutes' time over him—I stopped the motor, but immediately afterwards I wished I had not, for as soon as the driver had manoeuvred his pony past, instead of going on his way rejoicing, he pulled up, and, turning round to me, said, 'I'll have your name and address. Don't you know that *that* is a locomotive?' I replied that I did not, to which he said 'Yes. That is a locomotive, and you know you ought to have a man with a red flag in front.' I immediately suggested he knew nothing about it, whereupon he assured me that he did—'He knew a lot about it,' to which latter opinion I assented with an emphasis upon the 'lot'. He further informed me that 'I ought to have stopped', and various other things, which were scarcely relevant, and then with further enigmatical remarks concerning name and address, resumed the uneven tenor of his way.

Ashley got down and started the engine, and I essayed to recommence my progress when the man in his shirt-sleeves, who had been a passive onlooker all the while, came up and said, 'Here. Not quite so fast, please. I want your name.' He informed me that he was the village constable, and further that I could have the name and address of the other fellow if I wished. To this latter I objected, saying that I had no desire to know the gentleman, but that I had no objection whatever to giving the constable the particulars he wanted if he wished. I accordingly told him my name, which he duly entered in his book, and then, said he, 'Where have you come from?' The question at once put the answer into my head, so I simply drew out one of my 'save-trouble' cards, and pointed to the last line but two, which stated 'We have come from John o' Groat's House'. He read it, looked wise for a few minutes, and then in a much bewildered way, said, 'But *where is John o' Groat's House?*' Pitying his ignorance, I explained that it was in the North of Scotland, and if the gentleman liked to come up there to find me, I had no objection, whereupon he wished me 'Good day', and I once more proceeded.

Tewkesbury was soon reached, the fine church attracting our attention, whilst the heaps of apples and pears lying in the orchards showed that we were now fairly in the apple country. Shortly after leaving the town, our pump again necessitated a stoppage, and then through the clouds which had been slowly gathering came a few drops of rain, which gradually increased until it was steadily descending. We donned our mackintoshes, and pushed forward as fast as the motor (which was going in its best form) would carry us. The road soon began to show signs of slipperiness, and by the time we struck the tramlines which took us into Gloucester, they were in just about as slippery a condition as could be imagined. However, I was anxious to get in and, as there was no traffic about, and the motor was working with tremendous *vim*, I kept going at full speed till I was suddenly brought up (having to make momentary departure from the lines) by finding the car sailing up the roadway broadside on, whereat some females on the sidewalk set up a fearsome screech. But we were soon straight again, and slowing down a point I ran into the Spread Eagle, only to find, however, that this hostelry was closed, whereupon I made for the Bell, and found comfortable quarters there. I had scarcely changed and sat down to dinner before I was besieged by interviewers for the local press, but was only able to give them a few hurried minutes, as I caught the night train for town, leaving Ashley instructions to occupy his spare day by soaking the chains in petrol and lubricating oil, putting on our spare pump in place of the refractory one, changing the leaky float for the new one, and giving the car a thorough brushing and general clean-up.

In London the next day I met the Hon. Evelyn Ellis, who was full of his exploit of climbing the Malvern Beacon the previous day, and mutual congratulations were the order of the hour. I also came across Mr Harry J. Lawson, who, in expressing congratulations upon the success of the journey asked me 'how many breakdowns I had had', and, upon my informing him that nothing which could be classed in this category had yet occurred, I was much amused by the solid seriousness with which, in a stage whisper, he said, 'Come now. Between ourselves, you know,' a question which, perhaps, Mr Lawson might be excused from asking when we recall the fact that, although an autocarist of considerable experience, he had not at that time had any experience of an English-built machine.

On returning to Gloucester in the evening, I found that, whilst it had been fine in London, it had been steadily raining all day there, so that on Friday morning (which was fairly fine, but showery) the roads were thoroughly wet, although they afforded good running for some miles by the side of the canal. The benefit of the attention which Ashley had given to the chains was at once apparent, for whereas the car on coming into Gloucester on Wednesday evening had been groaning and rattling like a veritable rattle-trap, it now ran as smoothly and sweetly as a new car. The road after leaving the canal ran through a fairly level, pretty and picturesque country, with snug little thatch-roofed farms scattered here and there, the brilliant colouring of the good old-fashioned flowers in the cottagers' gardens lending brightness to the scene, and the loads of apples, and occasional peeps at the cider presses at work, giving proofs of our presence in the 'West Countree'.

A few miles out of Gloucester we met half a dozen rosy-cheeked children with a little round ball of a pony in a pony-chaise, and they were full of fun and frolic, as, seeing the car coming, they quickly hopped out and formed a cordon round the pony's head, and then filled the air with merry laughter at the funny carriage without horses going by. As we left the level ground, the roads began to deteriorate considerably, affording very heavy going through deep mud and ruts, and after a dozen miles of this the chains were groaning as noisily as ever, though they were somewhat quietened by a thorough coating of thick grease which we gave them, stopping a few minutes for that purpose. Gradually the road rose until we were running along the tops of some very high hills, from which a misty view of the Welsh mountains could just be seen, and after a sharp turn through Horfield, we ran down into Bristol, striking bad road surface and tramlines at the same time a couple of miles out, and making the Full Moon in three and a half hours for the thirty-six miles, arriving in the rain. At two o'clock, when we were ready to start, it was simply pouring, the rain just descending like the proverbial stair-rods, splashing the pools into bubbles, and gathering in thick muddy streams at the roadsides. But it looked so much like set in weather for the rest of the afternoon that I scarcely thought it worth while waiting, and, as we had got pretty well used to travelling in all weathers, and were fairly certain of the usefulness of our capes, we donned waterproofs, and made a start. The very steep little pitch which took us into the centre of Bristol was successfully negotiated, and then, having crossed the Avon, we ran along an exceedingly rough road, necessitating slow speed to avoid being bumped to bits. Then the motor began to rebel, running very poorly for a mile or so, and then changing its mind, starting off again with all the strength we could desire, occasionally repeating the performance, and varying the monotony of the travel by its in-and-out running. However, there was no occasion to stop, and we made fair progress over good roads once we had got clear of the town. Shortly we left the main road, and struck a series of narrow winding lanes, giving heavy-going and exceedingly bad surface until we got within a couple of miles of Weston-super-Mare, for which place we were making for the night. Then, too, the rain, which had steadily lessened, ceased, and as we ran into Weston the sun came out and gave us a brilliant welcome. The motor was now running at its best, and in search of an hotel I ran up the beautiful level marine drive, then took a turn over the hill and back through the town, finally finishing at the Alexandra Hotel, and putting the car up at some adjoining stables, the hotel's own accommodation being just then under repair. The distance for the day was fifty-seven miles, and the weather had now become much warmer. Having made all snug with the car, I strolled down into the town to look up an old friend, and on my way passed the cabstand on the parade, and found that the drivers were all talking about the car, and animatedly discussing its merits, and I was pleased to gather by overheard expressions as I went by that the opinion was decidedly favourable. . . .

. . . The good people of Bodmin did not mean to miss anything in the way of a sight of the autocar if they could help it, so, when at 8.30 the next morning I went down to see if the car was ready, I found quite a respectable crowd gathered. A photographer, too, was in readiness, and, as soon as we got the machine out of the coachhouse, we 'posed for a picture,' and then started to get up the hill in the yard. This was a big task with the motor only just started, and, as luck would have it, Ashley had got some oil in the cylinders, and the motor did not start off at its best, the consequence being that, when we got nearly to the top of the incline, the motor stopped, and the car began to run back against the brakes. Not relishing an increasing velocity to the right-angled turn at the bottom, and the car having started backwards before I had let the devil loose, I promptly turned the steering handle at right-angles, and backed her gently into the covered shed in which I had at first placed her for the night, and then, once more starting up the motor, drove straight out and up to the hotel door without any further trouble, and getting our baggage on board, got away at 8.50 to the tune of a ringing cheer from an immense crowd outside the hotel. After driving up the long incline through the town, we found ourselves running down a steepish hill of a mile or so in length, and, as the roads were wet, I deemed it advisable to keep the car well in hand. It was a good thing I did so, for towards the bottom a large beanfeast party were met, some five or six brakes and wagonettes coming slowly up the hill, the occupants for the most part walking by the side. As the car dropped slowly by a few of the party raised the cry, 'Now we *shan't* be long', to which Ashley very promptly responded, 'Well, anyway, *we shan't have to walk.*' Ascending the next slope, further vehicles evidently belonging to the same party were met, and, the horses in a brake objecting, I found it necessary to stop the motor before they could be induced to come by. The road now considerably improved as regards surface, and we should doubtless have enjoyed magnificent views from the hill tops but for the heavy rolling mists with which they were covered. A steeply undulating road followed, some of the rises being very sharp. The general trend was, however, downhill, until, running down a long steady declivity, we ran beneath a railway bridge on to the Goss Moors, finding a somewhat narrow road running straight away almost dead level for a mile or two parallel with the railway. The surface for the most part was not of the best, and in places was quite slippery, and this, with the narrowness of the road, made it ticklish steering at top speed, but I just managed to keep the motor at it without the necessity of slackening, as no traffic of any kind, save one solitary cyclist, was encountered, unless I except a flock of geese which ran gabbling before us for a hundred yards with outstretched necks and flapping wings. Then more undulating road followed, and we ran into the long straggling village of Indian Queens, and it was then at once evident that our fame had preceded us, and that the newspapers had done their work, for not only here, but even in the smaller hamlets, we found the people already at their doorsteps and windows waiting for us to go by, whilst in one place we passed a village school, with the whole of the children massed against the railings in the playground in front.

Taking the somewhat hilly road via Mitchell and Zelah, with surface for the most part of an excellent character, and the scenery chiefly composed of mining shafts and chimneys, with various immense but unattractive pit heaps, I found myself running down the long descent through and into Redruth. This hill has a gradient of about one in nine, and is fully a mile in length, and, as it runs straight through the town, forming, in fact, the principal street, it would be exceedingly dangerous if anything happened to place a car out of control; indeed, the C.T.C. route book in dealing with it says that on Fridays—that is, market days—the descent should not be *attempted* by cyclists. With the experience of Ambleside before me, I confess to having felt somewhat nervous as to the result, and, consequently,

I relied as far as it was possible upon my tyre brakes, keeping these jammed on tight, and applying the foot brake only as little as I possibly could compatible with keeping the car closely in hand. Here, too, the people were out in great force, and our passage through Redruth was one of some considerable excitement for the population. However, nothing untoward happened, and in due course, somewhat to my relief I admit, I found myself clear of the town. We ran over a somewhat rough road—along which quite a number of traction engines with their trains of loaded trucks were encountered—*en route* for Camborne, which is but three or four miles farther on. We arrived here at 12.15, a crowd of rapidly-increasing density being encountered. When I ran into the yard of The Hotel (*The* Hotel, mind, for that is the name of it), a surging mass of humanity closed in behind. Seeing in front of me an open doorway, which I judged to be just about big enough to let us through, I went straight at it, and with only about a couple of inches on each side to spare, and barely room for our heads, shot straight in, to the utter astonishment of three horses that were stabled there, with their heads outwards, the car running in directly under their noses. However, they were good about it, and beyond an astonished sniff, took very little notice of us. There was just room for the car and nothing to spare, but it gave Ashley the opportunity of filling his oil tanks in peace and quietness.

We got under way for Penzance at two o'clock, the mists of the morning having by this time rolled away, and the weather being gloriously hot and brilliantly fine. After a couple of fairly steep hills, some magnificent long runs down were encountered, the surface being simply superb—in fact, I have never run upon anything like it, save the sandpapered surface of a cycle track. The road was just dry, and without a single impediment to mar the smoothness of running, or interfere with the perfect freedom of steering, the car moved away with great alacrity, and I simply, to use a colloquialism, 'let her wuzzle' to the tune of considerably over twenty to the hour and the run into Hayle was made in splendid time, the sea level being reached here. We were not long in passing this place, and were soon heading for Penzance, which we reached at 3.15, the approach to the town running parallel with the railway for a couple of miles over a nearly dead-level road, with, however, a very rough surface. Here numerous signs of activity in view of our arrival began to make themselves apparent, a quickly-gathering escort of cyclists, including more than one lady, making their appearance. These rode some in front and some behind us as we progressed, one youth in particular distinguishing himself with a hand camera, and, after taking a snapshot at us, doing a lightning sprint for another half-mile, then hurriedly scrambling off to get another shot.

As we reached the town and commenced the long ascent, our ride became a triumphal procession. The elevated footways, as well as the road, were crowded with sightseers. Every window had its occupants, and a perfect roar of applause greeted us as we progressed. One excited little man stepped out in front of us, and, waving his hat wildly in his hands, shouted, 'That's *my* way, that's *my* way.' The very steep winding top of the hill into the centre of the town was simply packed with people and, apparently, all the available police force of the town engaged in keeping a narrow way for our progress. After a few minutes' stoppage we again set forth on the last ten miles of our journey, accompanied by a number of cyclists. The first five miles were exceedingly rough, as well as very steep and very muddy, the gradients being mainly in the ascendant, and then having reached top ground, we ran along over roads which were fairly level, and, although better in surface, still bad and very narrow. With the sun straight in my eyes it was somewhat difficult to steer, and at one place I had to drive one pair of wheels into the ditch and stop the motor to enable a horse vehicle to just scrape by.

Soon the tower of Sennen Church came in view, and in a few minutes I stopped at the Post Office to send telegrams announcing my arrival. The old lady in charge was greatly interested in the car, and asked 'if she might get up in it', to which I gave assent, and delighted her by taking her a couple of hundred yards up the road. Another two miles and we had completed our day's run of sixty miles, and finished the principal portion of our historic run, drawing up at the Land's End Hotel at 4.35, with a score of 929 miles to our credit, and the journey from end to end successfully accomplished.

As we stopped in front of the hotel, which is a plain and unpretentious building, a magnificent sunset greeted our view, a heavy bank of rose-tinted clouds running parallel with the horizon a short distance above it. In the brilliantly-lighted space between, the faint outlines of the Scilly Isles— forty miles away—were clearly seen. The car was put up for the night in a small coachhouse just big enough to hold it, and whilst Ashley went off in a donkey cart with one of the hotel servants to the nearest blacksmith's with our float spindle, which had worn down and wanted knocking up a little, I rambled about on the tops of the magnificent rugged cliffs until the last roseate rays of the setting sun had disappeared, watching the line of terrible rocks with the Longships Lighthouse fade away into the darkness, and the warning light shine out like a meteor amongst the starry host which were ere long twinkling in their places in the unbroken canopy of heaven.

When I returned to the hotel I found two telegraph clerks from the Atlantic Telegraph Station, who had walked the intervening four miles to see the car, having been informed by wire of its departure from Penzance. A calculation showed that the motor had consumed sixty-seven and a half gallons of petrol for the 929 miles from John o' Groat's, and that the average travelling speed, taken throughout, worked out at a shade less than ten miles to the hour, the actual travelling time being ninety-three and a half hours.   From *The Autocar*, 1898

Britain's roads in 1908, with 'infected routes', or roads in which police traps were in operation, clearly marked as a weekly warning to readers of *The Autocar*

Northward on a Rolls-Royce

We have now another account of a long journey, this time undertaken to test a new model of a famous make. The car is the 20 horsepower Rolls-Royce, the date 1923. A quarter of a century has passed since Sturmey's great drive from 'end-to-end'. The motor car is now a commonplace. The main roads at least are usually tarred. The red flag has long since gone, with the stampeding horses it was chiefly designed to protect. But, you will notice, Kirkstone Pass, tackled from the opposite to Sturmey, still could not be conquered without a halt. Hill-climbing powers, especially on loose-surfaced roads, remained an important consideration.

By this date, of course, the motor car had almost grown up. Much remained to be learnt of suspension and brakes (the Rolls-Royce had them only on the rear wheels) in particular, but 50 to 60 m.p.h. was not an uncommon speed for the higher powered machines. Only past owners of Rolls-Royce Twenties (of whom the writer is one) will doubt the claim that the acceleration is rapid 'in a positive crescendo of speed'—even by 1923 standards.

The controversy the introduction of this model aroused, mentioned in the opening paragraph, can be followed in Part Five.

WHEN, LAST October,* details of the design of the new 20 h.p. six-cylinder Rolls-Royce were divulged, the storm of discussion that followed testified to the high esteem in which this famous *marque* is held. Probably no other make of car is possessed of what may be termed prestige to a sufficient degree to arouse so much controversy. That correspondence will be fresh in our readers' memories, and will go down to history as not only one of the most illuminating series of contributions on a matter of current interest, but as an indication of the intelligent interest of the mechanically-minded motorist— an intelligence acquired largely by reason of careful study born of enthusiasm for the features adopted in modern automobile practice.

Since the introduction of the smaller model Rolls-Royce we have enjoyed several trips aboard the car, and the opportunity recently occurred of a long journey over the Border, and through the Rob Roy country, a distance of over 500 miles being traversed in three days of delightful motoring.

A breakfast-time start from London, a finish of the day's journey in comfortable time for dinner with 282 miles intervening, and an entire absence of fatigue, formed the opening day's achievement. Our objective

* 1922

was the Scottish Show in Glasgow, and since Glasgow is an easy two days' road journey from London we elected to deviate from the usual route in order to include the famous Kirkstone Pass from Ambleside.

We set out along the Great North Road in perfect sunshine on a day in January, creeping stealthily through Barnet on top gear. Once clear of traffic we sped along the tarmac road surface with a fleetness and a silence only impaired by the hiss of the tyres on the hard highway and the tick, tick—yes, remarkable though it may seem!—of the speedometer mechanism to attract attention. Though later, owing to extensive road improvements north of Norman's Cross involving new foundations for the whole width of the road, we were to be diverted from the course we had set ourselves, we were, nevertheless, able to avail ourselves of Dick Turpin's famous highway, now wide, magnificently surfaced, and comparatively deserted in the winter months.

Silent, effortless speed sums up the real qualities of the Rolls-Royce. One watches the speedometer needle creeping slowly round the dial—20, 30, 40, and so on—with never an increase of noise or fuss from under the bonnet or from any part of the chassis: no axle hum, no timing gear clatter— just a sense of luxurious floating along the road with a ghostly silence and ease that are well-nigh uncanny.

How curiously appropriate the name 'Rolls' is! No word better expresses the sensation experienced. Most motorists know only too well what coasting or rolling implies; those who do not should declutch their engines at the top of a moderate incline, slip the gear lever into neutral, and experience the difference in the smoothness of operation when coasting, as compared with ordinary running. It forms an indication of the future possibilities in motor car luxury, and the Rolls-Royce is among the very few that approach to that consummation.

As if to demonstrate quite early all the good qualities of this much-talked-of model, our driver, without warning and when travelling at full speed, thrilled us to the extreme by applying the foot brake only, and without jar, squeak or skid, bringing the car to rest in an almost incredibly short distance. Certainly few cars can boast a foot brake possessed of the power of that of the Rolls 'Twenty'.

To take over the steering wheel is to enjoy a new sensation in motoring, seasoned though the driver may be. Nothing more delightful than the Rolls worm and nut steering could be imagined; finger operation best describes it, and yet it is not too sensitive, and does not set up that to-and-fro action sometimes associated with light steering.

The gear changes, when starting from rest, are easy and are accomplished silently without practice or special attention. Each control lever operates freely and with equal resistance throughout the range, *but* the brake pedal, to the power of which we have already alluded, requires rather more exertion

1923 20 h.p. Rolls-Royce, with Mulliner tourer coachwork,
recently in the Editor's possession

to operate than we had imagined. As for the 'side' brake—the controls on the car are centrally arranged—we found that in a long day's run it was never operated either by the Rolls-Royce driver or ourselves except to hold the car when at rest. In some measure this was due to the difficulty of reaching the lever readily in an emergency. But the docility and sweetness of action of the car proved our chief delight. Once having taken over the driving we frankly confess we were never happy out of the driver's seat.

A more desirable ladies' car one could hardly imagine. Even before we reached Grantham (116 miles) for lunch, and after having twisted and twirled among by-lanes until we had executed what seemed to be a perfect figure eight in the neighbourhood of Eaton Socon and Wansford, where road repairing is going on, it had been borne in upon us that the smaller model Rolls is a single-speed car, of one-lever control, with ample power, docile as a kitten, and infinitely more manageable.

Engine knocking or pinking must be a rare experience, never a suggestion of it did we hear, despite the fact that with coil ignition an engine may be very responsive to timing control. The provision of an automatic advance range of 15 degrees, with a 20 degrees' range governed by the lever on the steering wheel, is undoubtedly a contributing feature. One may, if desired, start from rest on top, thanks to the silky clutch action, and quite regularly the test drivers used the second gear for starting, engaging top at little over walking pace. Thereafter one progresses through traffic, merely governing speed by the accelerator pedal alone, and never touching the clutch pedal for an instant, though one's progress may be reduced to a crawl. With the road ahead clear, one may stamp on the car's 'loud' pedal, and with a mighty initial gulping sound from the carburettor the engine immediately responds, accelerating smoothly and rapidly in a positive crescendo of speed, 3,000 r.p.m. being well within the range of the new engine. At this speed over 50 h.p. is developed.

Your intelligent Midland yokel, incidentally, knows his Rolls-Royce. Frequently along the route town and village urchins were heard to ejaculate 'Rolls' in appreciative tones as the good car sped past.

There is a perfect array of instruments on the dashboard of the Rolls-Royce, all black finished and therefore suggesting the need for luminous figures—this by the way—the temperature recorder forming the most arresting fitment after the essential speedometer. No thermostat is provided, a knobbed lever projecting through the dash operating the shutters fitted to the radiator as standard. A normal running temperature of 80–85 deg. Centigrade is recommended, and such is the efficacy of the radiator that the shutters had to be kept practically closed to maintain this temperature; still, we found it quite easy to forget the temperature control altogether, and some automatic device to watch over it for the absent-minded would, we think, be a sound addition.

The controls on the 'Twenty' are differently arranged from those on the 40–50 h.p. model. Although the Rolls feature of jet control of the carburettor from the driving seat is retained, the lever on the smaller car is mounted on the instrument board, whereas on the '40–50' it is arranged on the top of the steering column.

After tea in Leeds we struck out for the Lakes, *via* Ilkley, Settle and Kirkby Lonsdale, accepting the advice of a policeman to 'Follot'ramlines', which incidentally spread within two hundred yards in different directions! On the outskirts we replenished with petrol, noting roughly that we required ten gallons of petrol to replace that used on the 215 miles recorded— $21\frac{1}{2}$ m.p.g. We found an opportunity to change down on a long winding hill outside Settle, which we approached in the dark, and noted the fact since gear-changing, as already indicated, is generally something exceptional on the latest three-speed Rolls-Royce.

Arriving at Kendal in the rain about 7 p.m., we found hotel accommodation (as usual in our experience) already taken up, and accordingly telephoned to Windermere, where at Rigg's Hotel ample and comfortable accommodation awaited us. Just as well, perhaps, since two well-known motorists who had recognized the car and intended ordering, endeavoured to inveigle us into an argument anent the respective merits of three and four speeds and central controls.

In sunshine we set out next morning for Ambleside in company with an Arrol-Johnston saloon bound for Glasgow, the intention being to put 'paid' to the account on Kirkstone Pass (1,470 ft.) with its 1 in 5 gradient. At the foot we touched first speed occasionally, employing second for the most part and coming down again for the long crucial stretch after about a mile of steady climbing, with its three-inch coating of slimy mud, in which our all-rubber driving treads spun round merrily. Dropping back a few yards to pick out a more favourable part of the road, a restart was made with ease on the 1 in 5 gradient. It was simply a question of tyre tread—the car was shod with straight-side cord tyres—for our saloon companion with Dunlop Magnum covers, who followed, suffered no such experience, the pronounced knobs of the tread leaving clean and definite imprints in the red clay. At the summit of the Pass the Rolls-Royce temperature meter showed 95 deg. Centigrade, the radiator shutters having been opened wide at the foot of the hill. Slipping down into Patterdale through typical Lakeland scenery, we sped alongside the shores of Ullswater, turning aside for Penrith and Carlisle and Lockerbie, where we tarried for lunch.

Over the Border in the afternoon, on the deserted moorland road, we amused ourselves testing the road-holding qualities of the car on open bends. Curiously, with a confidence born of increasing experience, one felt that there was no limit to the speed at which corners could be negotiated without skid. Just why some cars should seemingly remain glued to the ground when making a perfect swoop round a corner, and others should suffer from back axle dither and consequent sidling over the road, it is hard to say. Mr Royce emphasized the road-holding qualities of the new 'Twenty', ascribing his achievement to the design and proportions of the units and the position of the spare wheel at the rear of the chassis.

The fact remains that cornering is ridiculously easy with this car, thanks mainly to the ease of the centre point steering and the extraordinary road-holding qualities of the chassis. One would like to witness a competitive event in the matter of road-holding without skid on corners, since successful design cannot be said to have been achieved without steadiness and real stability in such circumstances.

Glasgow was reached in daylight, our stealthy crawl along the tramlines once again emphasizing the complete mastery of the innate powers of an internal combustion engine, since in that 3,127 c.c. of engine capacity we had compressed energy sufficient to propel this car of approximately 30 cwt., with its roomy Barker five-seater touring body, at nearly a mile a minute, yet so well curbed that a mere crawl on the same gear of 4·82 to 1 is equally easy to accomplish.

To sum up, the new 'Twenty', though fast, is not designed as a racing car, nor is it remarkable on hills; its real virtues lie in the exceptional degree of comfort provided (shock-absorbers are combined with semi-elliptic springs of generous dimensions), the remarkable flexibility of the engine, its power of rapid acceleration, its road-holding qualities, its extraordinary silence—in short, its perfect road manners. Overhead valve mechanism is not easy to render inaudible, but in the 20 h.p. Rolls Royce, with its camshaft enclosed within the crank-case, the nearest approach we have encountered to absolute silence, whether the car be stationary or moving, has been here attained. Piston slap—the Rolls has aluminium alloy pistons—is simply non-existent, even when starting up from cold, but an almost imperceptible tap proceeds momentarily from the region of the rear cylinders when first starting; this, however, disappears as soon as the engine has been warmed up and the oil is circulating normally. *A fine car, indeed!*

From *The Autocar*, February 9, 1923

PART FIVE

CONTROVERSIES AND TROUBLES

The Controversial Rolls-Royce

Just before the London Motor Show in 1922, the Rolls-Royce Company announced a break with tradition. For some time there had been talk of a 'baby' Rolls to meet the needs of a new, and less affluent, motoring public: an economy model. The new departure was not so startling as many had imagined it might be. The price for chassis only was down from £1,850 to £1,100; the engine size from 7·4 litres to 3·1 litres; the wheelbase from twelve feet to ten feet nine inches. This, then, was scarcely an economy model designed for the new proletariat. The reputation for the ultimate in excellence, design, materials and assembly was not to be tarnished.

But there were some features in the new 'Twenty' that alarmed and even angered some people; and the cry of 'retrogression' rose loud above the motoring firmament. Centre change? Three-speed gearbox? Only a week later a letter appeared in The Autocar *above the name of Leslie Northcott. Others followed, including opinions from some of the most respected men in the industry. The storm raged for months. Here are some of the contestants' contributions.*

Sir,

As an admirer of the 50 h.p. Rolls-Royce car, I have been looking forward with keen interest to the details of the new 20 h.p. model. On reading the article last week, my impression was one of disappointment. A British motorist, I like to think of the Rolls-Royce as being the best of its class in the world, in both workmanship and *design*, particularly as a leading R.-R. motto is: 'Spend as much money in the construction as can be done wisely but not unnecessarily.'

Perhaps a brainier reader than I can answer the following queries, which I have written down in the order they occur in your article, and not in the order of importance. In fairness to the Rolls-Royce, let me add that I have not yet seen one of the new 20 h.p. models, let alone tried one on the road. Furthermore, I should think twice about spending £1,600 on a 20 h.p. *open* touring car of four seats.

1. Why *push-rod* operated overhead valves? I understand that maximum efficiency is obtained with overhead valves operated by an overhead camshaft, instead of using push-rods, as shown by the success of racing cars with overhead camshafts, and the use of this type of engine in aeroplanes. The chief disadvantage of overhead camshaft is cost of manufacture, which matters little in the case of the Rolls. A considerable number of cars may be

The maligned baby. 1923 Rolls-Royce 20, with open tourer body,
as shown in the company's first catalogue

mentioned, e.g. Napier, Lanchester, Wolseley, Hispano-Suiza, Leyland, Hotchkiss, A.C., showing that efficiency is not gained at the expense of quietness, reliability, ease of adjustment, and so on.

2. Is an oil consumption of 1,000 m.p.g. remarkably low for a 20 h.p. car costing over £1,000? What about a certain light six-cylinder of 18 h.p. and costing well below £1,000, which is reputed to have done over 13,000 m.p.g. in 10,000 miles?

3. Why are the radiator shutters operated by the driver, and not automatic (like those fitted to the six-cylinder Straker-Squire)? Considering that the shutters would be more efficiently operated by some kind of thermostatic device than by the average driver, and that automobiles are being made to run more and more automatically, I hardly see the use of driver control. Would the R.-R. designer ever think of selling a car with engine lubrication from an oil-pump operated by the driver, as fitted on some prehistoric cars?

4. Why *three* forward speeds? Is it not generally recognized that the less powerful a car the more speeds it should have? I cannot understand why the 50 h.p. model should have four speeds and the 20 h.p. model only three. Does the designer think that *all* owner-drivers are afraid of changing down to third occasionally? I notice that central control has been adopted for the gears. Is this on account of cheapness of construction, or because the designer does not believe in a four-door body with side control? Perhaps the owner-driver is *never* expected to carry more than the usual three passengers in addition to himself?

5. Why not front-wheel brakes? Does the designer think *all* owner-drivers

and chauffeurs are careless in brake adjustment; even so, what about R.-R. service? Perhaps he thinks that front-wheel (i.e. four-wheel) brakes will not be essential for a high-class car to sell well in a few years' time? If so, might I suggest that he should read the article on 'What the Salon will Reveal', with particular reference to a *small* car named the Lancia?

6. Why semi-elliptic rear springs? This question may be a matter of private opinion. Is not a well-designed cantilever rear spring more efficient than a semi-elliptic, or does the R.-R. designer fear roll on corners? If so, why not some anti-rolling device, such as that used on the Napier, to mention but one car? Perhaps Messrs Rolls-Royce Ltd. find the cantilevers on the 50 h.p. model not so good as they might be.

7. What about luggage for the 'touring' car? Since no mention of a luggage grid or carrier is made, I take it that one has not been fitted. If it has, these remarks are unnecessary. Does the designer think that a man who pays £1,600 for a touring car never intends to tour? I see the spare wheel is provided (without a weather cover) in a position to collect all the road dust, because 'its weight can be utilized to make the road wheels more effectively hold the road'. I should think that with a *good* set of rear springs, as well as the shock dampers provided as standard, the difference in the wheels holding the road would be quite negligible, particularly with a full load.

8. Why not a petrol gauge on the instrument board instead of on the rear tank? Is it because there is not a reliable petrol gauge on the market, or does the designer think the instrument board already well supplied with instruments? In the latter case, why not remove the chassis number plate, which the owner only wants to see about once in —— years? Would the designer ever think of fixing the speedometer to one of the road wheels, or the ammeter inside the accumulator box?

I am in no way connected with the manufacture of motor cars or accessories.

LESLIE NORTHCOTT

Sir,

Who is this Mr Leslie Northcott who has written you such a strange letter?

I feel very much tempted to take each of his queries and answer them in detail, but I do not want to waste your valuable space, which no doubt you could use to more advantage.

To every sensible person it is the road performance that counts, so why does Mr Leslie Northcott not try the new 20 h.p. Rolls-Royce first of all, then write about it afterwards?

This letter of Mr Northcott's nearly equals that of a well-known tyre manufacturer who rushed into print about his Rolls-Royce, but later had to apologize afterwards. Likes and dislikes are the outcome of so many contributory factors that to account for any preference for this or for that is a matter for the psychologist rather than the engineer.

Just and sensible criticism is always interesting, so I hope you will not inflict us with any more samples like the letter I complain about.

G. CAMPBELL MUIR

Sir,

Like your correspondent Mr Leslie Northcott, I, too, am greatly disappointed with the details of the new 20 h.p. Rolls-Royce.

Push-rod overhead valves, unit construction of engine and gearbox, imitation Delco ignition, central change, three-speed gearbox, straight-sided tyres, the whole specification has an American flavour which is, in my opinion, totally out of keeping with the reputation of Rolls-Royce. To older motorists with experience of numerous cars this new model will not, I am afraid, make any great appeal, for one feels there is a great deal wanting in the specification of this chassis at £1,100.
Whitehead, Co. Antrim.

DISAPPOINTED

Sir,

One would suppose, on reading Mr Northcott's letter, that he was being pressed by this excellent concern to purchase one of these cars, or that his opinion was of value to the motor world, otherwise I cannot see why he should have written such a letter, for at least he admits he has never seen or tried the car.

The armchair critic is a perfect trial, and is frequently a man with very little knowledge of the subject about which he is writing. If I were Mr Northcott I should not criticize the work of a firm which has for so many years held the reputation of designing and manufacturing the best car in the world.

Before passing an opinion I shall wait, anyway, until I have seen the car, but I have no doubt that the new car will be a credit to its makers, and, incidentally, the British motor industry.

W. R. MORRIS,
Governing Director,
Morris Motors Ltd.

Sir,

I was most interested to read Mr Leslie Northcott's letter on the design of the new 20 h.p. Rolls-Royce because I felt that his criticism was a workmanlike one. As to myself, I have been a user of cars for over twenty years, and for the rest I was brought up an engineer, and I feel that the 20 h.p. Rolls-Royce might well have been improved upon in view of the price charged for it.

Let anyone note the new price of the 1923 Isotta-Fraschini, £1,400 chassis, 35·8 h.p., four-wheel brakes, eight-cylinder engine, plus good work-manship. But lest I should be thought lacking in belief in my own country's wares, let any mechanical person take the new 1923 3-litre Bentley, and learn what this country can do for a chassis price of £1,050.

I do not want to go into the 'fors' and 'againsts' of the new Rolls, but when one of your correspondents gets on to the question of lubricating oil, and says that 'since a number of small cars can only do about 1,000 m.p.g. of oil, the Rolls-Royce consumption is not excessive,' I can tell him that he is talking through his hat, for what may be good for a small car is exceedingly bad for a large one. Not that a 1,000 m.p.g. is bad, except that my old Lanchester in 1910 would easily do it, counting in the back axle lubrication as well, but it might be better. In view of the price, plus the engineering progress since 1910, I feel it ought to be, and so on with other points in the general design, especially with regard to the brakes. Both brakes on the back wheel drums may be a good point from a production point of view, but personally I have a dislike for putting all my eggs in one basket, especially in view of the fact that oil has a habit of getting into the back brake drums, in spite of all that makers tell us to the contrary. Had the Rolls-Royce designers made the cylinders in two blocks of three, in place of one block of six, I think they would have received the blessings of prospective owners, whereas now they certainly will not.

GEOFF. JALLAND

Sir,

I very much resent the type of letter appearing in your last issue from Mr G. Campbell Muir. It contributes nothing to the world's knowledge but a consciousness of increasing bad manners.

Mr Northcott's letter is a legitimate criticism of design from the man in the street, and is not answered in any way by Mr Campbell Muir side-tracking on 'road performance'.

I know exactly Mr Northcott's feeling. He expected a super-car 'out-bristling' the French even in originality of design; what he finds is a very excellent vehicle of somewhat uninteresting standard American type. He puts down a list of points on which he wants enlightenment and all he gets in answer is to be called a fool by Mr Campbell Muir.

Messrs Rolls-Royce may truly say 'save us from our friends': their reputation and position in this country, nay, even the affection all have for them, is such that the public feel there is reason for their every move, and when criticism is made and explanations are asked for, it comes as a shock to find their side taken by a letter not of explanation but of abuse.

J. T. C. MOORE-BRABAZON

Sir,

In order to correct any wrong impression which some of your readers may have formed from this correspondence, may I say that I have had the opportunity of examining the chassis and taking a trial run, when I had the pleasure of driving this delightful car myself. Taking Mr Northcott's points in order:

1. The new R.-R. engine is not designed for a racing car nor for an aeroplane, and the other makes of car which he mentions have all yet to establish reputations for the silent longevity of their new engines. Push-rod operation of the valves entails a simple pair of pinions for the camshaft drive, while the overhead shaft necessitates a long train of gears or two right-angle drives with a vertical shaft. Anyhow, what matters the means, when the end is all that can be desired?

2. I have no doubt that the oil consumption is really much less than the figure stated by Mr Royce, as Messrs R.-R. are always very conservative in such statements. My 40–50 h.p. R.-R. consumes oil at the rate of 2,400 miles per gallon, but this is not desirable as after 1,000 miles or so the oil has deteriorated and should be changed. Anyone who runs 10,000 miles on a gallon of oil deserves to spoil his engine.

3. On a car with radiator shutters thermostatically controlled, when the engine is stopped the water round the cylinder heads gets over-hot owing to the lack of circulation and the thermostat promptly opens the shutter. A pint of petrol has then to be wasted in warming up the bulk of the water again. The ideal arrangement would be thermostatic shutter control put into action only when the engine is running—but this might be rather a dreadful gadget! If the forgetful driver leaves the shutter open, no harm is done, he merely fails to get the best out of his engine. If he leaves it shut, the water boils, which reminds him to open it or—to quote Ian Hay—he can shave or have a cup of tea. Personally I think the hand control has it.

4. All R.-R. owners to whom I have spoken preferred the old three-speeders. With a powerful engine three are ample except for the speed merchant. To get any use out of four one has to be constantly changing gear, and it is unpleasant to be frequently running at 30 m.p.h. or so on indirect drive. Further, three speeds require a lower top gear ratio, with consequent better top gear performance, and top gear performance is the criterion with 90 per cent of car owners. Central control prevents the very occasionally required use of the front seat for three. But on the other hand it provides perpetual easy access to and from the driver's seat.

5. I believe that Messrs R.-R. have for some time been experimenting with four-wheel brakes, and no doubt when they have tried out a satisfactory design their cars will be so fitted. One serious accident, proved to be due to front-wheel brakes, might tarnish a car's reputation irrevocably. Your correspondent speaks airily about front-wheel brakes as though they could be fitted like a set of spring gaiters.

6. What does it matter whether the springs are semi-elliptic, cantilever, tetrahedral, colloidal, or anything else, so long as they provide easy suspension? The fitting of cantilever springs is by no means a short cut to success. Mr Coatalen has been pointing out that good springing can only be obtained by the empirical method—i.e. intelligent hit and miss. The suspension of the new R.-R. is admirable. It does not float in the priceless fashion of its big sister, but it has its sister beaten on corners and during braking. The back axle freezes to the road in a perfectly amazing way, never a dither on the roughest corner or when under maximum braking on really bumpy roads.

7. The spare wheel is undoubtedly in the academically best place at the rear. It is out of the way, and its weight is in the right place. But what is to prevent Mr Northcott or myself carrying it elsewhere, if we think it unsightly or in the way of luggage? I intend carrying two, one on each side of the scuttle as usual.

8. I think it would be folly to have indicators on the dash to show the amount of grease in each shackle and the temperature of each big end, and—best of all—to show when a letter like this one is too long. Incidentally, the chassis number plate is put on the instrument board for Messrs R.-R.'s benefit, not for ours.

There are, I think, three doubtful points on this chassis, none of them mentioned so far. (*a*) The provision of a magneto as an optional extra only. I have yet to meet the battery which will provide starting and lighting current for more than 15,000 to 20,000 miles without giving up the ghost. (*b*) Autovac petrol feel. I have had immense and at first most baffling trouble, many of my friends have had trouble, and I have succoured stranded strangers in trouble with this most fickle device. (*Pace* Constant Reader who has run 10,000 miles, etc.) I admit that the Autovac fitted to the new car looks an aristocratic gadget only faintly resembling the usual can of mystery, so I must trust Mr Royce. (*c*) Most important, the mixture lever should be on the wheel. It could easily change places with the ignition lever, as with semi-automatic advance the latter need hardly ever be touched.

Mr Northcott considers £1,600 excessive for an open touring car. So do I. But the chassis is £1,100, and one can get an admirable body for £200.

May I say in conclusion that this little Rolls-Royce is quite the most charming car I have ever driven, and that I am in no way connected with the motor trade.   OLIVER LYLE

From *The Autocar*, 1922

Automotive Passacaglia

BY HENRY MILLER

This part of the book is concerned with motoring not literary controversy. In this chapter one of the most controversial writers of the day, and a man whose work Lawrence Durrell describes as 'one of the bravest, richest and most consistent ventures . . . since Jean-Jaques Rousseau', enters the nightmarish world of the jinxed automobile: a territory that most of us have explored at some time or another.

Henry Miller's car is clearly a mass-produced, well-worn one that was never intended to survive the mileage it had already endured. He is concerned here with what happened to him and his automobile on a long trip in the South, more especially in Albuquerque with 'the painless Parker of the automotive world', Hugh Dutter.

Automotive Passacaglia: there are few drivers who have not observed these ritual movements about ailing, ageing automobiles in remote garages; and experienced the complex of frustration, admiration, disappointment and yet undying confidence that they inspire in the anxious owner and beholder.

I FEEL like doing a little passacaglia now about things automotive. Ever since I decided to sell the car she's been running beautifully. The damned thing behaves like a flirtatious woman.

Back in Albuquerque, where I met that automotive expert Hugh Dutter, everything was going wrong with her. Sometimes I think it was all the fault of the tail wind that swept me along through Oklahoma and the Texas panhandle. Did I mention the episode with the drunk who tried to run me into a ditch? He almost had me convinced that I had lost my generator. I was a bit ashamed, of course, to ask people if my generator were gone, as he said, but every time I had a chance to open up a conversation with a garage man I would work him round to the subject of generators, hoping first of all that he would show me where the damned thing was hidden, and second that he would tell me whether or not a car could function without one. I had just a vague idea that the generator had something to do with the battery. Perhaps it hasn't, but that's my notion of it still.

The thing I enjoy about visiting garage men is that one contradicts the other. It's very much as in medicine, or the field of criticism in literature. Just when you believe you have the answer you find that you're mistaken. A little man will tinker with your machinery for an hour and blushingly ask you for a dime, and whether he's done the correct thing or not the car runs, whereas the big service stations will lay her up in dry dock for a few days, break her down into molecules and atoms, and then like as not she'll run a few miles and collapse.

There's one thing I'd like to advise anyone thinking of making a transcontinental journey: see that you have a jack, a monkey wrench and a jimmy. You'll probably find that the wrench won't fit the nuts but that doesn't matter; while you're pretending to fiddle around with it someone will stop and lend you a helping hand. I had to get stuck in the middle of a swamp in Louisiana before I realized that I had no tools. It took me a half hour to realize that if there were any they would be hidden under the front seat. And if a man promises you that he will stop at the next town and send someone to haul you don't believe him. Ask the next man and the next man and the next man. Keep a steady relay going or you'll sit by the roadside till doomsday. And never say that you have no tools—it sounds suspicious, as though you had stolen the car. Say you lost them, or that they were stolen from you in Chicago. Another thing—if you've just had your front wheels packed don't take it for granted that the wheels are on tight. Stop at the next station and ask to have the lugs tightened, then you'll be sure your front wheels won't roll off in the middle of the night. Take it for granted that nobody, not even a genius, can guarantee that your car won't fall apart five minutes after he's examined it. A car is even more delicate than a Swiss watch. And a lot more diabolical, if you know what I mean.

If you don't know much about cars it's only natural to want to take it to a big service station when something goes wrong. A great mistake, of course, but it's better to learn by experience than by hearsay. How are you to know that the little man who looks like a putterer may be a wizard?

Anyway, you go to the service station. And immediately you come smack up against a man dressed in a butcher's smock, a man with a pad in his hand and a pencil behind his ear, looking very professional and alert, a man who never fully assures you that the car will be perfect when they get through with it but who intimates that the service will be impeccable, of the very highest calibre, and that sort of thing. They all have something of the surgeon about them, these entrepreneurs of the automobile industry. You see, they seem to imply, you've come to us only at the last ditch; we can't perform miracles, but we've had twenty or thirty years' experience and can furnish the best of references. And, just as with the surgeon, you have the feeling when you entrust the car to his immaculate hands, that he is going to telephone you in the middle of the night, after the engine has been taken apart and the bearings are lying all about, and tell you that there's something even more drastically wrong with the car than he had at first suspected. Something serious, what! It starts with a case of bad lungs and ends up with a removal of the appendix, gall bladder, liver and testicles. The bill is always indisputably correct and of a figure no less than formidable. Everything is itemized, except the quality of the foreman's brains. Instinctively you put it safely away in order to produce it at the next hospital when the car breaks down again; you want to be able to prove that you knew what was wrong with the car all along.

After you've had a few experiences of this sort you get wary, that is if you're slow to catch on, as I am. After you stay in a town a while and get acquainted, feel that you are among friends, you throw out a feeler; you learn that just around the corner from the big service station there's a little fellow (his place is always in the rear of some other place and therefore hard to find) who's a wizard at fixing things and asks some ridiculously low sum for his services. They'll tell you that he treats *everybody* that way, even those with 'foreign' licence plates.

Well, that's exactly what happened to me in Albuquerque, thanks to the friendship I struck up with Dr Peters who is a great surgeon and a *bon vivant* as well. One day, not having anything better to do—one of those days when you call up telephone numbers or else go to have your teeth cleaned—one day, as I say, in the midst of a downpour I decided to consult the master mind, the painless Parker of the automotive world: Hugh Dutter. There was nothing very seriously wrong—just a constant high fever. The men at the service station didn't attach much importance to it—they attributed it to the altitude, the age of the car and so on. I suppose there was nothing more that they could repair or replace. But when on a cold, rainy day a car runs a temperature of 170–80 there must be something wrong, so I reasoned. If she was running that high at 5,000 feet what would she run at 7,000 or 10,000?

I stood in the doorway of the repair shop for almost an hour waiting for Dutter to return. He had gone to have a bite with some friends, never dreaming that there would be any customers waiting for him in such a downpour. His assistant, who was from Kansas, regaled me with stories about forcing flooded streams back in Kansas. He spoke as though people had nothing better to do when it rained than practise these dangerous manoeuvres with tin Lizzies. Once he said a bus got caught in the head waters of a creek, keeled over, was washed downstream and never found again. He liked rain— it made him homesick.

Presently Dutter arrived. I had to wait until he went to a shelf and arranged some accessories. After I had sheepishly explained my troubles he leisurely scratched his head and without even looking in the direction of the engine he said: 'Well, there could be a lot of reasons for her heating up on you that way. Have you had your radiator boiled out?'

I told him I had—back in Johnson City, Tennessee.

'How long ago was that?' he said.

'Just a few months back.'

'I see. I thought you were going to say a few years ago.'

The car was still standing outside in the rain. 'Don't you want to look her over?' I said, fearing that he might lose interest in the case.

'You might bring her in,' he said. 'No harm in taking a look. Nine times out of ten it's the radiator. Maybe they didn't do a good job for you back in Cleveland.'

'Johnson City!' I corrected.

'Well, wherever it was.' He ordered his assistant to drive her in.

I could see he wasn't very enthusiastic about the job; it wasn't as though I had brought him a bursting gall bladder or a pair of elephantine legs. I thought to myself—better leave him alone with it for a while; maybe when he begins to putter around he'll work up a little interest. So I excused myself and went off to get a bite.

'I'll be back soon,' I said.

'That's all right, don't hurry,' he answered. 'It may take hours to find out what's wrong with her.'

I had a Chop Suey and on the way back I loitered a bit in order to give him time to arrive at a correct diagnosis. To kill a little time I stopped in at the Chamber of Commerce and inquired about the condition of the roads going to Mesa Verde. I learned that in New Mexico you can tell nothing about the condition of the roads by consulting the map. For one thing the road map doesn't say how much you may be obliged to pay if you get stuck in deep clay and have to be hauled fifty or seventy-five miles. And between gravel and graded roads there's a world of difference. At the Automobile Club in New York I remember the fellow taking a greasy red pencil and tracing a route for me backwards while answering two telephones and cashing a cheque.

'Mesa Verde won't be officially open until about the middle of May,' said the fellow. 'I wouldn't risk it yet. If we get a warm rain there's no telling what will happen.'

I decided to go to Arizona, unless I had an attack of chilblains. I was a little disappointed though to miss seeing Shiprock and Aztec.

When I got back to the garage I found Dutter bending over the engine; he had his ear to the motor, like a doctor examining a weak lung. From the vital parts there dangled an electric bulb attached to a long wire. The electric bulb always reassures me. It means business. Anyway, he was down in the guts of the thing and getting somewhere—so it looked.

'Found out what's wrong yet?' I ventured to inquire timidly.

'No,' he said, burying his wrist in a mess of intricate whirring thingama-jigs which looked like the authentic automotive part of the automobile. It was the first time I had ever seen what makes a car go. It was rather beautiful, in a mechanical way. Reminded me of a steam calliope playing Chopin in a tub of grease.

'She wasn't timing right,' said Dutter, twisting his neck around to look at me but, like the skilful surgeon, still operating with his deft right hand. 'I knew that much before I even looked at her. That'll heat a car up quicker'n anything.' And he began explaining to me from deep down in the bowels of the car how the timing worked. As I remember it now an eight cylinder car fires 1, 3, 5, 7 with one cam and 2, 4, 6, 8 with the other. I may be wrong on the figures but the word cam is what interested me. It's a beautiful word and when he tried to point it out to me I liked it still better—the cam. It has a down-to-earth quality about it, like piston and gear. Even an ignoramus like myself knows that piston, just from the sound of the word, means something that has to do with the driving force, that it's intimately connected with the locomotion of the vehicle. I still have to see a piston *per se*, but I believe in pistons even though I should never have the chance to see one cold and isolate.

The timing occupied him for quite a while. He explained what a difference a quarter of a degree could make. He was working on the carburettor, if I am not mistaken. I accepted this explanation, as I had the others, unquestionably. Meanwhile I was getting acquainted with the fly-wheel and some other more or less essential organs of the mysterious mechanism. Most everything about a car, I should say in passing, is more or less essential. All but the nuts underneath the chassis; they can get loose and fall out, like old teeth, without serious damage. I'm not speaking now of the universal —that's another matter. But all those rusty nuts which you see dropping off when the car's jacked up on the hoist—actually they mean very little. At worst the running board may drop off, but once you know your running board is off there's no great harm done.

Apropos of something or other he suddenly asked me at what temperature the thermostat was set. I couldn't tell him. I had heard a lot about thermostats, and I knew there was one in the car somewhere, but just where, and just what it looked like, I didn't know. I evaded all references to the subject as skilfully as I could. Again I was ashamed not to know where and what this piece of apparatus was. Starting out from New York, after receiving a brief explanation about the functioning or non-functioning of the thermostat, I had expected the shutters of the hood to fly open automatically when the heat gauge read 180 or 190. To me thermostat meant something like a cuckoo in a cuckoo clock. My eye was constantly on the gauge, waiting for it to hit 180. Rattner, my then side-kick, used to get a bit irritated watching me watch the gauge. Several times we went off the road because of this obsession on my part. But I always expected that some time or other an invisible man would release the trap and the cuckoo would fly out and then bango! the shutters would open up, the air circulate between the legs, and the motor begin to purr like a musical cat. Of course the damned shutters never did fly open. And when the gauge did finally hit 190 the next thing I knew was that the radiator was boiling over and the nearest town was forty miles away.

Well, after the timing had been corrected, the points adjusted, the carburettor calibrated, the accelerator exhilarated, all the nuts, bolts and screws carefully restored to their proper positions, Dutter invited me to accompany him on a test flight. He decided to drive her up through Tijeras Canyon where there was a big grade. He set out at fifty miles an hour, which worried me a bit because the mechanic at the big service station had said to drive her slow for the next thousand miles until she loosened up a bit. The gauge moved slowly up to 180 and, once we were properly in the pass, it swung to 190 and kept on rising.

'I don't think she'll boil,' he said, lighting himself a cigarette with a parlour match. 'Up here the principle is never to worry until she boils over. Cars act temperamental up here, just like people. It could be weather, it could be scales in the engine box . . . it could be a lot of things. And it mightn't be anything more than altitude. The Buicks never did make big enough radiators for the size of the car.' I found this sort of talk rather cheering. More like a good French doctor. The American physician always says immediately—'Better have an X-ray taken; better pull out all your back teeth; better get an artificial leg.' He's got you all cut and bleeding before he's even looked at your throat. If you've got a simple case of worms he finds that you've been suffering from hereditary constriction of the corneal phylactery since childhood. You get drunk and decide to keep the worms or whatever ails you.

Dutter went on to talk in his calm, matter of fact way about new and old Buicks, about too much compression and too little space, about buying whole parts instead of a part of a part, as with the Chevrolet or the Dodge. Not that the Buick wasn't a good car—oh no, it was a damned good car, but like every car it had its weak points too. He talked about boiling over several times on his way from Espanola to Santa Fe. I had boiled over there myself, so I listened sympathetically. I remember getting near the top of the hill and then turning round to coast down in order to get a fresh start. And then suddenly it was dark and there were no clear crystal springs anywhere in sight. And then the lizards began whispering to one another and you could hear them whispering for miles around, so still it was and so utterly desolate.

Coming back Dutter got talking about parts and parts of parts, rather intricate for me, especially when he began comparing Pontiac parts with parts of parts belonging to the Plymouth or the Dodge. The Dodge was a fine car, he thought, but speaking for himself he preferred the old Studebaker. 'Why don't you get yourself a nice old Studebaker?' I asked. He looked at me peculiarly. I gathered that the Studebaker must have been taken off the market years ago. And then, almost immediately afterwards, I began talking about Lancias and Pierce Arrows. I wasn't sure whether they made them any more either, but I knew they had always enjoyed a good reputation. I wanted to show him that I was willing to talk cars, if that was the game. He glossed over these remarks however in order to launch into a technical explanation of how cores were casted and moulded, how you tested them with an icepick to see if they were too thick or too thin. This over he went into an excurses about the transmission and the differential, a subject so abstruse that I hadn't the faintest notion what he was getting at. The gauge, I observed, was climbing down towards 170. I thought to myself how pleasant it would be to hire a man like Dutter to accompany me the rest of the way. Even if the car broke down utterly it would be instructive and entertaining to hear him talk about the parts. I could understand how people became attached to their cars, knowing all the parts intimately, as they undoubtedly do.

When we got back to the laboratory he went inside for a thermometer. Then he took the cap off the radiator and stuck the thermometer in the boiling radiator. At intervals he made a reading—comparative readings such as a theologian might do with the Bible. There was a seventeen degree difference, it developed, between the reading of the gauge and the thermometer reading. The difference was in my favour, he said. I didn't understand precisely what he meant by this remark, but I made a mental note of it. The car looked pathetically human with the thermometer sticking out of its throat. It looked like it had quinsy or the mumps.

I heard him mumbling to himself about scales and what a delicate operation that was. The word hydrochloric acid popped up. 'Never do that till the very last,' he said solemnly.

'Do what?' I asked, but he didn't hear me, I guess.

'Can't tell what will happen to her when the acid hits her,' he mumbled between his teeth.

'Now I tell you,' he went on, when he had satisfied himself that there was nothing seriously wrong. 'I'm going to block that thermostat open a little more with a piece of wood—and put in a new fan belt. We'll give her an eight pound pull to begin with and after she's gone about four hundred miles you can test her yourself and see if she's slipping.' He scratched his head and ruminated a bit. 'If I were you,' he continued, 'I'd go back to that service station and ask them to loosen the tappets a little. It says ·0010 thousandth on the engine but up here you can ride her at ·0008 thousandth —until you hear that funny little noise, that clickety-click-click, you know —like little bracelets. I tried to catch that noise before when she was cold but I couldn't get it. I always like to listen for that little noise—then I know she's not too tight. You see, you've got a hot blue flame in there and when your valves are screwed down too tight that flame just burns them up in no time. That can heat a car up too! Just remember—*the tappets!*'

We had a friendly little chat about the slaughter going on in Europe, to wind up the transaction, and then I shook hands with him. 'I don't think you'll have any more trouble,' he said. 'But just to make sure why don't you come back here after they loosen the tappets and I'll see how she sounds. Got a nice little car there. She ought to last you another twenty thousand miles—*at least!*'

I went back to the big service station and had the tappets attended to. They were most gracious about it, I must say. No charge for their services this time. Rather strange, I thought. Just as I was pulling out the floor-walker in the butcher's smock informed me with diabolical suavity that, no matter what any one may have told me, the pretty little noise I was looking for had nothing to do with the tightness or looseness of the valves. It was something else which caused that. 'We don't believe in loosening them too much,' he said. 'But you wanted it that way, so we obliged you.'

I couldn't pretend to contradict him, not having the knowledge of Hugh Dutter to fortify my argument, so I decided to have the car washed and greased and find out in a roundabout way what the devil he meant.

When I came back for the car the manager came over and politely informed me that there was one other very important thing I ought to have done before leaving. 'What's that?' I said.

'Grease the clutch.'

How much would that be, I wanted to know. He said it was a thirty minute job—not over a dollar.

'O.K.,' I said. 'Grease the clutch. Grease everything you can lay hands on.'

I took a thirty-minute stroll around the block, stopping at a tavern, and when I got back the boy informed me that the clutch didn't need greasing.

'What the hell is this?' I said. 'What did he tell me to have it greased for?'

'He tells everybody that,' said the boy, grinning.

As I was backing out he asked me slyly if she het up much on me.

'A little,' I said.

'Well, don't pay any attention to it,' he said. 'Just wait till she boils. It's a mighty smooth running car, that Buick. Prettiest little one I ever did see. See us again sometime.'

Well, there it is. If you've ever served in the coast artillery you know what it's like to take the azimuth. First you take a course in higher trigonometry, including differential calculus and all the logarithms. When you put the shell in the breech be sure to remove all your fingers before locking the breech. A car is the same way. It's like a horse, in short. What brings on the heat is fuss and bother. Feed him properly, water him well, coax him along when he's weary and he'll die for you. The automobile was invented in order for us to learn how to be patient and gentle with one another. It doesn't matter about the parts, or even about the parts of parts, nor what model or what year it is, so long as you treat her right. What a car appreciates is responsiveness. A loose differential may or may not cause friction and no car, not even a Rolls-Royce, will run without a universal, but everything else

L

being equal it's not the pressure or lack of pressure in the exhaust pipe which matters—it's the way you handle her, the pleasant little word now and then, the spirit of forbearance and forgiveness. Do unto others as you would have them do by you is the basic principle of automotive engineering. Henry Ford understood these things from the very beginning. That's why he paid universal wages. He was calibrating the exchequer in order to make the steep grades. There's just one thing to remember about driving any automotive apparatus and that is this: when the car begins to act as though it had the blind staggers it's time to get out and put a bullet through its head. We American people have always been kind to animals and other creatures of the earth. It's in our blood. Be kind to your Buick or your Studebaker. God gave us these blessings in order to enrich the automobile manufacturers. He did not mean for us to lose our tempers easily. If that's clear we can go on to Gallup and trade her in for a spavined mule. . . .

From *The Air-Conditioned Nightmare*

A Speech from the Dock

BY PATRICK CAMPBELL

Among all the conflicts and nightmares engendered by the automobile, surely none can match the frustrated horror of the man at the wheel, wronged or even damaged, facing the injustices of police action or litigation. There is no parallel in human experience—as Patrick Campbell magnificently reminds us in this little tale: or advice on how to speed your way into the law's jaws without actually trying.

AT ONE time, while I was still parting my hair in the middle, I used to think that there was nothing more important than absolute truth in human relationships. I used to break in on people at parties and shout at them: 'Chatter, chatter, chatter! What's it all about? He said and she said, and I always do my new potatoes with a little sprig of mint. Can't we get down to something *important*?'

Personal revelation, and the soul bare right down to the boots—that was what I liked. I used to be able to clear a room in about twenty minutes. It got so bad that a number of people—quiet folk interested in gardening and bridge—knowing their own limitations, used to try to find out whether I would be there before accepting an invitation to something as harmless as a lunch. This business went on for several years, but did not achieve its final flowering until I appeared in an Irish court.

There had been an accident. I had run into the back of another car. The owner sued me for damages.

My father briefed counsel. 'It's absurd,' I said, 'there's no need to go to all that expense. The facts are perfectly straightforward. I was driving at 38 m.p.h. along a main road. This man comes shooting backwards—*backwards*—out of a side turning, lighting a cigarette. What do I want counsel for? I can handle this case myself.'

My father said he thought we might have counsel anyway. The law was a complicated business. It might do us no harm to have responsible advice.

When we arrived in court I was pleased to see that I knew the judge. He even nodded as we sat down.

The driver of the other car gave his evidence. I must admit I was surprised by what he had to say. He said he'd blown his horn twice before starting to reverse, looking carefully up and down the main road as soon as his view became clear, sounded his horn again, and then backed round slowly and carefully on to his own side. He was suddenly run into without warning. The only intimation he had received that some other vehicle was approaching was the roar of a racing-car being driven at high speed. He had been driving for twenty-two years, had never before been involved in an accident, and had lost a week's work as a result of being run down.

I stepped into the box. I was very angry. It seemed incredible that anyone could so distort the truth, and in a court of law, too, where—it seemed to me—it must have a specially sacred quality. My principles had been outraged. I resolved that my own evidence would be the truth, the whole truth, and nothing—of any sort, shape or description—but the truth.

My counsel rose to his feet. 'I suggest,' he said to me, 'that you tell the court what happened, in your own words.'

I stood up. I took a deep breath. 'You may be seated, if you wish,' said the judge. I sat down again.

'What happened was this,' I said. 'I'd been playing golf. I had one bottle of lager afterwards, because I was going on to a party, and didn't want to get full before the fun started.'

The other man's solicitor stood up. 'May I, my lord,' he said, 'put a question to the witness?' The judge seemed surprised, but he gave his assent.

'You are accustomed to drink heavily?' the solicitor asked me.

I considered it. 'I certainly do get pretty high now and then,' I said, 'if there's a party on.'

'Thank you,' said the solicitor. He sat down. I caught a glimpse of my counsel's face. His mouth was wide open.

'Well, to continue,' I said, 'I was driving more carefully than usual. I'd had a couple of bad smashes already, and I didn't want another one. Didn't want to miss the party, you know,' I explained to the judge.

He nodded. He was leaning forward watching me with a rapt expression.

'But suddenly,' I said, 'a small family saloon shot past me. It was full of children, with a pram on the luggage-grid, and a mattress strapped across the roof. I couldn't let that go, of course, so I put my foot down.'

The solicitor was up again. 'You mean you increased your speed?' he said.

'That's it,' I said, 'put my foot right down. I caught the saloon in the next half-mile, and passed him.'

My counsel stood up. 'Mr Campbell,' he said, 'your car is a twelve-year-old, seven horse-power, two-seater. What speed would you say you were doing when you passed this other vehicle? I suggest, in view of the age and size of your machine, that it could not have been very much more than 35 m.p.h.'

'Thirty-eight,' I said, 'thirty-eight miles an hour. I was watching the clock all the time. But probably it was a bit more. The speedometer is slow.'

'I see,' said my counsel. He seemed to be about to go on. Then he sat down again. He loosened his collar.

'Well,' I said, 'I came to this straight bit of road . . .'

'You were on your own side, of course,' said the judge. The normal procedure of the court seemed to have broken down. Everyone seemed to be asking questions as they liked.

'Nobody drives on their own side of a dead straight, empty road,' I said curtly. 'I was nearer the middle.'

'I see,' said the judge. 'Thank you,' he added, after a moment. He sat further forward in his chair. 'Go on, please,' he said.

'Well,' I said, 'I was travelling fairly fast, watching the speedometer, when all at once I saw this other car coming out of a laneway backwards.'

'Excuse me,' said the judge, 'when you say "at once" do you mean that this other car suddenly appeared in front of you without warning?'

'Oh no,' I said—'I must have been a hundred yards or so away when I first saw it.'

'But you did nothing to avoid a collision,' put in the solicitor, 'you didn't slacken speed, or blow your horn, or take any other reasonable precaution?'

'Well, no,' I said, 'I was too busy watching the clock. I'd never got up to forty before on that particular stretch.'

The judge cleared his throat. 'Mr Tennant,' he said, addressing my counsel, 'have you any question you would like to ask? I cannot help feeling that your client is not, perhaps, doing himself full justice.'

Tennant got up—reluctantly, I thought. 'Mr Campbell,' he said, 'what, in your opinion, was the cause of this accident? Take your time before replying. We are all here to help you, and—er—to see justice done.' He looked rather helplessly at the judge. The judge nodded. Tennant sat down. He began playing with his collar again.

'It's perfectly obvious how this accident happened,' I said. 'This other damn man came shooting out of the lane backwards, lighting a cigarette, without looking where he was going. How could I help running into him?'

They considered it in silence. The judge looked at Tennant. Tennant looked at the solicitor. The solicitor looked at the roof.

'I don't see that there's anything more to be said about it,' I added. 'The facts are perfectly plain.'

The solicitor pulled himself together.

'My lord,' he said, 'may I respectfully suggest that you give judgment in favour of my client. The defendant, by his own admission, is of an unstable nature, accustomed to taking alcohol, has already been involved in a number of other accidents, has stated on oath that he was driving at an excessive speed, and furthermore admits that he was actually looking at the speedometer at the time of the . . .'

'I said I was looking at the speedometer all right,' I broke in, 'but if you knew anything about cars you'd know that you can look at the speedometer

165

and sort of peep out under your eyelids at the road at the same time.'

Nobody said anything. The judge made a gesture. 'Please,' he said, 'just one moment. You were saying, Mr Marshall . . .?'

'Well,' said Marshall, 'I don't think I have anything more to add.'

'Thank you,' said the judge. He looked at Tennant enquiringly. Tennant shook his head. 'Nothing, my lord,' he said, 'we have nothing to add to our—ha—case.'

The judge sat back. He fiddled with some papers, and then whispered something to the clerk. The clerk shook his head.

'H'm,' said the judge. He cleared his throat again. 'Before I pronounce judgment in this case,' he said, 'I should like to say that it has been one of the most difficult matters that has been brought before me for some time. Without wishing to offer what might be deemed unwanted criticism I should like to point out that the attitude adopted by the defendant has gone a considerable way towards complicating what appeared at first to be a comparatively simple issue.'

He stopped, and looked round the court. Nobody said anything.

Suddenly the judge snapped out, 'I award the plaintiff £150 damages, the costs to be borne by the defendant.'

He turned to me. 'Mr Campbell,' he said, 'in view of the fact that we have already had the pleasure of doing so on several occasions it is probable that we will meet again socially in the near future. I shall then explain to you, even without your consent, why this case has gone against you. It appears to me to be a matter of some importance.'

'Me too,' said I. 'I've told you the truth. I'm two-thirds innocent. Now I have to pay a lot of damages. Why?'

'There are ways and means,' said the judge, 'of presenting evidence. You have hit upon the one least likely, under the present judicial system, to succeed. I shall go into this matter at greater length on a less formal occasion.'

He stopped. 'The court,' he added, 'will appreciate that no precedent is being set. Next case!'

'What was all that about?' I said to Tennant, as we made our way out. 'He lets us in for a hundred and fifty quid, and now he wants to explain why he did it. What for?'

'I think,' said Tennant, 'he wants to save you from getting hanged.'

From *A Long Drink of Cold Water*, 1949

PART SIX

THE AUTOMOBILE GROWS UP

When that distinguished British motoring writer Owen John went to the 1906 London Motor Show at Olympia, only four years had passed since Charles Rolls had advised his fellow automobilists on the vagaries of the petrol engine (see page 22). The capriciousness of internal combustion had not much reduced in the interval. Motoring was still an adventure. But the horizon's shape was sharply etched, for those who cared to glance towards it. The automobile had already won. With the advantage of hindsight we can already descry the momentous influence of the work of Ford in America, Benz in Germany and Royce in Britain. At Olympia, John was clearly shocked to notice that the top hat was no longer being worn. This disturbance of established custom had, of course, more than social significance. Another twenty years were to pass before the lower middle classes bought their bullnosed Morris-Cowleys by the thousand, and by hire purchase, from William Morris. But, as John reflects, business intentions in 1906 were serious: the motor industry was growing up. We like to flatter (and frighten) ourselves today with the boast that we are in the throes of the swiftest technological revolution of all time. Never has the pace of modern . . . and all that! I think this is open to dispute; and I think Laurence Pomeroy will agree with me. In all fields of engineering—most of all those directly relating to marine engineering and those branches connected with armament manufacture— the rate of development immediately before the First World War was astonishing. Numerous examples can be cited. Let us take submarines. A mere ten years separated the small precarious coastal and harbour defence craft, despised by all but a handful of visionaries in 1907, and ocean-going vessels of ten times the size, carrying battle-ship calibre guns in some cases, dominating the war at sea and coming near to bringing Britain to her knees. Only eight years separated the completion of the first tubby, slow, reciprocating-engined German Dreadnought, and the commissioning of the swift, devastatingly efficient, turbine-powered battle cruiser Hindenburg, *which incorporated in its design a multitude of refinements and prodigies of power never contemplated at the designing stage of its predecessor. In the automobile world, the years 1909-14 revealed some of the finest and most advanced work of Birkigt, Pomeroy Sen., Porter, Delage, Porsche, Henri and Bugatti.*

The state of automobile development in the full throes of revolution in 1910–14 is fascinating and deserves special attention. It also deserves to be seen from both sides of the Atlantic, with all their very evident contrasts. We continue, then, with an address delivered by C. Y. Knight (of sleeve valve fame) before the Chicago Motor Club on December 28, 1909, on the state of the European automobile industry, ' seen through the eyes of an American engineer'.

This is followed by the views of S. F. Edge, one of Britain's most colourful and loquacious motor car promoters, on the state of automobilism in America at the same period: a paper delivered before the Coventry Engineering Society on January 14, 1910.

The emphasis remains across the Atlantic with a brief statement of facts and figures on the American Automobile Industry in 1910 (offered by Hugh Chalmers to Detroit College); and an account of the beginnings of standardization and mass production in the United States.

So far this is all contemporary writing. But this Part would not be complete without the inclusion of the chapter by Laurence Pomeroy (whose father's genius was then in full flower) entitled 'New Men and New Methods', from his joint work with Kent Karslake, Veteran to Vintage. *This is a useful and reasoned summary of the achievements of some of the men who brought about an engineering revolution as important as that accomplished by Watt, the Stephensons and the Brunels; and in a few years rather than a few decades.*

Finally, we conclude with statistical data and comment on twenty makes of motor car from England, Scotland, Austria, Germany, America, France, Belgium, Italy, Switzerland and Holland—a brief sampling of some of the great number of models at the London Motor Show in 1913. The motor car had indeed grown up by then, both technically and numerically, and had become industrially important in numerous countries.

The Olympia Show, 1906

BY OWEN JOHN

I HAVE got into the habit of dating the beginning of winter from the opening of the motor show. Last year I started off in a snowstorm to visit it, and this year I got home in another. Last year I got badly stuck up coming home, but this year my little trip of over three hundred miles was as uneventful as my former two thousand since September except for the weather. The first thing that struck me was an adventure with a would-be robber at what he was pleased to call a *garage* about three-quarters of a mile from Olympia. I fortunately asked him his terms outside his shed, and when he told me they were a shilling an hour and five shillings a night I turned and fled to the yard of a public house, which gave me a separate shed for eighteenpence for the twenty-four hours. When I arrived on the scene of action my first impression was the wonderful state of readiness that was visible—hardly a sign of unpreparedness or haste. The next was the startling absence of the top hat. This shows serious business intentions, for it is well known that top hats are now only worn out of the city, at weddings, social functions in the season, and by persons in search of clerical employment. Of course, there may be other reasons, but I am speaking generally, and make my position absolutely safe by coupling frock coats to them. This does not apply to the Brewers' Exhibition.

This is the distinction I have got into the habit of drawing between the body and chassis of a motor vehicle. It is a regrettable fact that nowadays, however pure your soul (which means excellent is your chassis), the ordinary person will not stop and admire unless there is something bizarre and extraordinary about your body. Let us take the James and Browne six-cylinder touring carriage as an example, and I trust the firm will not be annoyed if I mention my dislike to their familiar title of 'J. and B.' I am old-fashioned enough to say 'telegraph', and not 'wire', and go so far as to prophesy that the Great Central Railway would become a more fashionable line if the general manager signed himself 'Samuel' instead of 'Sam' Fay. But this is very much by the way.

To return to the James and Browne stand and cars, I have not the faintest notion at present whether the engines are vertical or horizontal, or indeed of anything that happens under the 5 ft. long *mauve* decked bonnet, because my eyes never got beyond the same prevailing delicate boudoirish tint, the glitter of decanters, and the silver and walnut of the cigar boxes that focused the attentions of the untechnical many. Fancy all these perfections colliding and jamming with a cart conveying the staple industry of Brentford,

169

and why not? Then on the Rolls-Royce stand I beheld a gloriously striped chariot, with pendant bronze torches holding electric bulbs inside, sumptuously furnished and adorned with marvellous port-holes. Surely this firm of all firms stands not in need of such extra embellishments? I take it that almost every visitor came to the show fully intending to inspect the Rolls-Royce exhibit. If good wine needs no bush, surely this brand of car needs no extraneous attractions? But I expect they know their business best, and their meteoric rise into the position of one of the three first firms in England is a proof of it. With regard to the big Daimler, that looked as if it had been trying to pass the mustard and run into it, the inscription that it was to the order of an Indian potentate disarmed criticism, and, like the Rolls-Royce, the other exhibits on the stand made one glad they were so easy to find, which may have been the intention.

Why are most American cars called by their exhibitors 'incomparable'? I asked someone as to this, and he said that he thought it was because they could not be compared with English ones. But I think he was unkind. Certainly, their bodywork (excepting the White) has unaccustomed lines, and the new four-cylinder Cadillac engine, crowded with loose wires, looked like the inside of a motor boat trawled up in a torpedo net. At the same time, I admire the exhibitor for displaying all his wires and pipes—there is far too general a habit of disposing of all these contraptions on a show chassis, and pointing out the extreme simplicity of the engine, and the accessibility of its parts, with the result that the beginner hardly recognizes his purchase when it comes home to him in full panoply for travel.

The Humber, Argyll, and Talbot stands were so well patronized that it was as difficult to get near them, and, generally speaking, if there were any anti-motorists about they must have gone back sadly shaking their heads and resolving no longer to try to stop a tide that apparently is doubling its volume every year. I have not said much about the foreign cars, and, indeed, it is a curious reversal of things that used to be, to look around and see how lost they are amongst the crowd of home-made ones. And yet they are there, and a goodly show they make.

With regard to the galleries there is not so much to say, and the difference year by year, though it exists, is not so apparent as down below. Perhaps the greatest change of all was in the roof, which was gaily decorated with pink and yellow silk extinguishers and garlands. I could not help momentarily expecting them to disgorge showers of confetti and coloured paper ribbons on all below, in which case the band would certainly burst into the maddest and merriest music, and stallholders, general public, and the press, would have joined in the giddy revels. Perhaps this will happen on the closing night, for the volume of orders recorded on the books and faces of nearly every exhibitor certainly necessitates some such outlet to mark the festive occasion.

From *The Autocar*, November 24, 1906

The European Motor Car in 1909

BY C. Y. KNIGHT

THE STATUS of the automobile business abroad today is considerably improved over that which has prevailed during the preceding two years, but conditions are by no means as favourable as they are in America, nor need it ever be expected that Europe will to any extent parallel the United States in eve production of motor cars. The natural resources of Europe have to a very great extent been exhausted through centuries of use by man. The proportion of people who have it within their power to purchase a motor car is very small. Despite the fact that the roads, as compared with those that exist upon this side, are practically perfect in almost every one of the first-class countries, motor cars are not met with to the extent one would naturally expect. As a matter of fact, it is surprising how few cars one will encounter in a drive through France, the roads of which are almost perfect and most plentiful.

Taken as a whole, France, of course, may be classed as the centre of the industry upon that side. There are probably a greater number of large manufacturing concerns in that country than in any other across the water. But these concerns do not in any measure compare either in number or magnitude with those in America. In fact, with one notable exception, I might say that, were the largest establishments of France set down in America, they would be called only moderate-sized concerns, and compared with a number of leading establishments on this side, even small. I do not believe there is more than one concern in France—and I might say in England or Europe—whose annual output exceeds 2,000 cars, and even this concern's production is made up largely of taxicabs, the value of which does not count much in the aggregate.

In Germany, so far as I have been able to ascertain (and I have seen the statistics), about the largest production amounts to 1,200 cars per year, and this is of what we would call a comparatively small type on this side. There are dozens of concerns in this country making a larger output than the largest in Germany. The German industry, as a whole, is noted for the high class of its workmanship, quality of materials and general efficiency of the combination rather than for number of cars produced or number of makers.

The condition in Italy is deplorable. It would seem that the country went motor mad as the result of the success of one of the well-known Italian cars which through the splendid achievement of a number of its drivers in races won world-wide reputation and for a while threatened the supremacy of France. This was a signal for dozens of concerns to spring up all over the

171

country, to which the people rushed wildly to invest their money, and the puncturing of the boom by the last financial stringency has resulted in practical bankruptcy for almost every concern throughout the unfortunate kingdom. From the best information which I have at hand, I would say that very few, if any, of the Italian manufacturers are doing any great amount of business, and I might say that the interest taken as a whole could safely be classed as insolvent.

In Austria there are but few manufacturers and those are small and have not been successful in producing a great many cars, nor have these cars been fortunate enough to win distinction through any particular feature or achievement.

The Belgians are marvellously ingenious and good mechanical people, and in this small but busy country several cars have won distinction in one way or another. There are but few manufacturers, yet those few appear to be resting upon a particularly solid foundation. Holland manufactures one or two makes of cars: Switzerland has one or two, and there is a growing interest in Russia which promises well for the future of that country as a market, if not a manufacturing factor.

The northern countries, such as Norway, Sweden and Denmark, have practically no motor interest, roads not being so suitable to its development, whereas, the people of Spain, on account of the miserable roads and impoverished conditions of both, have done very little along this line, and all that has been said of Spain may be applied to Portugal.

When we cross the Channel, coming this way, we encounter a condition different from any on the Continent. While England, as a country, is not wealthy in minerals, with the exception of coal, nor productive in agriculture, except to some extent in live-stock, it is a nation of shop-keepers and manufacturers and of marvellously wealthy people. The first ambition of the educated Englishman is to acquire a competence, and he is most careful and frugal from the beginning of his business career until he is ready to retire from active trade, which is at a much earlier age than the business men of any other nation in the world. He lays by a proportion of his earnings or profits against the day when he may rest on his oars and enjoy the fruits of his early endeavours. As careful as the Englishman is, however, to acquire a competency which he may enjoy in later life, he is afterwards wonderfully liberal in spending his money up to a certain point. He differs from the Continental in the respect that he will spend his money to within a narrow margin of his fixed income, and nearly always in proportion, therewith, while it is characteristic of the Frenchman that it makes little difference what his resources, disbursements will not be greatly increased, though his income grows rapidly. He is wonderfully frugal and conservative. The Englishman is conservative, but may not be called frugal to the extent of his French brother.

England from early days has been a progressive nation in the matter of commerce. It may be said that it is a nation of merchants. For hundreds of years this people spread its energies over the world, and established able connections in the most productive regions of the various countries, where thousands upon thousands have investments which bring them fixed and steady incomes. As a matter of fact, the English people might be compared with an octopus, the body being England and the tentacles the various lines of commerce with which they reach all over the world. It is said in England that when railroads pay dividends in America, English people will increase their purchases. The Englishman controls the goldfields of South Africa, which pour into London millions of dollars of treasure every week; he is interested in rubber plantations all over the world, and, in fact, always ready to lend his resources to the development of any field of commerce which looks promising. England is naturally a nation of speculators. Almost every man, woman and child dabbles in stocks to a greater or less extent. The result is that they have both means and leisure for enjoying motor cars, and all Europe depends to a great extent on England as a dumping ground for its products.

Belgium, for instance, expects to market at least 50 per cent of its product of motors in England, while it is probable that nine-tenths of the thousands of motor cabs which ply the streets of the cities of Great Britain are produced in France. I presume that even a greater percentage than one-half of Germany's cars come to England for market, and Italy certainly also looks to that country to absorb a great percentage of her output, there being no home demand of consequence for Italian cars.

It is because of the start which the Continental manufacturers secured over the English industry, as a result of the Tom-fool red flag law, which remained in force in the United Kingdom until the motor car became finally established on the Continent, that the English manufacturer was tardy in the field of development. When this four-mile limit was repealed there were no English manufacturers of consequence to fill the demand for cars, and the English buyer naturally turned to France and Germany, both of which, because of the unhampered home markets they had enjoyed for years, had created a capacity which served as a basis for filling the demand. It was not until the repeal of the fanatical law that the English manufacturer had an opportunity for experience in the production of cars. His creation was looked upon, in comparison with the more finished product of the Continental maker, in much the same light as were the early efforts of our American manufacturers by our wealthy citizens, and the high-class people of England looked upon the home-made cars with a feeling akin to contempt. This condition, coupled with the fact that England's exports were hampered by tariff barriers at the gates of all other countries, whereas the Continent could ship cars to England without money and without price, so far as taxes were concerned, operated to hold the English manufacturer back. However, while it may possibly be said that the Englishman is slow to move, conservative to act, and not strikingly original, he does have one characteristic which is valuable enough in the long run to more than make up for that short-coming, and a trait which is responsible for England's commercial greatness, namely, his staid and persistent steadiness. His methods may be somewhat slow from our point of view, but they are safe and sure. He may not originate a new thing, but he will take it and improve upon it along safe and conservative lines. He will succeed in production when others would fail in effort. For instance, a few years ago American-made machine tools were almost universally used in the shops of England. Today the English manufacturer has not only improved the American tool, but gone the originator one better by adapting the design more properly to the English requirements. So with the English motor car. In the early days it was constructed along the well-known English practice of enormous weights and bulky strength. Latterly, through slow but painstaking evolution, weights have been reduced, the quality of material improved, and the product generally refined. I believe today that the product of the leading manufacturers of England is of as high a character as that of the manufacturers of any other country in the world. The English people are a people of high business morals and unquestioned integrity. Whatever they manufacture partakes largely of these sterling qualities. Cars are not produced for mere selling purposes, without regard to what may become of them after they leave the works. In fact, I think the very limited area of the country has something to do with the care with which our English cousins put the machines together, because one can start from any corner of the land at daylight and reach the farthest portion by sunset on a summer's day, and the British owner has a very annoying habit when his car is not up to concert pitch of jumping into it and driving to the factory, there to confront the powers that be, as there are no such things as bad roads to protect the shop engineers from unpleasant calls from any point. I picture some owner of an American car in California driving it across the continent to Buffalo to see about a defect in the rear springs or the intermittent action of a trembler coil! I have a large, boudoir-sized photograph of this!

Manufacturers in England, however, are a most conservative lot, and it may be said that, while business has improved to a remarkable extent during the past two years, there are few, if any, new concerns springing up. As a matter of fact, last year four of the leading institutions had very narrow escapes from bankruptcy because of their great proportions when compared with their available market. Three of these have not as yet recovered from their perilous financial condition, and I doubt if they ever will. It may be said that there are only two establishments in England which may be called fairly large. The Daimler Co. at Coventry is one of the most important of all English concerns, and is at present employing 3,200 men about fifteen hours a day, the working hours at this time for the machine shop being 6 o'clock in the morning until 9.15 in the evening. The production for the coming year, however, will not exceed 2,000 cars.

It is a noticeable feature of European business that few concerns are confined to one or two models. The Mercedes Co., of Germany, will produce twelve different sizes and types of cars during the season of 1910. The Daimler Co., of England, will turn out seven types; Panhard and Levassor, of France, will probably produce as many types as the Mercedes Co., of Germany; and even a small Belgian firm whose output does not exceed five hundred cars will make at least three models. The result of this great number of models is to increase the cost of production to a great extent. Taking down and setting up tools for so many parts necessitates having a great multiplicity of patterns, jigs, dies, etc., and the necessity of accumulating a great variety of supplies handicaps production tremendously.

I am asked to compare foreign cars in detail with those produced in this country. This is a most difficult proposition, for the reason that conditions under which the cars are used in Europe are entirely different from those under which American cars are used here. I have stated that, so far as I can observe, our best American cars are as good as the best cars produced in any other country in the world. Yet it would be difficult to say how American cars operated under the same conditions would stand up, compared with those produced upon the Continent. Americans repeatedly draw attention to the miserable roads upon this side as evidence that superior chassis and general design is necessary to withstand the stresses thereby produced. It is possible that this may be the case with regard to certain elements of the cars, such as axles and springs, but motor cars on the Continent and in a large portion of Europe are used in a manner never contemplated by the American manufacturer. In France, in particular, the most perfect design in construction is required to withstand the tremendous speeds which are attained upon the long stretches of straight roads encountered in nearly every section of that country. The motor which in America might be used for years, with no suggestion of difficulty, is liable to be broken to pieces within a limit of twenty-five miles in France. The French driver especially is a most reckless and daredevil sort of a fellow. He opens his throttle regardless of conditions, and does not consider for a moment that the motor is entitled to the slightest bit of consideration. The lubricating mechanism and other features of the car are supposed to be foolproof, and at the tremendous speeds attained the usual warnings which an abused mechanism sends forth are entirely drowned out through the rush of air and vibration of the car. A French smash is usually a bad smash.

The failure of American and English manufacturers in the racing game in

175

France is very largely due to the lack of comprehension of these conditions. As a matter of fact, I believe that France is the only country in the world where a motor car can be tested out to a point which will ensure its operating successfully within the borders of that country. Even England, which has 157,000 miles of improved roads, has very few stretches where more than five miles straight away can be had for testing the motor at full speed. No test upon the bench or brake can be depended upon to reveal weaknesses which might be brought out upon these roads at top speed. Very few manufacturers of fair-sized motors pretend to test them above 1,200 revolutions per minute. Then, when this motor goes on the road in the chassis and the operator opens up his throttle to sixty miles an hour or more for a long stretch, as great as he can find, the motor may be delivering its full power at 1,700 or 1,800 revolutions per minute, and a lubricating mechanism which is arranged to supply the cylinders at an average speed of 1,200 is inadequate at 1,700 on account of the great heat generated in the cylinder, which increases much more rapidly in proportion than the speed of the motor. It is my opinion, based upon general observation, that because of the strenuous work that the foreign cars are called upon to do, the average efficiency of the Continental motors, as far as the production of power is concerned, is in advance of the motors of this country, the difference lying very largely in carburation and dimensions of gas passages.

It is my observation that, while the American manufacturers of motors so time the opening and closing of their valves as to produce the quietest effect in operation, the Continental maker, with few exceptions, does the reverse, and designs his motor for power and speed. You may take it that with the poppet valve motor quiet running is invariably obtained at the sacrifice of efficiency, whereas the strength of the valve springs and the character of openings required for the greatest development of power carry with them the necessity for noisy valves and tappets.

It is my firm conviction that the French manufacturers have made two very great blunders within the past two years. First was their decision to abandon the Paris Salon, and the second the dropping of the Grand Prix. Great pressure was brought upon the Society of Motor Manufacturers of England to induce them to abandon the Olympia Show. This, however, they refused to do, and the unlooked-for and unprecedented success of the Olympia just closed has fully justified their attitude. The fact of it being the only show of consequence on the other side this year resulted in the huge success of that one show, and the foreign buyer who in former years visited the Continent but once a year, at the advent of the Paris Show, this time visited Olympia, giving the English manufacturers a chance to do business with him. The great success of the Olympia Show is encouraging for the motor business of the entire world, as it demonstrates the fact that even in those countries where automobilism has been indulged in by the people the greatest length of time, there is no evidence of waning interest, the fact being that such interest is growing.

The great feature of the recent Olympia Show was the general rush of trade toward the small-sized cars. However, in that this does not necessarily mean small price. It is the general desire of the Continental and English motorist to reduce the cost of upkeep of his car to the minimum. With the tremendous advance in the price of rubber, the advent of a six per cent per gallon tax upon petrol, and a yearly revenue tax amounting to $50.00 on a 40 h.p. car, and $200.00 on a 60 h.p., makes motoring much more expensive than ever before. Yet I must say that the general opinion at the close of the show was that very many more larger cars than anticipated were disposed of, and the pendulum, having been rushed precipitately to one side through sheer weight of numbers, seems to be swinging in the other direction to some extent.

Indications of two most radical mechanical departures are plainly apparent upon the English motor horizon and cannot be ignored by the remainder of the motor world, because they are undoubtedly in the right direction and tend toward economy and efficiency.

The first has been in evidence for several seasons, but the latter has attracted little attention until during the past few months.

Quickly detachable wire wheels have undoubtedly come to stay. While they were apparent only upon two or three makes of two years ago, few English concerns for 1910 will care to go into the market with a car without provisions for supplying this important improvement. In 1908 the Daimler Co. put out probably six cars with removable wire wheels. Last year almost 75 per cent were thus equipped, while for 1910 at least nine out of ten Daimler cars will carry the quickly detachable wire wheel, and every wheel upon every chassis will be removable, though the spokes may be of wood. It is the general experience of those who employ the wire wheels that they add life, as well as speed and smoothness, to the car, while the tyre bills are unmistakably greatly reduced. Personally, I would not care, as a permanent thing, to drive a car with wooden wheels after my two years of contact and year of experience with the detachable wire wheel—the former appear most clumsy and useless weight to me.

While the equipment has not found as much favour on the Continent, because of the fact that it originated with England, the fact that foreign makers who supply cars to English buyers are compelled to meet their wishes in this connection is an entering wedge which is rapidly introducing the wire wheel into Europe, not, however, without considerable resistance upon the part of the Continental manufacturers who two years ago barred the employment of the removable wire wheel from the Grand Prix, and at the same time eliminated the most promising British competitor. Americans object to the wheel upon the ground of washing difficulties, but practical experience has proven that this is more fancied than real.

M   177

The second undoubted evolution, which was unmistakably heralded at the recent Olympia Show, is the substitution of the worm drive for the bevel propulsion for small cars. This practice has for many years had two successful adherents in England, and for 1910 there will be no less than a half-dozen recruits. The cause of the evolution is the general tendency to produce enclosed cars for town use with large bodies and small motors. This means a further increase in the ratio between the pinion and crown gear in the rear axle, and corresponding increase of difficulty of production. It is well known to engineers that when the ratio between the driver and the driven bevel goes lower than three-to-one the problem of producing quiet gears increases to a maddening extent. And if I were asked today what is the outstanding obstacle to the production of the car as demanded by the purchaser, who yearly becomes more discriminating, I would answer the production of quiet gears.

The worm gear is always quiet, and lends itself particularly to low ratios. It has been until very recently considered less efficient than the bevel. But investigation and experience have demonstrated that this deficiency is more in workmanship than design. Properly constructed, the worm gives results quite indistinguishable from the bevel. So far, however, such perfection has only been attained by worms produced on one particular machine which so cuts the tooth that the greatest possible bearing surface is obtained, and thus the tendency of the oil to squeeze out at low speeds because of the abnormally high pressures is avoided. Speed tests on Brooklands between worm and bevel-driven 15 h.p. Daimler cars leave no room for choice, and the silent and smooth effect in the tonneau of an enclosed car is as pleasing to the customer as the ease of manufacture and adjustment of the worm gear is to the maker. I know that several American makers are testing the worm for small town cars.

The six-cylinder proposition is no longer discussed upon the other side. There seems to be a general admission that up to a certain horse-power the four-cylinder answers every requirement, and that above those sizes the six is desirable. The problems of construction naturally increase with multiplicity of cylinders, not, however, upon the basis of numbers or in proportion thereto, these problems being of an entirely different character and concern the designer almost wholly. A six-cylinder motor built upon the basis of the simple addition of two more cylinders to the four, having no regard for increased dimensions of certain parts, or attention to carburation spells six-cylinder failure, and this almost every designer has had to learn through most expensive and nerve-racking experience.

From an address given to the Chicago Motor
Club, December 28, 1909

The American Automobile in 1909

BY S. F. EDGE

CURIOUSLY ENOUGH the first hint that automobilism in America was different from automobilism in this country was given to me on board the steamer which took me from England to America. Before I had been on board many hours I was spoken to by an American who asked me if I was Edge the motorist, and I replied that I certainly was a motorist, and that my name was Edge.

This gentleman was an exceedingly keen automobilist and a highly intelligent man, and so before we reached the American shore I had learnt quite a lot about motoring in America and American motoring from this very kind friend. His knowledge of the motor, motoring industry, and motoring topics all over the world was extraordinarily good, and at once set me wondering and asking him questions, so that I might find out why it was that a man in his position—he was a stockbroker in Boston—had such a very thorough knowledge of motoring in all its branches in many parts of the world, covering manufacturing, driving, and the technical side, and after many discussions which I had with him, I arrived at the following conclusion:

That in America much younger men than in England were able to afford high-class motor cars, and this frequently caused them, therefore, to drive themselves, and by driving themselves they, of course, got a very clear technical knowledge. Another reason that caused them to drive themselves was the fact that a chauffeur in America generally had to be paid at least £5 a week, and the procedure that many automobilists in America in the large towns adopt is that they have automobile clubs which put in the forefront the advantages of a large garage, where their cars are washed, stored, and cleaned, so that the owner only had to go round to his automobile club and there find his car ready for use, filled up with petrol, and cleaned ready for the road, he himself doing all the driving and ordinary little technical adjustments that are necessary and desirable if a motor car is to be kept in its best possible condition.

Another reason I found so many people drive their own cars in America is that, as a whole, as I mentioned before, people are much younger who are able to afford cars, and not only do they appear to make their money earlier than is the case in this country, but even those who are more advanced in years seem to keep a much younger mind and a more sporting mind, at any rate as far as automobilism is concerned, than is the case in this country. The bulk of the cars, owing to their owners driving, are still open cars, and I would certainly say, from the point of view of personal driving and enthusiasm in motoring matters, that America is now where we were in this country, say, five years ago.

When I arrived in New York, even after a few hours I began to notice the differences of automobilism in New York from, say, London or any other large British city.

The taxicabs were to be seen, generally speaking, in a very poor condition compared to London taxicabs, not that they were necessarily worse cabs, but because they were badly kept up, and it was quite evident that they were not sent out by such well organized cab companies as exist in this country.

I heard terrible stories of the class of driver employed on these taxicabs, and how badly they drove, but my own experience did not confirm this. I used a good many while in New York, and I found the drivers exceedingly obliging and civil, and I also found that they drove quite nicely.

The police regulations seem most excellent, and should be copied by this and other countries. The system of only allowing the vehicles to draw up by the side of the pavement on the near-side, whichever way one might be proceeding, was most excellent, and added a great smoothness to the traffic. Also I found that the control by the police was exceedingly good and effective. Here again, I had been led to believe that the police in New York were exceedingly arbitrary and rude. My experience—and I went out of my way to ask questions of them at times—was that they were quite as civil as the London policemen, they were highly intelligent, and I never saw traffic under more perfect control. Undoubtedly their methods of dealing with delinquents for breaking the traffic regulations are severe and quick, because the breaker of the regulations is immediately stopped and taken away to the police station. It does not seem to matter who the driver is, no preference is given to the rich man over the most ordinary driver, and there is no difference made between horse-drawn vehicles and motor cars—all are treated in the same impartial manner.

While I was in the office of a well-known legal gentleman he had a telephone call, which he told me was from his wife, who was out driving in their horse brougham. A woman had run off the pavement and got underneath the horse. The coachman was immediately arrested and taken off to the police station, where he was waiting for some responsible person to bail him out. This summary method no doubt had its disadvantages, but it certainly had a splendid effect on the way roads and streets in New York were used.

I did not come across one single case of inconsiderate driving in New York; it apparently had a good effect on automobilism as a whole.

There is a peculiarity in New York and other large American cities, and that is outside a number of hotels and squares you find standing large 40 h.p. pleasure vehicles plying for hire. There is also a great difficulty in the establishment of taxicabs in New York, because the system of running about the streets and picking up fares wherever the taxicab drivers can is not allowed in the same free manner as is the case in London and other English cities. The taxicabs are generally attached to some hotel or some special rank, and their licence is so indicated, and therefore they are at this disadvantage: if they pick up a fare at one end of New York and travel to the other end they cannot pick up a fare off their own rank, but have to travel back to their original standing place empty. Also owing to the fact that one end of New York is residential and the other end business, and that New York City is built on a long narrow piece of land, and that the traffic is one way in the morning and another in the evening, there is not the chance for taxicab drivers to roam about the streets to pick up a fare, but they have to stop in the city end to bring them back to the residential end if they have travelled to the city end in the morning, and for this reason taxicab proprietors find it more beneficial to attach themselves either to an hotel or some special stand, even with the disadvantage of which I have told you.

Every method of getting about New York, except by the trams, or trolley cars as they are called there, and the overhead or underground railways, is exceedingly dear. The horse cabs are practically prohibitive, and hardly anyone except strangers or people with a large amount of money use them. The taxicabs, however, are creating a new class of user, the class who has been to Europe and seen the comfortable way in which people with money can travel about London in a taxicab, and he is beginning to find it is not conducive to best work when he gets to his office to have first had a fight on the overhead or underground railway, or even on the street car to get on board, and then stand there hanging to a strap, because owing to the vast number of people that travel from one end of New York to the other end at certain times in the day, their methods of transport, although very good, are not adequate for the terrific strain put upon them for a couple of hours each way each day. I therefore look forward to the time when the New York man, or, at any rate, the man with money, will use the taxicab to a greater extent than he is doing today, and the taxicab is growing in most cities throughout America for the simple reason that there are such an enormous number of people with sufficient money to use them. The vast crowd of Americans who come over to Europe every year from cities in every part of America find the great convenience of the taxicab in European cities, and they go back home and expect to have them there.

Now in regard to motor cars in America in general, there are two great classes of users there:

1. The man who buys a motor car for pleasure, and he is at present buying a car modelled more or less on European lines, who generally drives it himself, and has a fairly powerful vehicle, as a rule 30 h.p. to 60 h.p. R.A.C. rating. A couple of years ago this class were chiefly buying these powerful cars with seven-seater bodies; today they are buying either two-seater

runabouts on the same type of chassis, or little four-seater tonneaux, which they call baby tonneaux. This class are keen and relatively young, and appear capable of absorbing at least five times the number of motor cars per head of the population as is possible in this country. Most of these people use the automobile purely for pleasure, and it has not entered into their business life from a point worth considering, whereas, already in this country, and in Europe generally, the bulk of the people who are buying motor cars today are using them purely and simply as a method of conveyance and not merely as a method of pleasure.

2. The other great class in America who are using motor cars are the class who are simply forced to use them through the fact that they have no other method of transport that would enable them to live on their farms in out of the way places, considerable distances from the towns and railway centres, but with the addition of an automobile they can pursue their work, which extends over large tracks of country with a population very widely divided. This class means a permanent and fixed trade for the automobile, because:

(i) It brings the old farmer into touch with civilization in a way that he could never be if he had to depend upon horses.

(ii) It has made farming possible for a man with an intelligent mind who requires the mental stimulus that mixing with his fellow men gives, as he is enabled to live on his farm during the week, and for week-ends with the aid of his motor car he can get into touch with the civilization of the town.

This class are buying automobiles of a light cheap type, that have enabled the motor car factories of the West to get the colossal outputs which we hear of working up to 20,000 cars per annum from one factory. These outputs are achieved by merely assembling parts bought from large part makers. They are not a type of motor car that commend themselves to our ideas; they go, and they appear to give satisfaction, and I believe the reason for this is that the conditions under which they are used are so different from what we are accustomed to. In this country, and on the Continent, motor cars, even quite a small cheap type, are habitually driven at speeds from twenty to thirty miles an hour, but these cheap American cars are used over rough country, where although the strains may be more severe in some directions, owing to ruts and holes, the speed at which they travel does not set up the kind of vibration that is put upon them in Europe. I think the best proof of this is to see the motor cars with all the steering joints held together merely by clips, such as are used to clip a seat-pillar and hold this firm on a bicycle. How many people in England would care to drive in a motor car in which the steering connections were held together by bicycle seat-pillar clips?

I have often wondered when reading the American papers, and seeing the very big list of motor car casualties that seemed to be recorded from day to day when I was there, in which the driver was blamed for taking the corner too fast, or something of that sort, whether they are really caused by these methods of joining the steering. It seemed to me, if most of the cars were driven at all fast, sooner or later it would lead to disaster.

Now automobilism amongst these two great classes in America is making most extraordinary progress. As I have already said, at least five times as many people motor in America, *pro rata* to the population, as is the case in this country, and I believe this percentage will be enormously increased in the near future amongst the first class of man who motors for pleasure, by the fact that it will be augmented by the man who motors from necessity for business purposes and for saving time, and these two classes will be again augmented by the man who motors from necessity owing to the fact that more and more are learning the possibilities, and also with America's present financial progress, many more of both classes can afford to motor in America than can afford to motor here.

Arising out of this I cannot help thinking there is a very serious menace growing up in America against the motor trade of this country, which would particularly affect the city of Coventry. The class of motor user, whom I term the pleasure-using class, who generally live in the East of America, where there are thousands of miles of good roads, as good as in Europe, roads which extend from city to city, and which are being extended with great rapidity: this class of user is calling for an automobile which fulfils European conditions, and with the vast market that the American manufacturer has before him I cannot help thinking that as soon as he has got level with the American demand he will turn his attention to shipping his surplus product to this country, and when he does this you will find, as I did, that there are American motor cars which will bear comparison with any made either in this country or any other country in Europe and I believe that they can be landed here at a price that will be, commercially, very difficult for us to compete with, and it will be well worth the American manufacturer's while to send 25 per cent of his output here, if only for the purpose of reducing his establishment charges over the 75 per cent which he will be keeping for the American market, and thus, although selling to England at cost, reduce his standing charges over the whole of his output.

I know that many people ridicule this idea and point to the bicycle business, for which Coventry is so famous, but the conditions, in my opinion, are different between the motor car and the bicycle, because the bicycle which was called for in America was unsuitable for use in this country, but the motor car which they are now making in certain factories there is suitable for use and sale in this country, and I hope everybody interested in this industry will watch most carefully the trend of affairs in America. It may, of course, be that, owing to the wonderful natural resources of the country, for many years to come they will absorb all the motor cars they can make, but once they get to the point when they have a surplus stock of motor cars I believe that serious injury will be done to everyone connected with the motor car industry in this country, particularly the workmen who make motor cars.

I have heard it said that there are remedies for such a state of affairs within the power of this country, but I am told that this is a political point which is put forward on one side of the House of Commons, but not agreed by the other; and if this is the case, it would, of course, be most improper to refer to it at such a gathering as we have here tonight; but no doubt those who are politicians among this audience will know whether I have been correctly informed that an ordinary business defence against foreign-made articles is a matter of national importance, or merely a party politician's matter. When I first saw this difficulty, I thought it was one that the Members of Parliament, whichever party they belong to, would appreciate and deal with intelligently when the necessity arose. Those of you who are politicians might perhaps look into the matter of this statement of a business man, such as I am, and see what the remedy is for the trouble and damage to the British motor industry, which I see looming in the future from America, and no doubt elsewhere.

Now, dealing with some of the cars which stand out in America, and for the moment I am referring to the cars particularly used in the Eastern cities—powerful cars. The Packard is one that one sees most. These cars are exceedingly quiet. The users speak very well of them, and they have one peculiarity which is very rare in Europe, and that is that the whole of the change-speed gear mechanism is contained as part and parcel of the live back axle. This is a point which I think is worth considering, as they have this large amount of dead weight unsupported by the springs, but these cars hold a reputation second to none throughout America and Canada, and I feel sure it is a point that all members of your engineering society might well give some careful thought to, to find out why such a seeming bad point, for use over rough country, should in practice work out successfully, because you must remember the Packard is one of the most successful motor car companies in the States, and the firm has an exceedingly large output of powerful cars.

The other two cars which stand in a similar class to the Packard are the Peerless and Pierce-Arrow. The latter interested me very much, because it has a great reputation for very high-grade workmanship, and for the year 1910 this firm has pinned its faith entirely to six cylinders, which type of vehicle some of your members may remember I have had the pleasure of using more than once.

I called at their factory in Buffalo, and was most courteously received, and shown everything apparently that there was to see.

They were originally bicycle makers, and some four or five years ago, when they made up their minds they were going into the motor business, they went some little distance outside Buffalo, and built a large factory. The present output of cars is six per day, all six-cylinders, divided over three models— 36 h.p., 48 h.p., and 66 h.p., the smallest model being nearly 40 h.p. R.A.C. rating. Now this is a number of *powerful* cars which I believe no factory in Europe could make and sell in one year, so that will give you some indication of the absorbing power of the American market for big cars at the present time.

They told me one rather interesting thing, and that was in regard to bodies. I noticed that they were using a type of aluminium body which was quite different from what I had usually seen. I spoke to them about this, because the body was large aluminium castings, and I raised the question as to its strength. The strength seemed so enormous to that which one might reasonably require in a motor car body, and the reason they gave for it was that when people had accidents they seemed so pleased, if their car had turned over and the people were able to put it on its wheels, to find the body was very little distorted. I thought this information most interesting, and wondered exactly what it indicated. Perhaps some of you, when you have thought it over, could give me the answer.

The most remarkable part about this factory and its organization is that as early as the beginning of December of last year the whole of its output for 1910 was already sold, and the firm would actually begin to start on its 1911 machining. I can imagine that many works managers would think they had reached a place something like heaven if their output for this year's trade were all sold last December and if they were commencing to machine for their 1911 trade.

To give you another illustration of the way manufacturers in America seem able to tackle these great outputs. When I was there they were telling me that they were going to build what they call commercial trucks, viz. commercial vans, capable of carrying 3 or 4 tons, and they are now laying down works, alongside of their pleasure vehicle works, to make 1,200 4-ton trucks per year. It is difficult to realize such progress unless one has seen it, and it is more and more difficult to realize that there is a country that can absorb such outputs, because, of course, this I have mentioned is only one of many.

America claims that it is going to build up 180,000 motor cars for 1910. Personally, I have no method of proving such a statement as this, but I did see quite sufficient to show me clearly that they might comfortably turn out ten times as many motor cars in America during 1910 as we shall do in Great Britain, and as an Englishman I do not enjoy it, because I realize that a country which can run its factories on such a tremendous scale must cause us very serious trouble in the future.

I cannot, however, believe that American motor car manufacturers, or any other manufacturers, can continue to discount the future in such a tremendous style, and, of course, while they have such gigantic factories and plants, if they do get a setback, it will be a most serious matter for them; but certainly, while things are going in their favour, our method of doing business seems very small and very conservative, but when the setback first comes there is no doubt America will look round for every market where it is possible to send its motor cars at almost any price, and there is no doubt that in its present position Great Britain does make an ideal country for delivering unwanted motor cars from any country that has more motor cars than it can do with.

To sum the matter up, America is the greatest motor-using country in the world, and I believe that it will continue to increase and get further ahead of the world in its capability to purchase and use automobiles, and it will do this for several reasons:

1. There is not the prejudice against the automobile, speaking generally, or even if there be such in a city or district, owing to the rapid expansion of the city or district through newcomers, the old objections are soon diluted by the newcomers with new ideas, or completely swept away.

2. The people per head of the population are better able to afford motor cars.

3. That the people as a whole are younger, and apparently have younger minds, and therefore enjoy the sport of automobilism, quite outside its utility side.

4. There is a vast section of America where the automobile for many years to come will be the one means by which the intelligent cultivated man can keep in touch with civilization, and by which the uncultivated man can also be kept in touch with the advantages of the city, while at the same time attending to his work in isolated situations.

5. Owing to the stupendous outputs of the factories, I believe that America will more rapidly than any other country bring the automobile within the reach of more and more people, and that America will use automobiles more rapidly than any other country for two distinct reasons:

(i) That there are more people with money able to buy motor cars.

(ii) That the automobile, owing to its cheapness in America, will be used by people with less money than in this country.

Thus, by creating this enormous demand, the prices will be brought down, and by bringing the prices of the cars down, the demand will be increased.

I cannot, therefore, at the moment see any method by which we can hope to compete with America in the quantity of cars turned out, or the prices at which they can be produced; and, at the top of all this, there is still the innate wealth of this great continent being brought out by the vast number of workers from other countries who are going to America at the rate of something like a million a year. In fact, unless some change takes place, it would not surprise me to see America double its population within the next twenty-five years, and what this must mean to a manufacturer of an article that must be used by everyone who values time does not require much imagination to conceive, when you will have a country of something like 140,000,000 people as possible customers sooner or later.

As many of you know, I have the cares of a very large business on my shoulders, and which today is successful, but one which requires great consideration from me when I see such a position, in the relatively near future, staring me in the face that I have indicated to you tonight, and I am one of those who hope that our rulers may see some way to safeguard the interests of British workmen and British manufacturers from the dangers that these great foreign countries, with their resources and population, can, and will, sooner or later, I am afraid, bring to bear on our country, of which we one and all are so proud, and strive, each in his own way, to do something to advance the interests and well-being of our people.

> From an Address before the Coventry Engineering Society, January 14, 1910

United States Automobile Statistics

BY HUGH CHALMERS

IT IS estimated that there are 150 automobile companies in the United States. There are thirty-five companies in Michigan with a total capacity of 140,000 cars annually; twenty-three of these thirty-five companies are in Detroit, with a total annual capacity of 85,000 cars, and a total capitalization of 30,000,000 dollars.

There are 39,000 people employed by automobile manufacturers in Detroit, and 19,000 employed by accessory manufacturers, making a total of 58,000 altogether engaged in automobile work in Detroit. This means that more than 200,000 people in Detroit are dependent upon the automobile business. Nearly 1,000,000 dollars weekly are paid out in wages here in Detroit by automobile and accessory manufacturers.

Nearly 10,000,000 dollars are invested in automobile factories in Detroit. The total value of Detroit-made cars this year will be about 200,000,000 dollars. Detroit manufactures about 60 per cent of the output of all manufactured products.

Detroit formerly was proud of the fact that it made more stoves, more pills, more paint, and more freight cars than any other city in the country. The volume of the largest of these products in dollars and cents—freight cars—amounts to about 18,000,000 dollars annually. The product of any two of the more prominent automobile companies in Detroit will easily total 20,000,000 dollars a year.

Detroit produces any kind of a car that anyone can want, from a 500-dollar runabout to an 8,000-dollar limousine.

The automobile business has made Detroit a great hotel town, and it also makes business better in every line. Think of the retail sales establishments and garages which the automobile business has brought into existence. Do you know that the automobile garage is the only new thing in architecture in several generations? Some of our new combination salerooms and garages are among the most handsome buildings in the city.

Detroit has more cars per thousand population than any other city in the world except Los Angeles.

People naturally ask, 'How long will the automobile business continue, and isn't it likely to be overdone?' Now, I am not a prophet, and cannot tell just what is going to happen, but I believe that the automobile is not subject to any comparison, because the automobile is the first improvement in individual transportation in centuries. The automobile has replaced the only thing in our civilization that has been the same throughout centuries, and that is the horse, so that I think the automobile will be with us as long as the horse has been with us. But whether or not the public can take the output of some 200 automobile companies is another question.

From an Address given at Detroit College, May 14, 1910

Late Edwardian cars, from Europe and the U.S.A.
1910 Cadillac and 1911 four-cylinder Léon-Bolée
Courtesy Montagu Motor Museum and Musee de l'Automobile,
Rochetaille sur Saone

189

American Mass-Production

BY FREDERICK A. TALBOT

AN EMINENT British automobile engineer characterized the American motor car as a 'glorified perambulator'. This seems a harsh criticism, but nevertheless it is not inappropriate and unjustifiable if one compares the rough-looking American product with the high standard of excellence to which motor-engineering has been raised in the Old World, and particularly in Great Britain. This situation arises from the fact that the United States producer is five years behind the times, and there appears to be a woeful lack of initiative to reduce this handicap. In matters pertaining to automobilism Europe leads, the United States follows.

Several factors have contributed to this condition of things. In the first place, the American temperament did not respond very readily to the idea of mechanical traction. The horse had entered so extensively into the upbuilding of the continent, and had become wedded so intimately with American life, that it was difficult to supersede. Consequently the foreign automobile invasion had made great headway before the American awoke to its possibilities and decided to manufacture for himself. Then, as has been related, just as the industry was launched, it was threatened with strangulation by litigation. It is only within the past two or three years that the incubus of a law suit has been removed from the American manufacturer, permitting him to grapple wholeheartedly with the issue and to make a bold plunge for world-wide acknowledgment.

The Americans are making a strenuous bid for supremacy in their characteristic manner. Quantity, not quality, is the guiding star, and the result is that factories on every hand are engaged in a vigorous race to secure the blue ribbon for the greatest output. The outcome is an automobile inundation, for cars are being produced far more rapidly than they can be absorbed. Such methods have brought about a staggering slaughter in prices; the competition today is so keen that factories in many instances are only able to show a profit upon the enormous output. If the latter were reduced by 50 per cent the establishment would have to close or be run at a loss.

It is the story of the bicycle, watch, and other trades over again; but the idea of applying watch-manufacturing methods to such an article as an automobile is somewhat amazing. The Americans, it must be confessed, apparently do not see the difference between the two products—that the one is a necessity, and that the other is a luxury. Still, by their methods the Americans certainly have solved one problem which has baffled European manufacturers: they have introduced the cheap motor car, and consequently that mysterious and much-discussed individual 'the motorist of moderate means', if he does exist, is able to obtain a wide selection of vehicles between $500 and $750—from £100 to £150.

How is it done? Why can the American automobile manufacturers accomplish things which the European producers declare to be impossible? These are obvious interrogations. The reply is to hand—by severe standardization. The American is the apotheosis of standardization; by him this process has been developed into a fine art. Every part of the vehicle, from the smallest nut to the colour of the body, is standardized and manufactured by the thousand. When one learns that one factory turns out sixty-four cars every twenty-four hours; that another establishment builds and delivers between five and six thousand cars per month in the busy season and that an output of 75,000 cars is the estimate of one company for a single year, one is able to glean something of the fruits of standardization.

Hand in hand with the development of standardization methods, the machinery for disposing of the product has been improved and improved until today it has attained its highest pitch. Take the Ford Company as a typical case in point. I mention it because it is one of the largest, and certainly the 'liveliest', automobile organization in the United States. In 1902 this car was not; early in 1903, Mr Henry Ford, a young American hustler, entered the manufacturing field; today there are over 100,000 Ford cars running the roads; while in 1911 alone over 36,000 cars were sold. During the summer months, when the factory is running at its maximum capacity, between 200 and 300 cars are turned out every working day, and high-water mark was reached when some 6,000 cars were built and delivered in a single month!

Manufacture is not spread over a wide range of types. Variety is the curse of standardization—a deadly brake on the output. Only one model of chassis issues from the Ford factory. The motor is of four cylinders and develops 20 h.p. Every chassis is like its fellow down to the linch pins. And this chassis serves for five standard models, ranging from a runabout selling at less than $600, or £120, to a five-passenger touring car for $690, or £138, and a light delivery car for tradesmen at $700, or £140, every vehicle being replete with all accessories, such as lamps, wind-shield, speedometer, etc., ready for the road. As the one chassis serves for all models, it will be seen that the whole plant in the factory, both mechanical and human, is concentrated upon the production of integral pieces by the thousand, by straightforward methods, to patterns. The testing and measurement of the parts to ascertain whether they conform to the specifications is reduced to a machine-like process, and there is no waste of time, no finicking work to make things fit. Then look again, what an overwhelming advantage the producer possesses when entering the market for his raw materials! By buying in enormous quantities he secures the very rock-bottom prices. For instance, the Ford factory set itself in order to produce about 75,000 vehicles during 1912. This meant that the buyers entered the markets for 300,000 wheels, 300,000 tyres, 75,000 ignition coils, 300,000 sparking plugs, 375,000 lamps, and so on, all of one pattern and size. Probably by purchasing in such bulk the buyers were able to secure from 30 to 45 per cent better terms over the competitor who acquired his necessities by the gross or hundred.

Economy in purchasing the raw materials, however, is only one step in the cheap production of the car. In order to keep the price down, time and labour-saving devices and system must go hand in hand with standardization. The most progressive American motor manufacturing establishments are practically machines in themselves. Wherever time or labour, or both, may be saved there is no hesitation. As a result, many highly ingenious appliances are to be seen. Automatic milling machines reduce production cost in the machining of such parts as crank-cases, transmission-cases, spring-hangers, fly-wheels, and so on; automatic gear-cutting tools turn out all transmission parts, camshaft, steering, and pump gears by the thousand; powerful milling machines finish three sides of ten blocks of four-cylinder motors, cast in one piece, at one operation, and so accurately that the error cannot exceed the one-thousandth part of an inch; and so on.

By means of standardization to jigs, templates, and patterns the finest degrees of accuracy are obtained. The Cadillac is an old American favourite among British motorists, and in this factory the insistence upon accuracy may be seen in its most perfect form. In this vehicle there are more than 250 parts, which demand more than 400 operations, not one of which is permitted to err more than the one-thousandth part of an inch from the prescribed limits of measurement. In other parts the deviation allowed is cut down to one-half of this limit. To realize what this permissible error means it may be mentioned that the one-thousandth part of an inch is less than one-half of the proverbial hair's-breadth! This minute adherence to measurements so small as to defy recording except by special apparatus is exemplified most strikingly in the wholesale manufacture of the cylinder heads and pistons, every one of which has to be submitted to the test before it is permitted to enter a chassis. For the measurement of the cylinder there are two gauges. One is marked '4·500 Go', meaning that the gauge is $4\frac{1}{2}$ inches *dead* in diameter, while the other is marked '4·502 Not Go', signifying that the diameter is just two one-thousandth parts of an inch in excess of the $4\frac{1}{2}$ inches diameter. The cylinder is submitted to this test after being ground. If upon testing it will permit the 'Go' gauge to enter, but is not large enough to admit the 'Not Go' gauge, it is passed. If it will not allow the 'Go' gauge to slide in, then the head is returned to the grinding shop to be bored to the correct size. On the other hand, if it admits the 'Not Go' gauge, then it is discarded and melted down. The pistons are tested in a similar way to obtain the same accuracy, a snap-gauge being used in this instance to measure the outside diameter of the cylinder. The fact that the cylinder and its piston are measured to the thickness of a hair affords some convincing idea of the pains to which the Americans will proceed in order to secure accuracy of fitting. The effect is obvious. Any piston will fit any cylinder. There is no need to adapt one to the other. If a cylinder head breaks through accident, frost, or from any other cause, there is no laborious work in fitting the new to the old part. It appears to be carrying accuracy to extreme limits, but it is one of the penalties and benefits of standardization.

All the other parts in this car are fashioned with similar precision and care. In this way an absolutely perfect fit is assured, and, what is far more important, a homogeneous and silent whole, without any wear and tear setting up at various places due to imperfect workmanship, is obtained. When it comes to the valve motion the Cadillac Company is even more particular. The correct operation and timing of the valves is vitally dependent upon the accuracy of the cams and camshaft, so in consequence the cams and the shaft are ground to the one two-thousandth part of an inch. To secure such fine perfection in measurement demands the use of first-class tools and equipment, and in this respect the Cadillac Company is second to none. In the manufacture of this car the parts pass through one or more of no fewer than 500 special automatic labour-saving machines, to ensure more delicate precision than emanates from the best of human aptitude. At the same time some of these machines will turn out ten times the volume of work, and more precise, too, than is possible by hand labour. As a matter of fact, the Cadillac equipment is among the finest in operation in America for the production of automobiles, the equipment including over 100,000 tools, dies, jigs, fixtures, etc., of which total some 20,000 were specially made for the production of this popular car.

Some critics are apt to scoff at standardization, but their ridicule receives a severe shock and refutal when a car is subjected to such a test as the Cadillac fulfilled. In this instance three vehicles of a similar type were given a long, heavy run upon the high roads of this country. When they returned to the garage the three cars were dismantled entirely. The integral parts of the three vehicles were then promiscuously mixed up, and from the resultant heterogeneous heap of shafts, gear-wheels, bolts, and nuts the three vehicles were re-erected and run out on the road once more. The result was astonishing, and one that is only possible from very high-class standardization. The three cars ran without the slightest click, and there was no sign whatever of friction or other trouble due to parts from each of the three cars being called upon to work together.

The criticism has been levelled against the American manufacturer that because his product is low in price inferior materials are used. This is a charge which investigation fails to substantiate. The materials employed in the American vehicle selling for $600, or £120, are not one wit inferior to those utilized in the English vehicle selling at ten times that price. The most rigid inspection and testing of materials are maintained in all the United States automobile factories producing a car worthy of the name. One may go into a factory, such as that from which the Overland emanates, and see a bar of metal taken from a pile awaiting the call into the works for the fashioning of some part or other, and then whizzed round at terrific speed, with a weight attached to either end, on a special testing machine. The revolutions are kept up until the bar succumbs to the strain, but by the time collapse ensues the number of revolutions it has completed have been recorded automatically. There is another machine in which the spring of the vehicle is compelled to betray its life and capacity for the purpose for which it has been designed. The spring is placed in the machine to be vibrated very rapidly, and the number of million oscillations it makes, which are similar to those arising when pounding along the high road, are recorded up to the moment it breaks, or assumes a permanent set or deformation. Another apparatus tests the twisting strain which the metal will resist. One end of a bar of metal is gripped tightly so that it cannot possibly move, and then the opposite end is twisted round by a set of gears until the bar gives way under the wringing action, when a calculation is made to ascertain how many degrees the bar has been twisted before snapping. Even the files which are used in the various departments are submitted to a searching test before being handed to the workmen, to determine their fineness, while another instrument, the impact tester, shows how many heavy blows per square inch the different metals will withstand. Even the oil is not permitted to be accepted on trust. The life of a motor car and its component parts are influenced very appreciably by the characteristics of the lubricant. One scale measures accurately to fifteen ten-thousandth parts of a grain; the specific gravity balance determines accurately to the one ten-thousandth; the combustion crucible affords conclusive testimony concerning the carbon content. The viscometer is a wonderful little device. At the base is a minute outlet drilled by a hair-drill through agate. Oil and water are passed through this orifice, and the quantity of oil that exudes therefrom in relation to the amount of water within a specified time provides the standard for the viscosity measurement upon which the oil is based.

Seeing that the parts are turned out automatically by the thousand, as may be supposed, the inspection and testing operations are of an elaborate character. Gauges of all descriptions are employed, so that if an error has crept in with regard to the fabrication of one of the many parts, it is detected and the defective piece is thrown out before it reaches the assembling-room. Thus, by checking and counter-checking step by step, a complete grip upon dead accuracy of manufacture in the parts is secured, and a careless workman can be traced and dismissed before he has wrought much damage.

As rapidly as the motors are assembled they are sent to the testing-room, where one may see as many as 5,000 or more engines being put through their paces on the bench, to show whether or not they conform to the specified horse-power, run smoothly and easily, or manifest defects in material which may, perhaps, have eluded the vigilant eyes of the inspectors lower down the manufacturing ladder. The engines are kept going for hours to see whether they can keep up the power, and brake tests are made at frequent intervals to determine this factor. Emerging from this trial satisfactorily the engine is caught up in a sling and whisked away to the assembling-shop, where it is deposited until required along with the hundred and one other parts of·the car, and all stored in large racks. When the assembling takes place the requisite components are drawn promiscuously from the respective stocks and put together. This is the advantage of standardization carried out upon true lines. It ensures that every part is true to the fractional part of an inch, is dead accurate with the specifications, is bound to fit its fellow, and can be interchanged just as much as occasion demands. Every part being so precise, when it comes to the erection there is no need to file this and pack that to secure a perfect fit; everything goes together smoothly and perfectly.

When the car is assembled, it is taken out on to the roads and given a hard gruelling in the hands of an expert mechanic. In the early days the testing operations of American motor manufacturers assumed rather the lines of circus performances—riding over stairs to determine the resiliency of the springs; driving up flights of steps to demonstrate the power of the engine and the gripping power of the brakes; balancing two on a see-saw; driving the car backwards over a smooth surface in such a way as to crack an egg, and no more, with the rear wheel, to demonstrate complete control; driving rapidly round a circular track obstructed with barrels and other formidable obstructions, which had to be dodged, in order to convince one of the steering control, and so on. In one instance the manufacturer of a car, to prove the steady running of his engine, placed a small-sized billiard-table on the tonneau and played '100 up' with the motor running full speed while the car was stationary. These extraordinary tests, however, have been abandoned for more conventional trials upon varying types of high road, and these are certainly far more conclusive, as the conditions comply more with those with which the average motorist has to contend.

In order to secure the very best results from the perfection of standardization methods the American manufacturer spares no expense in the acquisition of machinery for his establishment. A die for pressing a special part may cost $800, or £160, a dry kiln for storing over a million feet of lumber for the bodies possibly represents an outlay of $50,000, or £10,000; but if the manufacturer can see his way to profit from the outlay he does not hesitate. He may have a complete plant today doing its work with the greatest satisfaction, and the whole running as smoothly as a clock. But tomorrow someone brings along an idea to improve today's perfection. If it will secure the manufacturer any economy in time, labour, and expense, with equal quality of work, then it is adopted, although it may entail scrapping other machinery which has cost several hundreds sterling to install.

One might naturally ask, seeing the perfection of this system, why it is not practised in Great Britain or upon the Continent. It might and could be adopted, and yet the prices of British and Continental automobiles would not drop a single penny. Why? Because the Old World motoring public has been educated to such a high level in matters pertaining to automobilism, that it regards the American product with contempt—a cast-iron box of tricks. The motorist of the Old World, instead of standardization, prefers individualism, and, what is far more important and costly, he demands *finish*. This is the operation that runs away with the money. The British motor manufacturers, if they felt so disposed, and were convinced of the market, could turn out cars equal in every respect to those emanating from American workshops, and at prices ranging from 15–25 per cent cheaper, owing to the lower cost of raw materials, improved time, and labour-saving tools, and cheaper labour. But the British manufacturer has achieved his present high position through the excellent finish of his product. Finish demands hand-labour of the most skilled and expensive character, and this costs approximately the same the whole world over. In fact, it has been stated that finishing off a car represents about 50 per cent of its total cost. This is probably an exaggeration, but there is no denying the fact that finish is the most expensive detail in its construction.

I have heard many British motorists describe the American production as cheap and nasty. This attitude is quite unwarranted. The car is cheap, but it is not nasty. It is worth exactly what the manufacturer asks for it—no more, no less. The purchaser on his part gets full value for his money. On the other hand, the $1,250, or £250, car represents the limit of American value. There is no American car on the market today which is worth more than this figure —that is, if one compares it with the British vehicle for durability, sweetness in running, comfort, and life. The American car is built essentially to suit the American temperament, which differs very radically from the motoring tastes of the Old World. Indeed, the American motorist is a curious individual. His first investment probably will be a car costing, say, $600, or £120. He runs it to death, and never gives a thought to the possibility of being able to recoup himself upon its ultimate re-sale. His buoyant optimism fills him with the hope that his prosperity will increase to such a degree that within a year he will be able to scrap his first purchase and to buy another costing $1,000, or £200. This in turn will rattle like a coffee-mill after twelve months' service, to make way for a third car costing 25 per cent more than its predecessor. Finally, when the enthusiastic motorist has climbed the motoring ladder high enough in step with the advance in his prosperity, he will realize the height of his motoring ambitions, will become the possessor of a magnificent $5,000, or £1,000, European motor car, finished to his own tastes, replete with every refinement, and this he will treat more kindly and thoughtfully. He has become one of the motoring *elité*, the envied of all his neighbours and friends, and patriotism when pitched against vanity counts for naught.

The American manufacturer is only too fully aware of this failing on the part of his compatriot. An American high-priced car would not compel a moment's thought. Accordingly, the builder caters for the cheap market, and can only hope to recoup himself by turning out his product in prodigious quantities and by ploughing his own channels for their disposal. This is the reason why the United States laid itself out to produce 225,000 cheap vehicles within a year. The bogey of over-production stares the manufacturer in the face as the inevitable corollary of standardization and automatic manufacture. The Old World dreamed the same visions of conquest five years ago, but these commercial fantasies were shattered very speedily, and Britain settled down to build motor cars with the same care and individual study with which it produces ships. Will the American manufacturers do likewise? Far-sighted American motor engineers are bold enough to vouchsafe the statement that in the course of a decade motor manufacture in the United States will be a decaying industry unless there is a change in production methods. Standardization within certain limits is a blessing; but when those boundaries are crossed it becomes a curse.

From *Motor Cars and their Story*, 1912

New Men and New Methods

BY LAURENCE POMEROY

THE INTRODUCTION of the Mercedes car in 1901 set new standards for automobilism to match the new century. Nevertheless within five years any claim of the German car to offer the last word in silence and flexibility had been utterly confounded by the new values for these qualities which emerged in England as a result of the work of Montague Napier with his six-cylinder cars, and even more importantly the efforts of Henry Royce. Yet that Royce and his cars should be dealt with in this chapter at all is an anomaly.

It is impossible sympathetically to assess the work of the pioneers Benz, Daimler, Levassor and Maybach without remembering that the self-propelled petrol-driven vehicle did not exist until they were 40 years old, or more. Their formative thought was therefore conditioned by stationary engines or perhaps locomotive engineering. The early life of Sir Henry Royce, the technical influence of whose work was to continue deep into the twentieth century, was moulded by a similar upbringing. Born in 1863, he was 17 years younger than Maybach, 19 years younger than Benz, and 29 years younger than Daimler. Not until three years after Daimler's death did he have any connection with the motoring world, for at the age of 14 he was apprenticed to the Great Northern Railway Company where he soon showed his skill as a mechanic, and in 1889, at the age of 21, he founded Henry Royce Ltd. for the manufacture of electric cranes to his own design. But when he was 40 he was tempted to purchase a French Decauville, and it was the challenge which the imperfections of this car made to his engineering idealism which made him build a car of his own, and led, in the astonishingly small span of three years, to the alliance with Rolls and the production under the commercial guidance of Claude Johnson of the Silver Ghost which was to set standards of flexibility, silence and smooth running which stood as an ideal for the next forty years.

The strength of Royce lay in his combination of many virtues and the fact that like Levassor he brought a mind at once fresh and mature to bear upon the problems before him. He was himself a superb mechanic and well knew the benefits that could be obtained from perfect workmanship; he saw how the designer could profit from an assumption that work of this order would be available; and yet at the same time he tried to make the lot of the machinist or fitter as easy as possible. In addition, and most important, Royce did not dissipate his engineering energy by seeking new or unconventional solutions to the known problems; on the contrary he remained

Henry Royce's 'Ghost'. This is the car that ran from London to Edinburgh
and back with a dead load of 1,035 pounds, plus a passenger weight of 508 pounds,
all in top gear, with a petrol consumption of 24·32 miles per Imperial gallon.
It completed this famous run with a speed of 78·26 m.p.h. on Brooklands track

throughout his life convinced that the best results were to be obtained by
applying existing knowledge and proved practice to the best advantage. Thus
on his very first car the dimensions of the bore and stroke were determined
by taking the average of all the existing cars on the market!

Built in 1903 this was a two-cylinder model with overhead inlet and side
exhaust-valves but with a three-bearing crankshaft and three speeds, giving
7, 17½ and 30 m.p.h. at the maximum crankshaft speed of 1,000 r.p.m. With
the modest dimensions of 6 ft. 8 in. wheelbase and 4 ft. track, this model
showed little of the Royce designs to come, but it was so beautifully made in
detail, so excellently manufactured, that it made an immediate impression
on the Hon. C. S. Rolls when he first tried it in 1904. This was all the more
remarkable in that Rolls was one of the great car connoisseurs of the time,
and a leading agent for Panhard.

He set all this aside, and later in 1904 displayed at the Paris Show both a
four and six-cylinder Royce with a bore and stroke of 95×127 mm. in each
case. In the following year a 100 mm. four-cylinder '20' was made, and
despite brief flirtations with three-cylinder and V-8 models there arrived
for the Olympia Show of 1906 the first Silver Ghost with engine dimensions
of $114·5 \times 114·5$ mm. (soon modified to $114·5 \times 127$ mm.) and with a
capacity of 7·4 litres. This gave the modest output of 48 b.h.p. at 1,200
r.p.m. (6·5 h.p. per litre) with a maximum crankshaft speed of 1,500 r.p.m.
Thus, piston speed was but little over 1,000 ft. per min. and m.e.p. under
75 lb. per sq. in. These figures make it plain that Royce once more was not
endeavouring to march clear beyond known practice, rather was he following
his plan of applying existing knowledge to the best advantage. Yet it is just

on these very grounds that we must regard him as the final flower of the nineteenth century in automobile engineering although at the same time acknowledging that those who seek in motoring for *ordre, luxe, calme, volupté et beauté*, find these qualities combined in the Silver Ghost in a degree not rivalled by any other make or model.

Comparison has already been made between Royce and Levassor. Further ties can be found between him and many of the other pioneers. Like them, he came of a modest family, had to work desperately hard in his early days, and then set up for himself in a business completely divorced from road transport. Like them he made his way by a single-minded devotion to his affairs and lived a thoroughly sober and industrious life. Like them he was devoted to his work and business and was at once unworldly and unambitious. Like them, also, his engineering training was on the lower levels; all the early engineers were doubtless well versed in geometry and aquainted with algebra; it is highly improbable that any had the calculus. To complete our list of similarities, like the early pioneers Royce was an essentially modest man—a point brought out with startling clarity by a remark made almost at the end of his life. As he watched the Rolls-Royce engined Supermarine S6B's being prepared for their great victory in the Schneider Trophy contest of 1931 a journalist asked him (and the question itself seems astonishingly archaic as we write it today): 'Would it be a dreadful calamity if your designs were known in America?' Royce replied: 'Oh I don't think it would matter very much. The design is not the most important part of the business by any means. The design of this engine is really quite simple, but only the finest engineers could make it effective.'

There we have not only Royce's modesty, but also his essentially nineteenth-century mechanical outlook. What we lack is the measure of his ability as an engineer. Yet when one considers that Royce first began to think about the problems of automobilism in 1902–3, that he designed and built his first car on a modest scale as a 10 h.p. two-cylinder in 1904, and by 1907 had, unaided, designed and developed the Silver Ghost which not only towered above all contemporary designs but continued to maintain supremacy for wellnigh twenty years, it is scarcely possible to deny him the title of genius.

But whereas Royce produced the pinnacle of nineteenth-century mechanical design in the early part of the twentieth century, it was Frederick William Lanchester, LL.D, FRS, MICE, MIME, HON.MIAE, who designed the first scientific twentieth-century car in the latter part of the nineteenth century. Born in 1868 and thus some 20 years younger than Royce, Lanchester stood as a complete contrast with the man who cannot be called his rival in that their work and lives differed at almost every point.

Lanchester was a Colossus, a man of imposing stature and of giant intellectual capacity. But he would have thought anyone mad who called him modest, and as an example of characteristic *de haut en bas* I recall that when he was discussing some business associates he said: 'Well, they seem to change their minds pretty frequently, but then if I had a mind like theirs I would change it as soon as I could!'

He had indeed but one thing in common with the early motoring pioneers which was an apprenticeship in the gas engine business, that of T. V. Barker and Company of Saltley, Birmingham. Here he became Works Manager at the age of 22, and took out his first patent in the same year. When 25 he built a single-cylinder petrol engine (95 × 114 mm.) which gave 2 h.p. at the high speed for the time (1893) of 800 r.p.m.

In 1894 he showed his versatility by reading a paper to the Birmingham Philosophical Society on the subject of flight, and then in 1895, that is to say, when he was 27 years old, he turned his attention to the automobile world and with the assistance of his brother, George, produced a car of outstanding novelty. This was developed into the 1897 model which formed the starting-point for subsequent production types.

Designed from first principles in the light of existing scientific knowledge, it showed few features in common with any car produced up to then. A tubular frame was used, and to this wire wheels were attached to axles supported on true cantilever springs supplemented by radius arms which included ball and socket joints.

Two-cylinder engines were common enough in 1896, as was air cooling, but Lanchester went further by adopting not only forced draught (as predicted by Daimler on his first engine) but also in the use of horizontally-opposed cylinders and pistons. Moreover, each piston was provided with two connecting rods, the big ends being connected to two geared-together crankshafts running in opposite directions. By this means complete balancing of all primary and secondary forces was attained.

Equally ingenious was Lanchester's high-tension ignition system. The current was provided by a fly-wheel to which was fitted two permanent magnets revolving around a fixed armature, while an external contact was provided which broke momentarily before the break which took place within the contacts inside the cylinder.

The engine inspired mixture through the medium of a combined poppet and rotary valve which gave in effect one of the earliest mechanically-operated inlet valves.

Not content with all this Lanchester transmitted the power through a three-speed epicyclic transmission giving a direct drive on top to a *worm drive* live rear axle. The worm was mounted beneath the wheel and by this means the line of the propeller shaft was dropped by some 6 in., permitting a corresponding lowering of the floor level and overall height of the car.

Lanchester was probably the first man to realize the importance of spring rates and centre of gravity from a fundamental point of view. Writing on these subjects he said: 'If there were no practical limitations to the period attainable the slower the period the greater the comfort; it is therefore the object of the designer to obtain as slow a period in the suspension system as is compatible with the other conditions. If the centre of gravity is kept as low as possible in the design of the chassis and bodywork, and in the adaptation of one to the other, the difficulties (of soft springing) are minimized and a car may be produced with general all-round virtues not otherwise obtainable.' Even today these vital relationships are inadequately recognized! Lanchester's use of tiller steering (with a transverse tiller, lead-loaded to damp down road reactions) may be considered as poetic licence or an extraordinary example of conservatism allied to radicalism. But this would be wrong. He believed that such a tiller was a natural way of controlling a road vehicle; that one leant forward to go round right-hand corners and slightly backwards to go round left-hand bends.

The breadth of Lanchester's mind is shown by his insistence upon the ties between the human and the mechanical at many points. For example he claimed that the eye of the driver when sitting in the driving seat should be at the same height from the ground as when he was standing up and walking, for all his perspective and judgments would be based upon such a position. Moreover, he early pointed out that the rate of car suspension should as far as possible be the same as the oscillations imparted in the natural act of walking, and it was for this reason that elderly people, who took slow steps, preferred softly sprung cars, whilst children who took short and rapid steps preferred a harsher springing system and might even be made sick by a softer one!

Lanchester also realized far earlier than most the importance of the inter-relationship between road surface and suspension systems. In a paper he read before the Institution of Automobile Engineers in 1910 he said:

'I do not think that sufficient attention has been called to the need for uniformity in the character of the road surface. If a vehicle has to be constructed to operate for 20 per cent of its time on badly-built roads in a bad state of repair, it has to be designed suitably, and it is unable to take due advantage of a really well-made road when the opportunity occurs. In a sense this statement requires explanation; I will give an illustration. It is notorious that the main roads in France are some of the best in the world, straight and of good surface. At the same time the roads in the villages and smaller towns are abominable, badly laid and worn out *pavé* being plentiful. A French expert driver, reporting on three pleasure cars which we will call A, B and C, made comments as tabulated, the spring periods in each case being as given in column 1. Now we know that the criterion of the hardness of a suspension is the spring period, and the accuracy of the observations may be gauged by the complete agreement shown; these observations also, however, show how impossible it is to suit both kinds of road with one and

1911 Lanchester with Salmon body
photo: Philip Turner Esq.

the same car, and hence the importance of uniformity in the roads of the country.'

OBSERVATION ON SPRINGS

Type	Period *Vib. per min.*	Remarks
A	72	Springs rather too easy on main roads, but very good in towns.
B	88	Far too 'hard' on town *pavé*, but very good on main roads.
C	82	A good compromise, but still somewhat 'hard'.

In this paper Lanchester showed that in the past decade the weight of car engines had been reduced from 30 lb. to around 10 lb. per h.p. and he looked forward to weights of 3–4 lb. per h.p. which just about correspond with the best engines today. Also with his remarkable prescience he said, speaking of transmission systems:

'In the gearbox of the sliding gear type we have a piece of mechanism which we should most of us like to see abolished; it is a notoriously make-shift appliance and its survival is in the main to be accounted for by the fact that the h.p. commonly used in pleasure vehicles has been increased in extent but the direct drive is in operation for 99 per cent of the distance run and for the remainder we put up with the make-shift and make the best of it.'

He certainly did not think that the make-shift would still be used by the bulk of European cars nearly 50 years after!

The scientific merits of Lanchester's early cars were recognized by the award of a gold medal at the Richmond Motor Show organized in the summer of 1899 by the Automobile Club of Great Britain and Ireland.

Lanchester has the right to claim that he was the first to build a four-wheeled petrol-driven car in England. He was anticipated by others in the matter of production and sale to the public but the Lanchester Engine Company was formed in 1899 and from 1901 onwards cars based on the earlier type, but with water-cooled engines, were offered for sale. In 1905 under the aegis of his brother George the horizontal type of engine was replaced by a 20 h.p. four-cylinder vertical type which was claimed to have a road speed on top gear which could vary between 4 and 40 m.p.h.

An owner of one of the earlier 12 h.p. horizontal engines recorded that with an all-up weight of 27 cwt. he was able to travel between London and Birmingham at an average speed of 20·4 m.p.h. with a consumption of four gallons of fuel giving 34·6 m.p.g. This remarkable figure was aided by coasting down hills but the engine was never stopped.

The same owner, summing up his experiences, said:

'The special advantages of the Lanchester are silence in running, great comfort on account of the method of spring suspension, absence of chains, absence of vibration from imperfectly balanced engine, simplicity of driving and consequently but little fatigue, safety owing to broad wheel-gauge and low centre of gravity, its perfect brakes, and an ignition system which does not develop faults. In conclusion, I would like to say that I have never seen any piece of complicated mechanism, such as a motor is, better designed or with better material and workmanship than the Lanchester. It is a great pleasure to me as an engineer to see attention paid to the working out of details to the same careful extent as is given to the more essential parts of the work.'

Nevertheless despite the brilliance of Lanchester's scientific attainments, and in the face of such glowing testimony to the practical virtues of his car, neither his theories in the abstract, nor his products in the concrete, had any marked influence on the development of automobile design in the first part of this century.

They remain analogous to the biological 'sport' which has great scientific interest but lesser practical significance. There are three main reasons why this was so. One is that Lanchester's thought was so far ahead of his time that few people could appreciate and apply it. The other is that unlike Royce, Lanchester was by no means consumed with the desire to produce the perfect motor car. By the time the first Lanchester cars were in production he was already directing his vast intellectual apparatus to the problems of aeroplanes. His *Aerodynamics*, constituting the first volume of a complete work on Aerial Flight, published in 1907, was long the standard work on this subject and mentioned experimental work carried out since 1894; and in 1913 he considered the statistical problems inherent in air fighting and showed that the chances of each side were inverse to the square of the numbers engaged. This latter work incidentally was written long before aircraft were armed, let alone taking part in actual combat, and the former before any heavier than air machine had left European soil!

It would be wrong to infer from the foregoing comments on Lanchester's works that he was a dreamer and not a practical man. He had, by contrast, a high degree of manual skill and could not only design a motorcar but personally build it. He could even make and colour copies of Chinese pottery with such skill that Bond Street dealers would make serious offers for them as genuine antiques. However, this is but one example of how the variety of genius tended to divert him from the everyday problems of motor car maintenance and driving.

Thus, from 1904 onwards the practical direction of Lanchester's affairs in the motoring world fell increasingly upon the shoulders of his brother George and it was not until some years had passed that he in turn made his own complete contribution to the art of automobile engineering.

Meanwhile the sale of the earlier designs was limited by the nature of their conception and the time of their birth. In these respects, Lanchester, for all his great mental powers, could not escape being the child of his age. This led him inevitably to think in terms of the horse and in providing a vehicle which was at once self-propelled and capable of, say, twice the road speed of the horse-drawn carriage he felt that the automobile constructor had fulfilled his function.

Unlike the pioneers who sought this goal by methods of trial and error, Royce and Lanchester both believed that the utmost efforts should be made on the drawing board but when, subsequently, the design was built as well as they knew how it lay with the buyer to operate it with skill and circumspection. Hence from an early date Rolls-Royce ran a school to which it was customary for owners to send their chauffeurs so that they could be taught how best to drive and maintain this beautiful piece of machinery. It is worth digressing at this point to make it clear that in the period covered by this book the word 'driver' was commonly an abbreviation for 'paid-driver' and stood in contrast to the rarer individual specially designated as an 'owner-driver'.

Some idea of the responsibilities of the driver in maintaining the car, as well as in actually handling it, are given by Max Pemberton in *The Amateur Motorist** who says:

'Any novice may understand that a car should never be left overnight with the mud upon it, that it should be hosed down directly it comes in, that mud

* Hutchinson and Co. (Publishers) Ltd.

must never be rubbed or brushed off, that a spoke brush should never be used, that a sponge is the safest implement when a hose has been used, and after that a selvyt or a chamois leather. He should rigorously forbid his chauffeur to use petrol for paintwork. The commonest excuse of the motor-house is, "We cannot get the motor car clean this muddy weather unless we use petrol or paraffin." This is mere laziness—it means to say that the men will not be at the pains to do the work properly. I repeat that a novice can see that it is so done just as well as any expert.

'The engine of a car should be cleaned every morning. French drivers have a much greater care for their engines than English. When I was touring in the south of France last year this fact was brought home to me somewhat ironically. The English drivers would be smoking their morning cigarettes while the Frenchmen were, to a man, cleaning their engines. At Toulouse I saw an English car reeking with oil and filth. Very proudly the driver told us that he had never cleaned his engine since he had it, needless to say he was an Englishman.

'See that your driver cleans his engine every day, and pay, as it were, surprise visits to the gearbox, take the footboards up when he is least expecting you to do so, and see how much of this worldly goods you have gathered in your undertray. A liberal allowance of filthy oil mixed with road mud and small stones does not bear witness to that zeal which even a moderate enthusiasm may demand. Discharge the man on the spot who keeps his car in filthy condition, and you have done much to lessen the expense of keeping a motor car.'

Pemberton then goes on to lay down fourteen points (thus anticipating President Wilson) which he calls 'Rules for the Management of the Motor-house':

1. All mud to be hosed from the car immediately upon its return to the stable; but should the hour of that return be unreasonable, then washing to be done before breakfast next morning.

2. The engine, all paint and brass work to be cleaned every morning without fail.

3. The whole car, including gearbox, differential, and undertray to be thoroughly inspected and cleaned once a month.

4. All steering-leathers to be removed once a week, the bolts thoroughly greased, the pins examined, and the wheels tested for alignment.

5. All tools, when not in use, to be kept either on the car or in their proper drawers, to which they must be returned immediately work is concluded for the day.

6. The car to be covered whenever it is not in use.

7. All spare covers to be kept in canvas cases and hung up against the walls.

8. No leakage of water to be permitted from hose or taps. No oil to be left on the concrete.

9. No sale to roving dealers under any circumstances whatever. Immediate discharge the penalty.

10. No unnecessary racing of the engine under the pretence of adjustment.

11. No tinkering with the engine when it is running well.

12. One set of accumulators to be upon the charging-board, the other two sets upon the car. There is no excuse but carelessness for a discharged accumulator.

13. In cold weather, the water to be drawn off every night.

14. Tyres to be kept fully pumped and tried by the gauge. All small cuts to be attended to immediately.

Cleanliness the supreme rule both in the car and the house.

No one can have embraced this doctrine of customer responsibility with greater enthusiasm than Ettore Bugatti, but although he shared this outlook with names already famous when he was struggling to produce his first cars with the aid of a few men, he was unique both as a personality and as a designer. Moreover, although it has been estimated that the cars built under his own name did not exceed 10,000 in number the influence his designs had directly as a consequence of licensing other constructors, and indirectly as a general example, is of such importance that he well deserves his place in this book. Ettore Bugatti was born in Milan in 1881, the son of Carlo Bugatti who was an all-round artist who practised as a goldsmith, sculptor and architect. One of Bugatti's brothers was christened Rembrandt and became a well-known animal sculptor, and Ettore himself was nick-named 'little Leonardo' and in later life certainly shared a considerable part of the versatility and genius of the great da Vinci.

However, as a younger son it was borne in upon him that he was unlikely to rival his brother Rembrandt as an artist and it was in 1898, when only 17, that he turned to other things and made his first motor car.

This fact has often been recorded but no one has yet commented on the extraordinary nature of the event. The Fiat Company had yet to be founded, and the number of cars running in Italy must have been almost negligible. Nevertheless, Bugatti's first effort had a four-cylinder engine mounted at the back and as he was not very pleased with the results he soon built a second car with front engine mounting. In 1899, coincident with the founding of Fiat, this model fitted with a water-cooled engine 90 × 120 mm., and with a four-speed gearbox and chain drive, was exhibited at the first Milan Motor Show and received a gold medal in recognition of its merits.

It was doubtless this which aroused the interest of the Baron de Dietrich who asked for the rights to manufacture it. Bugatti was doubtless honoured by such wholly unexpected interest from the head of a large industrial concern, but as he was still only 18 years of age his father had to sign the contract on his behalf.

The de Dietrich industrial complex was centred at Niederbronn, a small town some 30 miles from Strasbourg, and naturally enough Bugatti made many visits there in the course of developing his designs.

In 1901 he showed his first signs of great originality in building a car with driving and passenger seats placed behind the rear axle and space for luggage between the pedals and the engine; and in 1903 he presented a car for the Paris–Madrid race which had such an extremely low seating position that the Minister of Mines refused to allow it to start on the grounds of impaired visibility. The car was later rebuilt with a higher driving position and in 1902 Bugatti celebrated his majority by producing another conventional chain-drive car for de Dietrich.

Although these early models had nothing about them 'to set the Thames on fire' the mere fact that Bugatti's association with the Baron continued for four years is evidence that they must have performed reasonably well, for the industrialist also built cars to the designs of such well-known figures in the motoring world as Bollée and Messrs Turcat and Méry. However, none of these Bugatti-designed cars was very successful commercially and in 1904 Bugatti looked around for some other backer.

It was at this time that he met Mathis who was an agent for the sale of de Dietrich cars and more importantly, as it subsequently transpired from the Bugatti point of view, concessionaire for Fiat in France. The two men soon came to an agreement, and Bugatti settled down in the Hotel de Paris at Strasbourg (which belonged to Mathis' father) and designed a car which was called the Hermes.

Called the Burlington when offered in the English market, this car was described and illustrated in *The Autocar* of 1905 in which it is stated that the chassis is designed to take engines of 40, 90 and 120 h.p. at the option of the owner. All are of the L-head type, but the beginnings of traditional Bugatti features are shown by the use of 'tappets' made out of curved square section bar and although the drive to the camshaft is at the front end of the engine there are skew gears at the back driving a low-tension magneto on the right-hand side of the crankcase and a typically Bugatti water-pump on the left-hand side. The clutch also appears to have the subsequently traditional Bugatti layout of multi-plates with the levers arranged to give supplementary loading on the plates by centrifugal force and the gearbox, which drives a countershaft to provide final drive by chain, has an indirect geared-up fourth speed.

The car was built at Illkirch Grafenstaden, about five miles from Strasbourg, and one of them ran in the 1905 Herkomer Trials for which the first prize was, appropriately enough, a statue of the god Hermes. Whether or not this inspired the name of the car is not known, but although the Bugatti-Mathis creation did not provide the winner it made an auspicious competition début and ran third in the 32–60 h.p. class.

About 25 Hermes cars were made and sold (only one is known to survive) and in *The Bugatti Book* there is a most interesting picture which shows one of them with Bugatti at the wheel, the great Felice Nazzaro in the passenger seat, and in addition the chairman of the Fiat Company, Ludovico Scarfiotti, together with managing director Agnelli, and two of his most famous racing drivers Lancia and Wagner. Supporting Bugatti, as it were, are to be seen Mathis and Rembrandt Bugatti. This picture is wrongly attributed to 1905 and wrongly placed at Hamburg. As Wagner did not join Fiat until 1907 it is likely that this great gathering was after the 1907 Kaiserpreis, which was won by Nazzaro on a Fiat and in which Mathis also entered and ran a Hermes; and that the purpose was to interest Fiats in a licence agreement.

It has long been apparent that the 1909 130×190 mm. S.61 Fiat, the Bugatti 100×160 mm. 'Black Bess' Type, and his 65×100 mm. Type 13 had a common design theme. Bugatti himself, speaking of the cylinder block design of the 'Black Bess' model, said that he had thought of it in 1905 and as we have seen the Mathis-Hermes car had a number of features later to be found both in the Fiat and Bugatti's own productions. Research has produced a 'missing link' between the Hermes and the later designs in the shape of a Bugatti-designed Deutz which was designed and built in Strasbourg between 1905 and 1906 with the support of the Darmstadt Bank and with the assistance of three draughtsmen and three workmen. This car was very fully described in the journal *V.D.I.* in 1908 and from the numerous engineering drawings it has been possible to build up a sectioned perspective view of the engine which shows some of its outstanding features.

The cylinders are cast in pairs and deeply spigotted into the crank-case, and the integral cylinder heads carry two overhead valves staggered slightly across the combustion space. Surmounting them is an overhead camshaft driven from the back of the engine by a split vertical drive with bevel gears. It is mounted within a tunnel to which are attached the guides to hold the beginnings of the quadrant type valve motion used earlier on the Hermes and later on the Type 13. It will be seen that in this case there are rollers which receive the motion from the cam and others which transmit it to the vertical valve stem, a small V-shaped quadrant being placed between them. The bevel gears at the base of the cam drive are also used to engage supplementary gears connected to shafts running forwards at an angle of 45 degrees, the left-hand one connected to the magneto and the right-hand to the water pump.

The crank-case is split along the centre line of the crankshaft and carries the top and bottom halves of the two end bearings and the top half only of the centre bearing and to which a conventional cap was fitted. Although a variety of cylinder bores and strokes could be used 150×150 mm. was normal, giving a capacity of 10·6 litres.

As on the later Fiat the rim of the fly-wheel embraced blades giving an air extractor effect from the closely-cowled engine compartment, and the clutch is of multi-plate type. As on the Hermes and on all later Bugattis the clutch plates on the Deutz were held in contact by pivoted levers giving centrifugal assistance with rising speed and pressure was released through the medium of a transverse bar swinging from one side of the car and opened up in a bow shape to pass around the withdrawal collar. The gearbox, with tunnel to the selector arms and external contracting brakes on the nose of the main shaft and a bevel drive to the countershaft immediately behind, is highly similar to the arrangement provided on both the Hermes and the Fiat, and there are also noticeable similarities in the chain drive and radius arm to the rear axle. These resemblances, interesting as they are, must be weighed against the undoubted fact that all the drawings for the Italian car were executed in the Turin works, but this is consistent with the S.61 being based on a general arrangement developed by Bugatti from the Deutz project.

It seems an astonishing coincidence that Bugatti should enter into contractual relations with a concern which had previously employed both Benz and Daimler, but it is a fact that following the delivery of the prototype to Cologne, Deutz entered into an agreement with Bugatti whereby they retained his services for five years up to 1912; and in 1909 a team of three Deutz ran without penalty in the Prince Henry Trial. Significantly, perhaps, Bugatti entered separately with a car bearing his own name. It was in fact in this year that the always difficult relations between the temperamental designer and the large commercial organization came to a head and Bugatti received a substantial sum as compensation for the breaking-off of relations.

Deutz continued to build cars to his designs up to the outbreak of the 1914 war, and it is worth mentioning that all of them had an elliptical name-plate similar in design and proportion to that which became the hallmark of Bugatti himself. It seems almost certain that it was with the capital sum received from Deutz in 1909 that he was able to set up in business in the production of cars under his own name for the first time.

However, even whilst he was under contract to Deutz, Bugatti had found a further customer to pay for one of the basic designs that he was afterwards himself to use, and he next designed some cars for Isotta Fraschini who started in business as a Dietrich subsidiary! These were run in the 1908 Grand Prix des Voiturettes.

These wheels within wheels are carried a stage further, if the metaphor be permitted, by a record in *The Autocar* of 1911 that Col. Dawson, the owner of the Type 13 Bugattis described in Part III of this book, himself owned at this time one of the ex-1908 *voiturette* de Dietrich racing cars. He was evidently highly delighted with it as converted to touring use and said that the small overhead camshaft engine would run up to between 3,000 and 3,500 r.p.m.

The engine clutch and gearbox and chassis were all remarkably similar to the Type 13: the bore and stroke are 62×100 (c.f. 65×100 mm.) and the single overhead camshaft operates the valves placed across the engine to form a Deutz-like head.

It was Christmas 1909 when Bugatti moved into the nucleus of the existing Bugatti works and in 1910 five cars were built there. In 1911 65 people were employed and in addition to the Type 13, which was second in the Grand Prix de France at Le Mans, they built a back-to-back version making a 2·8 litre straight-8. In this year also they designed and built the car which was licensed as the Bébé Peugeot. In 1911 75 cars were made, and in 1912 the first of the few production models of the 1905 cars were made under the Bugatti name.

In 1911 also the S.61 Fiat won the Grand Prix at Le Mans and if the foregoing hypotheses are correct, then Bugatti was in some measure responsible for the design of both the first and second place winners, as his small car won the up to 7·6 litre class! In 1913 output rose from 12 to 19 chassis a month and before the outbreak of the war in 1914 output was at the rate of 27 per month.

When World War I broke out Bugatti was still only 33; and so at an age when the pioneers had still been working with gas-engines or wood-working machinery Bugatti had produced cars of sufficient merit to be built under licence by de Dietrich, Deutz, Isotta Fraschini, Peugeot, and almost certainly by Fiat. He had, in addition, pioneered on his own account an engine mounted in a light but rigid chassis with exceptional road-holding which was to point the way for some of the most important developments in automobile design.

One of the best appreciations of Bugatti himself has been written by J. A. Grégoire in his book *Best Wheel Forward*. Here he says:

'The analysis of such an astonishing personality as Bugatti, the elucidation of his genius-like characteristics and also of his weak points is of absorbing interest. Bugatti was an artist pure and simple; his only scientific knowledge stemmed from ever-growing experience plus a natural mechanical bent supported by the gift of observation. He did not believe in calculations, formulae and principles. He joked about pages covered with figures and the integral calculus which he called the sound holes of a violin. Fortunately he was wise enough to surround himself with engineers of talent whom he paid very well, while demanding of them complete anonymity.

'This lack of scientific grounding enabled him to take mechanical liberties, although he made mistakes at times. Nothing seemed impossible to him. He even occupied some of his spare time with research into the question of perpetual motion. Yet in the realm of the possible he sometimes achieved solutions which no ordinary engineer would have dared to attempt.

'The natural tendency of such a man is to use his sight as the normal instrument of control. To check essential parts of his designs, Bugatti had wooden mock-ups made to natural size. He pared or enlarged according to the impression he received on looking at the model.

'In his later years he needed glasses. Obviously he could not content himself with ordinary spectacles and asked his friend the Duc de Gramont, who had interests in an optical firm, to have very special lenses made. These spectacles enlarged too much. Thus deceived by his sight, Bugatti arranged over a period of time for the systematic decrease in size of certain mechanical parts which later disclosed themselves as weak in use!

'As might be expected, Bugatti was proud of his eye. He loved engines that had straight lines with flat and polished surfaces, behind which manifolds and accessories lay hidden.'

Grégoire continues with a criticism of Bugatti's obsessions with classic beauty and thereby exemplifies the unbridgeable gulf between the harshly realistic Frenchman and the more sensitive Italian.

In fact Bugatti occupies a special niche in the hall of fame as being the first man to bring some architectural concept into engine design and one has only to contrast his 1905–8 Deutz-Fiat-'Black Bess' type layout with a typical high-output engine of the same period (the 1907 Fiat for example) to realize how much we are indebted to him in this respect.

With the great designer there is an inevitable link between the nature of the man and the work he produces (*le style est l'homme même*) and we see in the Rolls-Royce Silver Ghost the reflection of Royce's great virtues of modesty, integrity and single-mindedness.

Similarly, we see in the scientific concepts of Lanchester and the artistic balanced layouts of Bugatti a facet of their versatility and it is worth mentioning that unlike the earlier engineers, who were proud to claim the bourgeois virtues of hard work and simple living, Lancaster and Bugatti enjoyed life to the full, and in their appreciation of wine, women and song, one need perhaps only say that Lanchester, who had a fine voice and was a serious student of Wagner, was most expert in the last; that Bugatti, who kept his private cellar at Larue in Paris, was the more knowledgeable in the first-named, and that for the second we need not pry too far!

We have now considered the influence of a genius in mechanical engineering, of a superb scientist, and of a mechanically inspired artist on the development of motor car design in the first years of the twentieth century.

Let us take next the case of the first of a new type of professional man, the automobile engineer. Here I select my father as an example, because if not the first he was one of the first who could properly be so-called; because if not the best he was without question one of the best; because, with Lanchester, he was in his published work and contributions to controversy the most articulate; and last but not least, because I have in my possession many original papers which throw an interesting light on the technical problems of the time.

Laurence Henry Pomeroy was born in 1883 and was thus two years younger than Bugatti, still at school when Daimler had retired temporarily from business, when Royce was running a £20,000 p.a. electrical business and when Lanchester was busy building his first motor car.

So, like Bugatti, L.H.P. grew up amidst a world of motoring and I have in my possession a book he bought at the age of 21 which has some interesting comments on the significance of this. This is Professor Spooner's *Motors and Motoring* written in 1904, in which the author remarks:

'The petrol engine is used in the great majority of cars now running and this doubtless accounts for the kind of motor language that is heard at every turn by the man in the street, and, if the truth must be known, by the boy in the street; for, strangely enough, the schoolboy's allegiance to the locomotive has been wavering in favour of the automobile for some time, and now his school locker generally contains a rare collection of pictures, plates, postcards, technical journals, and parts of models relating to autocars and motorcycles instead of such things concerning the various types of locomotives that were formerly so much in favour. In this connection there cannot be a doubt that the great progress we are making in automobilism has had not a little to do with the astonishing increase in the number of boys whose greatest ambition is to be engineers.'

These remarks certainly applied to this particular purchaser of the book, but whereas Bugatti was building motor cars with his own hands at 17, L.H.P. at this age was following a rigorous training in both the practical and theoretical aspects of engineering generally.

He became apprenticed at the age of 16 to the North London Locomotive Works at Bow, and simultaneously commenced a four-year engineering course at the East London Technical College. In the three years 1900–3 he sat for 22 examination papers, gaining 15 seconds, 5 firsts and 2 Honours and on September 1st (incidentally four years to the day before I was born) he learnt that he had passed sixteenth out of thirty Whitworth Exhibitioners for 1903.

Later in life when speaking about the best training for young engineers he said:

'I think the ordinary apprentice, if he wants to become anything at all, should be prepared to put in evening classes three nights a week for two or three hours each night, and on the remaining nights he should be prepared to put in two or three hours' home work. If he is up at five in the morning and knocks off at six at night and puts in this amount of work at evening classes, he will not have very much time left for himself when the hours of rest are taken into account, but unless a lad is prepared absolutely to devote himself to the profession he does not deserve to get on.'

L.H.P. was reciting his early experiences in this matter, neglecting, however, to point out that in his case he had an hour-and-a-half travelling to fit

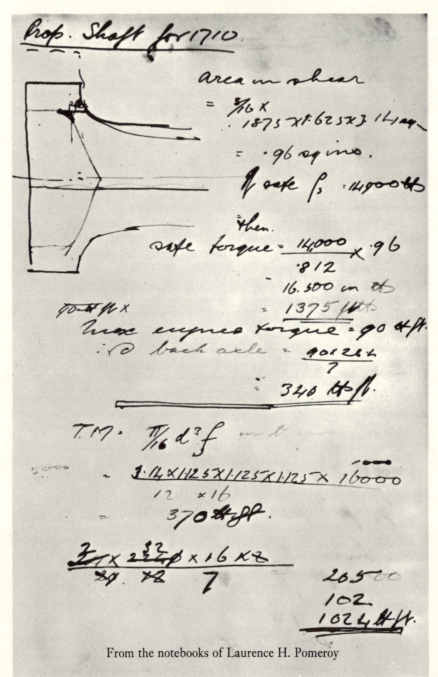

Prop. Shaft for 1710.

area in shear

$$= \tfrac{3}{16} \times$$
$$.1875 \times 1.625 \times 3 \ \text{sq.}$$

$$= .96 \ \text{sq ins.}$$

If safe $f_s = 14{,}000 \ \text{lb}$

then.

safe torque $= \dfrac{14{,}000 \times .96}{.812}$

$$= 16{.}500 \ \text{in lb}$$

$$= 1375 \ \text{lb ft}.$$

max engine torque $= 90 \ \text{lb ft}.$

$\therefore$ @ back axle $= \dfrac{90 \times 28.4}{7}$

$$= 340 \ \text{lb ft}.$$

$$T.M. = \tfrac{\pi}{16} d^3 f$$

$$= \dfrac{3.14 \times 1.125 \times 1.125 \times 1.125 \times 16000}{12 \times 16}$$

$$= 370 \ \text{lb ft}.$$

$$\dfrac{\tfrac{\pi}{4} \times 2\tfrac{3}{4} \phi \times 16 \times 2}{\text{sq. in}} \quad \dfrac{7}{} =$$
$$\begin{array}{r} 20500 \\ 102 \\ \hline 1024 \ \text{lb ft}. \end{array}$$

From the notebooks of Laurence H. Pomeroy

214

into the 24 hours, so that 'not very much time left for himself' was a masterly meiosis.

The result, however, was that by the time he was 20 L.H.P. had a formidable knowledge of mathematics, science and engineering and after taking his first paid job with the civil engineers Humphreys and Company in Victoria Street, London, he thereafter came in contact with road vehicles from a professional point of view at Thornycrofts of Basingstoke. He recounted later that when seeking his early jobs he found his academic qualifications considered of little account, and it was not until he mentioned that he was capable of working in the shops if necessary that he found himself acceptable.

These were the first steps towards the position which was to bring him fame and fortune. The next was an appointment to be assistant to the chief engineer of Vauxhall Motors at Luton, which he took up in 1906. The Company had been making cars of no particular distinction for the past three years, and this state of affairs continued through 1907. Then it was decided to build a new car for entry in the R.A.C. 2,000 mile Trial, to be held later in that year, and this started a series of remarkable coincidences which greatly influenced L.H.P.'s life and the commercial fortunes of the Company.

Seeking to remedy weakness in foreign languages L.H.P. devoted himself to the reading of French text-books on automobile design, and at this time the earlier supremacy of French engineers was reflected by an immense literature on the technicalities of automobile engineering in that tongue. One which particularly attracted L.H.P. was: *L'Automobile à l'Essence: Principes de Construction et Calcul*, by Heirman. This book, which is now in my possession, contains L.H.P.'s notes as he went along, and shows the evident impression that some of the chapters made upon him, particularly where the author stressed the need for high compression pressures for high piston speeds. Significantly, the top corner of page 147 is turned down where the text reads:

'The faster the engine turns the more it multiplies its capacity, and the more space it makes for the combustible mixture, but on the other hand the pistons in moving more rapidly increase the vacuum produced behind them. This depression has the effect of reducing the density of the carburetted mixture in such a way that although the volume of the mixture admitted into the cylinders grows in proportion with the speed of the engine, the mass introduced into each cylinder diminishes. The mass of the explosive mixture diminishing the power of the explosion naturally becomes weaker in consequence.

'From another point of view perfect scavenging of the products of combustion—the burnt gases—undergoes difficulties in the same way at high speeds and contra pressures are produced which still further diminish the output.

Early 'Prince Henry' Vauxhall, as delivered to H. W. Cook in March 1911

'The remedy for this situation is easy to sketch. It resides in the use of large valves, of inlet pipes of large diameter presenting a minimum of length and free from sharp curves; it resides also in the development of a carburettor working on a very small vacuum, and finally in the choice of a well-designed and free-flowing exhaust system.'

The opportunity of putting such theories into practice in 1908 arose from the fact that when the decision was made to build the new car, the chief engineer of the Company was on holiday in Egypt. By the time he had returned L.H.P.'s new design was well on the way towards completion, and the existing 92×95 mm. engine which gave $23 \cdot 5$ h.p. at 1,800 r.p.m. was replaced by a 90×120 mm. model giving 38 b.h.p. at 2,500, representing a 75 per cent step-up from $7 \cdot 36$ h.p. per litre to $12 \cdot 7$ b.h.p. per litre and of b.m.e.p. from 60 lb. per sq. in. to 73 lb. per sq. in.

Great attention was paid on this engine to crankshaft design, fully forced lubrication, and the choice of gear ratios, and the results of this few weeks of work in the drawing office can be rightly termed phenomenal. In the R.A.C. Trial which lasted for 13 days the car demanded no stops for lubrication, tyres or penalties. It averaged 26 m.p.g. including a finale of 200 miles on the recently opened Brooklands circuit; in the hill-climbs it had an aggregate of 37 seconds less time than any other car in its class, and at the end on a marking system which took reliability and m.p.g. into account it lost but 77 marks, the next lowest (achieved by a Silver Ghost Rolls-Royce) being 115 marks.

The *Auto Motor Journal* summed up by saying: 'That 1908 performance brought the 20 h.p. Vauxhall from a comparatively uninteresting background into the full glare of public interest.' In the next six years this basic design and the derivatives therefrom (the 95×140 mm. four-litre, which installed in a light chassis became known as the C Type Prince Henry model, and the 98×150 mm. E Type, popularly known as the 30-98) continued to attract public attention in a series of great competition successes.

Some of these have been mentioned already and in sum, between 1909 and 1913 the design had to its credit 17 class records and 18 world records, and in only one of these years at the hill-climbs of Aston Clinton and Shelsley Walsh did the car fail to gain first place on either time or formula. In 1913 the Company and private owners driving cars made by it gained first prizes for 35 hill-climbs, 23 races at Brooklands track, and in 14 reliability trials.

It is not the theme of this book to concern itself with the successes of various makes of car in competition but in this case they formed part of a larger theme for the essential contribution of L.H.P. to the development of the automobile industry was the demonstration that high-performance cars could be built which were simple in construction and profitable to sell.

In contrast to Royce, who had virtually to be banned from the works at Derby because his perfectionism prevented economical production, with Lanchester, whose pursuit of science contributed to the commercial collapse of the original Lanchester Company and to a reconstruction under the guidance of his brother George, and to Bugatti, who had the unique quality of making licensees pay for prototype work, and customers for development, L.H.P. combined in a high degree engineering attainment with a practical outlook. This contrast in personalities was highlighted during the 1911 session of the Institution of Automobile Engineers in which L.H.P. read a paper entitled *Engine Design for h.p. rating Rules.*

In this he summed up his approach to engine design in words which show clearly the influence which Heirman's book had had upon him, saying, *inter alia:*

'Having now dealt with the fundamentals of high-speed engine design, a few conclusions will be drawn before passing on to the consideration of horse-power rating. These are:

(*a*) That high mean effective pressures depend upon mixture strength;

(*b*) That high mean effective pressures at high speeds depend upon high volumetric efficiency and high compression;

(*c*) That high volumetric efficiency depends entirely upon large ports and valves;

(*d*) That lightness of moving parts is essential if high mechanical efficiency is desired.

'If these conclusions be true, then it follows that, given sufficient valve and port area, horse-power is directly proportional to the cylinder capacity and to the revolutions per minute. It then only becomes necessary to design for either a minimum rating for a given cylinder capacity, or a maximum cylinder capacity for a given rating. In competitions generally the range of engine size is not great. For instance, in a recent hill-climb the smallest engine was 68 × 120 mm., whilst the largest was 127 × 152 mm. bore and stroke respectively. The cases to be considered will therefore come within this range of cylinder capacity. If it can be shown to be reasonable that each of them should develop the same revolutions per minute and the same mean effective pressure at that speed, then rating by cylinder capacity is obviously just.'

Lanchester's academic conscience was scandalized by this approach and in the discussion of the paper he said:

'It seems strange to have to tell an engineer in the twentieth century that a large engine, other things being equal, cannot be safely run at so high a revolution speed as a small one; and considering how thoroughly it is established that piston speed is the criterion rather than revolution speed, it would seem almost an impertinence to offer to the Institution in a discussion a demonstration of the fallacy of any such doctrine as that which, it would appear, has the author's support. However, he deals with the whole question with apparent seriousness, with a certain patronizing pretence of exercising an exalted faculty of judicial criticism, and something has to be done.

'Let us take out two engines, one double the bore and stroke of the other; let them be designed for equal explosion pressures, then if equal skill, materials, and factors of safety are used, the weights of the moving parts of the larger engine will be, part for part, eight times the weight of the same parts of the smaller engine. And their motions are of twice the amplitude and executed in the same intervals of time, that is, their inertia effects per unit mass are twice as great in the larger engine. That is to say, the actual inertia forces are, part for part, $2 \times 8 = 16$ times as great in the larger engine. But the sectional areas by which these greater stresses are taken are only 2^2, that is, four times as great, consequently the stresses per sq. in. in the larger engine are 16 divided by 4, or four times as great in the larger engine as in the smaller; the fallacy of the author's assumption is therefore manifest.'

However, the last word in this matter remained with L.H.P. who replied:

'I am sorry Mr Lanchester is such a busy man—for I presume a certain part of the paper missed him. I will just read a portion of it again, because I knew Mr Lanchester would come along with exactly the words he has done, so I am not disappointed.

'"We know that, given adequate port areas, the limit of speed is determined as, in structures of all kinds, by the strength of materials. It is convenient to base the following argument upon the strength of the connecting rod. This at slow speeds is subject to compressive stress by the explosion pressure, and at high speeds to tensile and compressive stresses due to piston inertia. So long as the inertia stresses do not exceed the explosion stresses the rod cannot be overstressed. It should obviously be capable of taking all normal working stresses." My contention is that if the connecting rod is capable of taking the actual pressure put on it, then it should be capable of taking inertia stresses which do not stress it any more than the explosion pressure.

'The fallacy underlying Mr Lanchester's theory of inertia limitation of piston speed is that it does not apply to engines of the sizes used in motor cars. When the speeds of such engines are two or three times as great as they are now, or when the cylinders are two or three times as large as the largest now used, it will be time to apologize to the Institution for my impertinence in demonstrating the fallacy of the doctrine which I have referred to.'

In this respect L.H.P. was a true prophet, for in the subsequent year, 1912, a capacity limit was employed for the first time and in the subsequent 33 years of Grand Prix Regulations there has been a capacity limit on 25 of them.

At other times L.H.P. showed his differences in outlook with Royce by the remark: 'The Rolls-Royce is a triumph of workmanship over design', and by inference in the statement: 'No design is good unless it can stand a liberal dose of bad workmanship.'

But just as it would be wrong to underrate Lanchester's practical abilities as a consequence of his great intellectual capacity, so would it be false on the basis of these 'down to earth' statements to underrate L.H.P.'s gifts on the drawing board. These were demonstrated in dramatic form within two years of his first complete design, for by 1910 as shown earlier his 3-litre engine had been developed to give 60 b.h.p. at 2,800 r.p.m., the equivalent of 20 b.h.p. per litre, and a b.m.e.p. of 102 lb. per sq. in. at a piston speed of 2,050 ft. per min.

I have in my hands many notebooks filled with calculations which made this exceptional result, attained with the most rigorous simplicity of layout and construction, possible, and these show not only estimates of gas velocity, required valve diameter and lift, but also such details as the sketch of a piston, a complete analysis of the varying areas, and the weight of metal contained in them, and a final estimate that the total weight would be 2·2 lb. (2 lb. 3·2 oz.) or 'say 2 lb. 3 oz.' As a check upon the skill of these calculations, *The Automobile Engineer Reference Book* of the period shows that the weight of the production piston was 2 lb. 2 oz.!

This example may be taken as a typical illustration of the change which had taken place within a decade. In an earlier time we have one of the pioneers, Captain Ferber, remarking that to essay is all; now we have proof that the components of a car—indeed the complete car itself—could be set out on the drawing board so that before it was built, let alone tested, they would be very near to their final form, and a final form which reached a high standard of efficiency and flexibility.

The difference between the engineer-mechanic of 1903 and the designer-engineer of 1913 can be amusingly demonstrated by contrasting the stories of constant mechanical breakdowns which have been related in earlier chapters with an experience which befell my father when on a journey with a distinguished Danish engineer called Poppe. The firm of White and Poppe were proprietary engine manufacturers on a large scale in Coventry, sold one of the best-known carburettors of the time, and by producing the first power units for W. R. Morris played a prominent part in the successful foundation of the Nuffield empire.

Poppe's private car was a 35 h.p. Lancia and when he was driving my father in it the engine stopped firing. The young L.H.P. jumped out, quickly diagnosed slipped timing and began to suggest the procedure starting with the removal of the radiator which was necessary to effect a repair.

Both men were, of course, quite capable of bringing the car into running order with their own hands, but the more elderly Poppe epitomized the new outlook by staying resolutely put behind the wheel, saying: 'No, no, Pomeroy, dis is where we schmoke our pipes; dat is job for de mechanic, not fòr de expert.'

As one might suppose, however, this new breed of experts was few in number and there were only 385 qualified members of the Institution of Automobile Engineers in 1908. There were at this time some 81 British concerns putting their individual names to makes of motor car, so when one includes the demands of the component industry it will be seen that the trained engineers were very thin on the ground and certainly at this time a first-class man in the chief engineer's office could make a company's prosperity just as one with indifferent ideas, or weak personality, could quickly break it.

Between 1908 and 1914 Vauxhall built the modest number of 1,979 cars at prices varying between £350 and £750 (£1,000 up to £2,500 in modern values), but they made a net profit of about 10 per cent on the catalogue price of each car, the total profits between the years mentioned amounting to £78,864. Thus, Vauxhall Motors, as well as the Sunbeam Company which will be referred to later, found in this period of motoring history that an active competition programme was by no means incompatible with a very high return on the capital invested in the Company.

Returning now to the more personal theme, Milton has it:

> Fame is the spur that the clear spirit doth raise
> To scorn delights and live laborious dayes.

In the case of L.H.P. the extreme labours of his early life were certainly rewarded by rapid appreciation in his twenties. In 1909, he was made works manager of Vauxhall Motors Ltd.; two years later at the age of 28 he was elected a member of the Council of the Institution of Automobile Engineers, and awarded the Crompton gold medal by that same body; and he celebrated his thirtieth year with the design of the 30–98 and election as a full member of the Institution of Mechanical Engineers, the youngest man to have achieved this distinction.

To these honours were added cash rewards on a scale hard to conceive in Europe at the present time.

The social philosophy and negligible taxation of the Edwardian age made it possible for the successful man to both earn and enjoy a substantial differential above the average salary, and in L.H.P.'s case he had at the age of 24 a weekly wage of approximately twice that earned by the skilled mechanic, which was increased fivefold in five years. Thus at the age of 30 his net income was 10 times that of the skilled weekly worker, or he had shall we say the value of £200 a week net at the present time.

This had a technical as well as a personal and sociological importance. The chief engineers of the time lived on terms of financial equality with all but the richest of car users and could appreciate motoring from their customers' point of view. This led L.H.P. to build really fast cars which could be maintained by a new generation of young enthusiasts who did not enjoy the services of chauffeur-mechanics and which would also run for very large mileages without wear or the need for adjustment. To sum up, his standard of 20 b.h.p. per litre equalled, if it did not exceed, the results obtained by Bugatti with his considerably more complicated and fragile, but admittedly more elegant, engines, and looking back after forty years we can see that his cars were no less durable than the Rolls-Royce, which were quieter and smoother but built with little regard for cost in materials or man-hours.

In 1910 it might have seemed that automobile design would evolve along three main branches. One would be the *voitures de grand luxe* producing a superlative standard of refinement for the really wealthy man, another the car of exceptional performance obtained at considerable cost in construction, and with the penalty of frequent adjustment and renewals, and the third a purely utility machine, cheap to buy, simple to run, but with a maximum speed of not more than 45 m.p.h. L.H.P.'s conjunction of scientific training with practical knowledge enabled him similarly to synthesize something of all three branches and to foster a fourth line of development which finds expression today in that class of car which the Italians have so aptly described as *Gran Turismo* or *Turismo Veloce*.

Although L.H.P. could not claim to be as expert a musician as Lanchester or as much a connoisseur of wine as Bugatti he was a good judge of both, he could justly say that he enjoyed life to the full; and in one of those interviews between the adolescent and the parent which take place traditionally in the study I remember that his text might well have been taken from Terence: 'I am human and nothing is alien to me.'

This quality of character he shared with his great rival Louis Coatalen.

Coatalen was a Frenchman who came to England and achieved immediate

Louis Coatalen in 'Toodles 11', his 15·9 h.p. car which he drove
at 86·157 m.p.h. over the flying half-mile at Brooklands in April 1911

prominence as a designer for Mr Hillman—a relationship which he confirmed by marrying Hillman's daughter. He later joined the Sunbeam Company and here he acted more as *le patron* (a title by which he was commonly
called) than as an engineer in his own right. It cannot be said, either, that he
sponsored anything highly original in design; rather would one say that he
was acutely aware of the advantages and disadvantages of various new ideas
both from a technical and a commercial point of view. Nevertheless, his cars
were so·extremely successful both in road racing abroad and on Brooklands
track in England that he cannot be overlooked despite the fact that Sunbeams produced originally few cars of competition type for sale to the
private owner and their production models were comparatively commonplace. It is moreover significant to our theme that whereas in 1909 Sunbeams
made a profit of but £90, as the Coatalen programme gathered strength they
rose to £20,700 in 1910 and £41,000 in 1911. After the great Sunbeam
performance in the French Grand Prix of 1912 a profit of no less than
£94,909 on a capital of £120,000 was realized in 1913.

As has been indicated, 'Louis' used talented engineers, such as Hugh
Rose, to work under his direction. Other makes, designed by other men, also
played their part in automobile development at this time. In England the
25 h.p. Talbot designed by Ferrier Brown was the great competitor of
Vauxhall in straight sprints, and in outer circuit races at Brooklands; Star
and Crossley were strongly competitive in hill-climbs.

In the U.S.A., Leland was showing what fine production meant and pioneering the great boon of the self-starter; in France Henri was working under the direction of those three talented Peugeot racing drivers Zuccarelli, Boillot and Goux on the 1912 Grand Prix and 1913 3-litre cars which, with their inclined multiple valves worked by double overhead camshafts, were the very foundation of the modern high-speed engine. Italy had yet to make any notable contribution to motor car design, but in Spain Marc Birkigt was selling the Alfonso XIII type Hispano-Suiza which, by embodying the lessons gained in winning the 1910 Light Car race at Boulogne, stands with Porsche's overhead camshaft Prince Henry type Austro-Daimlers as cars which have a truly historic significance.

But the engineering developments in the Golden Age of motoring industry were fostered by no more than a score of men, and although it would be obviously untrue to say that it was wholly determined by the four whose character and work has been studied in this chapter, the pace and direction of progress was established by such as they.

So let Lanchester, Bugatti, Coatalen and Pomeroy stand as representatives of the new men who tackled new problems in a new way. In their struggle to eliminate rule of thumb and to reduce trial and error they transferred the work of the engineer from the road to the drawing board, the test-bed and the racing circuit; they 'killed the fox in the kennel'. They showed almost every conceivable difference in their approach to the problems of motor-car design, and correspondingly in the solutions which they produced; they shared a common belief in working hard and playing hard; and it was by their hard work that they achieved the means to play in the grand manner. They would not only have been bored by the somewhat humdrum life of the early pioneers, but equally would have been repelled by the suburban satisfactions which must perforce content most chief engineers of the present day. They had, in the words of Gibbon, 'The commanding superiority of soul, the generous clemency, and the various genius which could reconcile and unite the love of pleasure, the thirst of knowledge and the fire of ambition'; and they used these qualities not only to their personal advantage but also to found a new art and to establish a new profession.

From *From Veteran to Vintage*, 1951

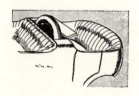

1913 Olympia Motor Show poster, and some examples of the coachworks and fittings on displa

Courtesy Montagu Motor Museum

224

Your Choice in 1914

ALBION
Country of Origin: Scotland
The Albion Motor Car Co. Ltd., Scotstoun, Glasgow (Stand 63).

Exhibit: One 15 h.p. four-cylinder Albion chassis; one 15 h.p. shooting car; and one 15 h.p. country house car, four cylinders, 79 × 127 mm., three speeds, worm drive.

Features: The engine on this model is an *en bloc* casting, with T-headed cylinders and enclosed valves on either side. Thermo-syphon cooling is employed, and a fan of large diameter is placed behind the radiator and driven by belt from the near-side camshaft. The carburettor is the Albion patent, and is attached to the off-side of the engine. The base chamber of the motor is extended to form a housing for the gearbox, with which it forms a rigid unit which is braced directly to the main frame. The clutch is of the Albion patent metal-to-metal type, and the gear change is on the gate principle. Behind the gearbox is a large diameter locomotive type foot brake. The propeller-shaft is unenclosed and carries a universal joint at the front end and a sliding joint at the rear.

An overhead worm drive is used. The back axle is supported so far as its torque is concerned by a pressed steel member which is anchored to a spring support carried on a special cross member of the frame. The drive is transmitted through the front part of the half-elliptic springs. Internal expanding brakes operate in drums on the rear wheels. Considerable road clearance is given to all parts of the chassis, which is of a particularly sturdy construction suitable for extended and hard use over difficult roads. Particular attention has been paid to lubrication, and the car embodies a thoroughly complete system, oil being fed separately to all the principal working parts of the engine. A special point in the control is the Murray governor, which has for many years been used in these cars.

ALLDAYS
Country of Origin: England
Alldays and Onions Pneumatic Engineering Co. Ltd., Birmingham (Stand 77).

Exhibit: One 10 h.p., four-cylinder, 59 × 100 mm. bore and stroke, touring car, three speeds, worm drive; one 12–14 h.p., four-cylinder, 76 × 120 mm. bore and stroke, four-seater touring car, four speeds, bevel drive; one 16–20 h.p., four-cylinder, 86 × 130 mm. bore and stroke, four-seater touring car, four speeds, bevel drive; one 16–20 h.p., four-cylinder, cabriolet; one 25–30 h.p., four-cylinder, 100 × 130 mm. bore and stroke, three-quarter landaulet, four speeds, bevel drive.

Features: A new model makes its appearance in this exhibit in the shape of the Alldays 10 h.p. The h.t. Mea magneto is employed in conjunction with a Zenith carburettor. A very up-to-date V-fronted gilled tube radiator is assisted in its cooling action by a fan efficiently designed on the lines of an aeroplane propeller, and the whole appearance of this little machine, with its tapered bonnet and scuttle dash, is advancedly modern without being *outré*. A most interesting point about it, however, is the springing. At the back inverted semi-elliptics are employed on the Lanchester system, pivoted midway of their length. These springs are not secured directly to the axle, but the position of the axle is assured by radius links connecting it with the front ends of the springs. The front springs, too, are inverted half-radius rods to hold the axle in position. Like the 12–14 h.p. and 16–20 h.p. Alldays touring cars, this little machine is turned out completely equipped with lamps, hood, screen, and detachable steel wheels and tyres, though it should be mentioned that in the equipment of the two larger cars a dynamo lighting system is included. As regards the other chassis, no great alterations in last year's practice have appeared, the attention of the firm having been mainly devoted to improvement rather than alteration.

ARMSTRONG-WHITWORTH
Country of Origin: England
Sir W. G. Armstrong, Whitworth and Co. Ltd., Newcastle upon Tyne (Stand 41).

Exhibit: One 17–25 h.p., four-cylinder, 85 × 135 mm., limousine car, four speeds, overhead worm drive; one 17–25 h.p. cabriolet coupé; one 20–30 h.p., four-cylinder, 90 × 500 mm., cabriolet, four speeds and worm drive.

Features: The latest model on the Armstrong-Whitworth stand is the 20–30 h.p. car. This has a *monobloc* engine of clean design. A chain-driven distribution gear is employed, and adjustment for this is obtained by means of an eccentric bush on the spindle which drives the water-pump. Lubrication is forced to the bearings by means of a gear pump. This pump picks up the oil from the sump, which delivers it to the main bearings and big ends, spraying to other parts. The sump is of an extra large size, and is ribbed beneath in order to gain as much cooling for the oil as possible. An oil filler is conveniently placed on the near-side of the crank-case, and beneath it is a level tap. This car, indeed all the Armstrong-Whitworth models, is fitted with an interesting multiple disc type of clutch, in which the discs are alternately of metal and Ferodo, and run dry. On the front of the gearbox is mounted a pump which maintains air pressure in the petrol tank, which is

Courtesy Montagu Motor Museum

carried at the extreme rear of the frame. The propeller-shaft is enclosed, and at the front of its casing is a Y-fork carried on brackets attached to the cross member and gearbox. Three-quarter elliptic springs are employed without radius rods. The other Armstrong-Whitworth models are practically un-altered from last year. On the 20-30 h.p. chassis is mounted a very nice double cabriolet built by the firm. It is fitted with a top, which is most easily raised or lowered. The front uprights fold along the back of the front seats; the centre and rear uprights fold backwards along the body after the fashion of a parallel ruler. There are no outside irons. A similar style of body is also fitted on the 30-50 h.p. six-cylinder car. Another body on the stand which is worthy of mention is a cabriolet coupé on the 17-25 h.p. chassis. The front seats are adjustable as to height, distance, angle, etc.

AUSTIN
Country of Origin: England
The Austin Motor Co. Ltd., Northfield, near Birmingham (Stand 47).

Exhibit: A 30 h.p. landaulet and one 30 h.p. chassis, four cylinders, 111×152 mm., four speeds, bevel drive; one 20 h.p. three-quarter landaulet, four cylinders, 89×127 mm., four speeds, bevel drive; one 10 h.p. touring phaeton and one 10 h.p. chassis, four cylinders, 76×89 mm., four speeds, bevel drive.

Features: The outstanding feature of all Austin engines is their separately cast cylinders and five-bearing crankshafts. The 30 h.p. Austin has a friction drive electric engine starter, and C.A.V. lighting set. The gearbox is three-

227

Courtesy Montagu Motor Museum

point suspended, and has particularly short shafts, thus tending to reduce gear noise considerably. A distinctly unusual feature is the provision of universal joints on the foot brake actuating shaft, which has a bearing on the chassis frame member, and thence passes directly across to the brake shoes. The brake drum is spring mounted on the propeller-shaft behind the universal joint, the shoes being carried on the propeller-shaft casing.

A torque tube encases the propeller-shaft, and at its rear end is fitted with a vertical trunnion block which allows for lateral movement of the rear axle. Full elliptic rear springs are employed, these being underslung. Details have been carefully carried out, and the brake gear is particularly substantial, The 10 h.p. model resembles the 30 h.p. in many details, but is not fitted with electric starter or lighting set as standard. The clutch of all Austin models consists of a Ferodo fly-wheel facing which is engaged by a very light pressed steel cone. The Ferodo facing is made up of six segments mounted on light steel pressings, each of which is capable of being quickly removed.

AUSTRO-DAIMLER
Country of Origin: Austria
Austrian Daimler Motor Co. Ltd., Great Portland Street, W.1 (Stand 28).

Exhibit: One streamline sporting model, 16–25 h.p., four cylinders, 80×110 mm., four speeds, bevel drive; one 16–18 h.p. limousine, four cylinders, 80×100 mm., four speeds, bevel drive; one 20–30 h.p. saloon, four cylinders, 90×140 mm., four speeds, bevel drive; one Prince Henry type chassis, 27–80 h.p., four cylinders, 105×165 mm., four speeds, bevel drive.

Features: The chassis of the Prince Henry type is a striking exhibit; the angular arrangement of the valves on the top of the cylinders (the overhead valve motion being enclosed) and the inclined position of the two magnetos which furnish the current to two sparking plugs in each cylinder are notable details. All the vehicles are fitted with Rudge-Whitworth detachable wheels, and, if one more than another can be picked out for individual mention, it is the 16–18 h.p. finished car, which has a neatly arranged *en bloc* engine and is of generally clean design right through. The C.A.V. lighting set is fitted on this model. The doors are lined with natural wood, finely grained, and the door windows are frameless. A small point to notice is the glass buttons cemented to the inner side of the window panes to provide a grip when raising or lowering the windows, thus obviating the objection to the frameless window type that they cannot be raised or lowered if they happen to stick slightly. It is evident that considerable care has been given to the lines of the front portions of these cars in order to secure harmony with the bodywork.

BENZ
Country of Origin: Germany
The Brompton Motor Co. Ltd., Brompton Road, S.W.1 (Stand 104).

Exhibit: One 100 h.p. chassis, four cylinders, 130×190 mm., four speeds, bevel drive; one 40–65 h.p., 130×160 mm., four-seater touring car, four cylinders; one 12–20 h.p., 72×120 mm., touring car, four cylinders, four speeds, bevel drive.

Features: Undoubtedly the most imposing item on this stand, in a way the most imposing in the Show, is the big 100 h.p. Benz chassis. This is the more interesting in that it follows the standardized lines of the smaller cars, the only material difference lying in the cylinders, which in this case are cast in pairs instead of *en bloc*. Forced lubrication is employed to the main big end bearings, whence the oil draining down is caught in scoops and carried by the centrifugal action of the crank to the big ends—a very simple system. Water circulation is by pump through a V-shaped radiator carried on trunnions. The brakes are water-cooled, and for the foot brake an additional pedal is provided so that it can be worked in conjunction with the clutch, the

Courtesy Montagu Motor Museum

clutch coming out before the brake goes on, or by the alternative pedal the brake can be applied independently. The propeller-shaft is carried in a torque tube, and strong radius rods are fitted on either side; their forward centres coincide with that of the universal joint. Such a car has almost unlimited possibilities with a large body on Continental roads where speed limits are non-existent. There is one point calling for particular attention in the steering gear as fitted on all Benz chassis, and that is that the stub axles are placed slightly behind the pinions on which they turn consequently they are always subject to a castor or trailing action which makes the steering exceptionally easy.

CADILLAC
Country of Origin: U.S.A.
F. S. Bennet Ltd,. Shaftesbury Avenue, W.C.2 (Stand 108).

Exhibit: One 20–30 h.p., 114×146 mm., sectioned chassis, four cylinders, six speeds, bevel drive; one 20–30 h.p. seven-seater touring car; one 20–30 h.p. two-seater; one 20–30 h.p. four-seater touring car; one 20–30 h.p. coupé.

Features: The principal feature of the Cadillac car is, of course, its extremely complete equipment, which comprises first of all electric self-starting, lighting and ignition installation of the Delco type, the motor being combined with the dynamo and carried in an accessible position under the bonnet. It rotates the engine for starting purposes through teeth cut on the rim of the fly-wheel. Another special feature is the use of a two-speed gearbox, incorporated in the rear axle, which, with the ordinary gearbox, gives six speeds forward, including two direct drives. The ordinary gate change gear is used for the main box change, but in the rear axle this is effected by pressing an electric switch and pushing the clutch pedal forward. The majority of ordinary running can be done on one or the other of the direct drive ratios. The clutch is of the cone type, and is fitted with a very neat adjustable brake. A good point in connection with the gate gear change is the arrangement of the lever in such a position that it does not interfere with the entrance on the driver's side. The dashboard is very completely fitted up with instruments, and presents a neat appearance. The propeller-shaft is of the unenclosed type, and a separate torque member is, therefore, employed. The equipment of the chassis includes detachable rims, which are of a particularly neat design and are easily operated. Both foot and hand brakes apply to the rear wheel hub drums, one being external and the other internal. The ignition is automatically variable, but also under the control of the driver. There is also a power-driven tyre pump.

DAIMLER
Country of Origin: England
The Daimler Co. Ltd., Coventry (Stand 76).

Exhibit: One 20 h.p., 90×130 mm., four-cylinder touring car; one 45 h.p., 110×130 mm., six-cylinder Selston limousine; and one 45 h.p. limousine, the latter being for Her Majesty the Queen.

Features: In the new 20 h.p. Daimler, which constitutes one of the features of the Show, the gearbox and back axle are incorporated in a single casing,

Courtesy Montagu Motor Museum

231

and from the front end of the gearbox the torque tube is brought up so that the front spherical joint fits into a spherical bearing on the centre of a cross member of the frame. This latter also supports the tail end of the clutch-shaft. The axle itself, which supports the frame on cantilever springs, is practically an enlarged edition of the B.S.A., triangulated rods extending from the outer ends of the axle casing to the torque tube. In this design a brake is fitted at the tail end of the wormshaft that drives the back axle, thus enabling braking effect to be transmitted in such a way that only the differential is affected. Three choices of equipment are afforded with these cars. Either chassis can be supplied with a three-speed gearbox, with oil side and tail lamps, or a four-speed gearbox can be substituted for an extra £20, the third choice consisting of a four-speed chassis with electric lighting equipment and lamps at £430; to this a self-starter can be added for another £20. Special attention should be given to Her Majesty's car with limousine body by Hooper, whilst the Selston landaulet affords a very fine example of motor manufacturers' bodywork.

DELAGE
Country of Origin: France
The London and Parisian Motor Co. Ltd., Davis Street, W.1 (Stand 34).

Exhibit: One 12 h.p., four-cylinder, 65 × 110 mm., three-seater car, with four speeds and bevel drive; one 14 h.p., four-cylinder, 75 × 130 mm., car, four speeds and bevel drive, with an all-weather body; one 14 h.p. four-cylinder, three-seater car; one 15·9 h.p. saloon, six cylinders, 65 × 130 mm., four speeds and bevel drive; and one 15·9 h.p. six-cylinder chassis.

Features: The Delage chassis is remarkable for its extremely clean design. The exhaust and inlet manifolds of the six-cylinder *en bloc* casting are both on the near-side and do not affect the accessibility of the valves. The distribution gear is driven by a silent chain, and the lubrication is maintained by means of a pump which draws oil from the the sump in crank-case and forces it to the main bearings and big ends, the remaining parts being lubricated by splash. A leather-faced cone clutch conveys the drive to the four-speed gearbox through two universal joints of block type, which are provided with leather covers to enclose the lubricant. A gate change is used and the shaft on which the lever is mounted is attached to the gearbox only and not to the frame, so that the possibility of binding is removed. The drive to the back axle is taken through an unenclosed propeller-shaft, the front end of which has a block type universal joint, the rear joint being of star type and enclosed in a metal case. The rear springs take both the drive and torque. On this car the pedal applies the two expanding brakes on the rear wheels; each of these being provided with separate hand adjustment. The side lever brake is on the counter-shaft and is of internal expanding type. The saloon body on the other 15·9 h.p. six-cylinder chassis presents a very striking appearance. It has one door on each side, access to the back seats being afforded by swinging the front passenger's seat.

DELAUNAY-BELLEVILLE
Country of Origin: France
Delaunay-Belleville Automobiles (England) Ltd., Pall Mall, S.W.1 (Stand 50).

Exhibit: One 45–50 h.p. limousine, six cylinders, 103 × 160 mm., four speeds, bevel drive; one 37 h.p. dome-roofed landaulet, six cylinders, 100 × 140 mm., four speeds, bevel drive; one 30 h.p. chassis, six cylinders, 88 × 150 mm., four speeds, bevel drive.

Features: Several alterations have been embodied in the latest type Delaunay-Bellevilles. One of these is the two-jet carburettor, the design of which allows both jets to be removed simultaneously and without special tools. The inlet leads are taken through the cylinder castings, and each jet supplies mixtures to three cylinders. Each set of three cylinders has a separate exhaust branch, leading into a common pipe. An electrical engine starter may be fitted inside the fly-wheel, or else the Barby air starter, which consists of a four-cylinder air engine on the front end of the crankshaft. The clutch is of the single plate type with steel surfaces in contact with asbestos, the plates working without oil. The gearbox is now fitted with helical constant mesh wheels and helical teeth for the third speed wheels. A large internal expanding brake is fitted directly behind the box. The propeller-shaft is unenclosed, and the bevel wheels have also helical teeth. The rear springing is of the three-point suspension type, each spring having a very large number of thin leaves. Rubber spring buffers are fitted on the axles. The arrangement of radius and torque rods is somewhat unusual, both being of 'I' section, the torque rod being carried on the off-side of the chassis and the radius rod on the near-side. The bodies shown are by D'Ieteren Frères, the limousine on the 45–50 h.p. being exceptionally well finished and embodying several interesting features; the rearmost seats, for instance, are adjustable as to tilt, and the extra emergency seats fold quite flat against the panel behind the driver's seat.

EXCELSIOR
Country of Origin: Belgium
H. M. Hobson Ltd., Grafton Street, W.1 (Stand 43).

Exhibit: One 14–20 h.p., four-cylinder, 85 × 130 mm., two-seater, complete car, with four speeds and bevel drive; one 14–20 h.p. four-cylinder car with a side entrance body; one 20–30 h.p., six-cylinder, 85 × 130 mm., chassis, three speeds and bevel drive; one 20–30 h.p., six-cylinder, 85 × 130 mm., car with landaulet body.

Features: The 20–30 h.p. chassis presents but few alterations since last year. The six-cylinder engine has its cylinders cast in blocks of three. The inlet and exhaust branches and the valves are on the near-side, and a carburettor is fitted to each three cylinders. The water circulation is by thermosyphon. Lubrication is effected by means of a gear pump, which raises oil from the sump and forces it to the main bearings and big ends. The correct level in the crank-case is maintained by a bird fountain system from a tank attached to the front of the dashboard, and therefore easily replenishable. The timing gear is chain-driven. An Eisemann electric lighting dynamo is fitted, the spindle of which in turn connects with and drives the magneto. The engine and gearbox are bolted together to form a single unit, which is carried by the flared underflanges of the longitudinals. The clutch is of the internal leather cone type, the clutchshaft connecting to the gearshaft by a flexible box coupling. The gearbox brake is actuated by the side lever, the internal expanding brakes being connected up through a compensating device to the right pedal. Both brakes are very easily adjusted. In the rear of the gearbox brake drum is a star universal joint, from which the propellershaft continues to a box coupling in front of the bevel pinion. The propellershaft is encased in a crutch-headed tapered torque tube, pivoted to brackets on a cross-member. The rear axle casing is of steel cast in halves. Three-quarter elliptical springs are fitted to the rear axle. The worm and segment steering gear is adjustable for rake. The accelerator pedal is adjustable for slow running by a knurled knob at the top of the steering column. The 14 h.p. car is very similar to the above model, with the exception that the engine is cast *en bloc*. Provision is made for a lighting dynamo if desired.

HISPANO-SUIZA
Country of Origin: France
Hispano-Suiza Cars (G.B. and I.) Ltd., Shaftesbury Avenue, W.C.2 (Stand 123).

Exhibit: One 30–90 h.p. chassis, four cylinders, 100×180 mm., four speeds, bevel drive; one 25–50 h.p. chassis, four cylinders, 90×150 mm., four speeds, bevel drive; one 15·9 h.p. three-seated sporting type body, four cylinders, 80×180 mm., four speeds, bevel drive; and one 15·9 h.p. with three-seated boat body.

Features: The overhead valve gear of the 30–90 h.p. and 25–50 h.p. models is very neatly carried out. A vertical skew driving shaft is used to transmit power to the camshaft. This camshaft operates the valves through rockers which may be detached without the use of any tools. The valves are inclined towards the centre of the cylinders, and the valve stems are of very large diameter so as to render breakage practically impossible. One of the most interesting features of the valve gear is the provision of dummy cams and spring tappets to obviate a snatch on the camshaft when not compressing a valve spring. Oil is forced direct through the camshaft into troughs in which the cams dip, the surplus oil being led through ducts to the main crankshaft bearings of which there are four. Another delivery pipe feeds troughs below the big ends, which are constructed deeper at the back than at the front so as to retain a high oil level when hill-climbing. The fan is skew gear driven from the vertical valveshaft, and is fitted with a plate clutch which may be thrown out of action instantly should the weather be cold. Water circulation is by centrifugal pump driven by skew gear across the front of the engine, the high tension magneto lying on the opposite side. On the gearbox is mounted a small air pump which is utilized for inflating tyres. The propeller-shaft is surrounded by a tube which does not act as a torque tube but merely as a stiffener to prevent whip to the driving shaft, the torque being taken by the forward end of the broad, flat semi-elliptic rear springs. A feature of these models is that the radiator filler cap is placed inside the bonnet. Other Hispano-Suiza models follow the above description in the main except for the fact that the 15·9 h.p. model has opposed valve chambers.

ITALA
Country of Origin: Italy
Itala Automobiles Ltd., St James's Street, S.W.1 (Stand 59).

Exhibit: One 14–20 h.p. coupé, four-cylinder engine, 77 × 120 mm.; one 18–30 h.p. convertible, two or four-seater, 80 mm. bore × 130 mm. stroke; one 35 h.p. landaulet, 105 mm. bore × 150 mm. stroke; one 50–70 h.p. chassis, 130 mm. bore × 160 mm. stroke. All have four speeds and bevel drive.

Features: The three larger models are fitted with rotary valves. Considerable improvements have been effected in the 14–20 h.p. model, which is now fitted with C.A.V. dynamo and C.A.V. engine starter as part of the standard equipment. The latter consists of a series-wound motor carried level with the gearbox, and a driving friction wheel which is brought by a pedal into contact with the fly-wheel. The dynamo is driven from the clutch-shaft. The engine has four cylinders cast *en bloc*, the valves being neatly enclosed. The carburettor is of the special Itala type, and is carried on the off-side of the cylinder casting, the inlet ducts being integral. The lubrication is of the forced feed type, the supply of oil being carried in the crank chamber sump and raised therefrom by a mechanically-driven pump. A belt-driven fan is fitted behind the radiator. The rotary valve models are practically unchanged from last year's type, with the exception that the valve ports are placed at 135 degrees apart. This practically prevents any possibility of leakage, and also improves the appearance of the engine. The valves are driven by skew gear from the half-time shaft, and are independently and efficiently lubricated. The clutch is of the disc type, and the final drive from the four-speed gearbox is through an unenclosed propeller-shaft universally jointed at each end.

LANCHESTER

Country of Origin: England

The Lanchester Motor Co. Ltd., Montgomery Street, Birmingham (Stand 67).

Exhibit: One 38 h.p. six-cylinder coupé-limousine; one 38 h.p. six-cylinder touring torpedo de luxe; one 38 h.p. six-cylinder landaulet, bore and stroke 101 × 101 mm., three forward speeds by epicyclic gearing, worm drive.

Features: Few changes of note have taken place in the distinctive Lanchester design. The engine has its cylinders cast in pairs, the water joints between the cylinders being effected by a neat arrangement of india-rubber rings. The valves are on opposite sides of the combustion chambers, lie horizontally, and are fitted with flat return springs. The gearing is of the epicyclic type, and is actuated by a form of gate change. The 38 h.p. cars are this year fitted complete with electric engine starters and electric lighting installations of the Delco type; the dynamotor for this purpose is carried in the centre of the chassis, where it is driven as a dynamo through an enclosed silent chain from the front end of the propeller-shaft. When used as a motor, a long flexibly-joined shaft connects the armature spindle with the small spur pinion, which is brought into mesh with a rack cut on the fly-wheel rim by pushing forward a lever. A neat point in connection with the change speed gear is the employment of an interlocking device, whereby it is made impossible for any gear to be put into action without taking the clutch out first. Needless to say, the chassis incorporates the well-known Lanchester system of suspension, in which the whole of the weight of the springs both fore and aft is suspended from the chassis instead of being carried on the axle, and in which the axle is given a parallel vertical motion. The final drive is by under-worm.

MORRIS-OXFORD

Country of Origin: England

W. R. M. Motors Ltd., Cowley, Oxford (Stand 9).

Exhibit: One 10 h.p. chassis, two 10 h.p. two-seater cars, four cylinders, 60 × 90 mm., three speeds, worm drive.

Features: The excellence of this light car impresses one immediately on inspection. The engine is coupled up to the gearbox by a casing enclosing the fly-wheel and clutch, and the whole of this unit is constructed by Messrs White and Poppe, who also manufacture the carburettor. The frame is of simply designed pressed steel construction on semi-elliptic springs in front and three-quarter elliptics at the back. The water passages of the thermo-syphon cooling system are exceptionally large, and the radiator is of the vertical tube convex pattern. The propeller-shaft is enclosed in a tube having a spherical joint at the forward end, the mechanism, in fact, being completely enclosed from the starting handle to the back wheel. Both brakes act on the rear wheel drums. The cars have taper bonnets with scuttle dashes and torpedo bodies and ample length is provided for two full-sized passengers. Detachable artillery wood wheels are used with 700×80 tyres. The wheelbase is 7 ft. 6 in. and the track 3 ft. 9 in. Such details as the combined spring bolts and lubricators are characteristic of the excellent detail design and workmanship conspicuous throughout these cars, which are exactly of the type to make light cars as a class a success.

PICCARD-PICTET
Country of Origin: Switzerland
Donne and Willans (1909) Ltd., Gillingham Street, South Belgravia, S.W.1 (Stand 103).

Exhibit: One 16–20 h.p. touring car, 85×130 mm., Argyll single sleeve valve engine, four speeds, bevel drive; one 16–20 h.p. V-fronted four-seater torpedo touring car; one 20–30 h.p. four-cylinder chassis, sporting type, 90×170 mm., four speeds, bevel drive; one 30–40 h.p. four-cylinder Argyll sleeve valve engined chassis, 100×150 mm., four speeds, bevel drive.

Features: Three out of four vehicles on this stand are fitted with engines operated by the single rotary Argyll sleeve valve with forced circulation for both oil and water. In both types of engines the magneto and the water pump are driven by a skew gearshaft lying transversely across the front of the engine, and the cooling is assisted by a fan behind the radiator. Apart from the difference in engine, the Piccard-Pictet practice is similar in its main essentials for both models. In both cases the fly-wheel runs in a cast aluminium well connecting engine with gearbox and practically making them one unit. On the 20–30 h.p. poppet valve car, the connection between clutch and gearbox is enclosed in an aluminium sleeve. In all cases a little air-cooled single-cylinder pump is embodied with the gearbox, and this can be worked at will for tyre pumping. Notice, too, should be taken of the frame, which is a beautiful example of pressing, the lower webs being extended inwards to connect the supporting flanges of the gearbox; thus the whole mechanism is enclosed from underneath, and no apron is necessary. No torque or radius rods are employed, the long underhung springs taking the torque and drive.

SPYKER
Country of Origin: Holland
Spyker Cars (I.M. Trompenburg), Long Acre, W.C.2 (Stand 33).

Exhibit: A 20 h.p. chassis, four cylinders *en bloc*, 90×135 mm., four speeds, bevel drive; a 12 h.p. special doctor's coupé with four-cylinder *monobloc* engine, 72×110 mm., three speeds, bevel drive; a 14 h.p., 80×120 mm., sporting torpedo, *monobloc* four-cylinder engine, four speeds, bevel drive; and a 20 h.p. landaulet; also sectional model of engine.

237

Features: The 20 h.p. chassis shows the unit construction of the engine and gearbox, and demonstrates how much thought and care has been brought into play to secure a clean and efficient drive to the centrifugal water circulating pump and the magneto shaft, which is transversely arranged in front of the crank-case. A C.A.V. dynamo is belt-driven from a pulley behind the clutch, the belt passing through a slot in the casing cover enclosing the fly-wheel. The exhaust pipe arrangement is particularly neat and has only one outlet casting of triangular shape fitted at the centre of the left-hand side of the engine, the pipe passing straight down through the crank-case web to the exhaust box. The whole of the mechanism is so well cased on both above and below that it is impossible for any dirt to get into any of the exposed working parts. Particular care has been paid to bracing the rear axle by long radial rods which extend from the forward part of the casing and the propeller-shaft to bosses just inside the rear spring brackets.

SWIFT
Country of Origin: England
The Swift Motor Co. Ltd., Coventry (Stand 42).

Exhibit: One 11·9 h.p. four-cylinder, 69 × 120 mm., chassis, four speeds and bevel final drive; one 11·9 h.p. four-cylinder two-seater complete car with a dickey seat; one 13·9 h.p. four-cylinder, 75 × 110 mm., complete four-seater touring car, four speeds and bevel drive; one 15·9 h.p., four-cylinder, 80 × 130 mm., chassis, four speeds, bevel drive, and lighting dynamo; one 15·9 h.p. complete car with a touring body.

Features: The two chassis shown on this stand share three features in common—that is, splendid workmanship, really clean design, and a thorough attention to detail. The 11·9 h.p. chassis has a *monobloc* engine, the carburettor being fitted on the off-side and the exhaust pipe high up on the near-side. The valves are readily get-at-able. The distribution gear is chain-driven, but the magneto is operated by skew gear and a cross-shaft. It is placed across the front of the engine, and stands well out. It has a very neat form of flanged joint with a leather disc centre. Lubrication is by means of a gear pump; this lifts the oil from the sump, and passes it round the main bearings and big ends, and thence onwards by splash. A large diameter filler is provided on the near-side of the engine, and placed close to it is a tap for indicating the level in the crank-case. A leather-faced external cone clutch of a substantial design is used, and this conveys the drive to the gearbox through a box coupling. The gearshafts are castellated, and the layshaft gears are pressed on, so that a renewal is very easily fitted if necessary. The oil filler for the gearbox protrudes from the side of the box at such a height that it is rendered impossible to introduce too much oil. A band-brake, which is easily adjustable, is placed at the rear of the gearbox. The drive is taken from this point to the rear axle through an enclosed propeller-shaft, having a universal joint forward, and a square nut sliding coupling at the back. A spring-anchored torque rod is used. Half elliptic springs are fitted, and the spring pads are free to rock on the axle casing. The rear axle shows the same forethought as regards lubrication as the other parts of the Swift car, and the case cannot be overfilled. A turn-buckle is provided for adjusting the rear internally expanding brakes.

The details of the 11·9 and 15·9 h.p. chassis are very similar, save that the latter has cylinders cast in pairs with no sacrifice of accessibility. Above the magneto in the front of the engine is mounted a Rotax dynamo for a lighting set, and both this and the magneto are extremely easy of access. The gate change lever on this car is of the hinged variety. Both these new cars are fitted with smart taper bonnets and scuttle dashboards, and the front edges of their radiators are bevelled. The 13·9 h.p. four-seater car exhibited on this stand is an instance of the type with which the Swift Co. have been very successful during the past year. It has a nicely proportioned streamline grey body.

VAUXHALL
Country of Origin: England
Vauxhall Motors Ltd., Great Portland Street, W.1 (Stand 91).

Exhibit: A 25 h.p. seven-seated Sutherland cabriolet by Mulliner, four-cylinder *monobloc* engine, bore and stroke 95 × 140 mm., four speeds, bevel drive; a 25 h.p. open touring car, Newmarket model; a 25 h.p. Prince Henry type open car and a 35 h.p. six-cylinder limousine by Regent Carriage Co., with cylinders cast in two blocks of three each, bore and stroke 95 × 120 mm., four speeds, bevel drive.

Features: A model which attracts considerable attention is the Prince Henry, which is tastefully finished in brown and presents a very racy appearance with its V-fronted radiator. This model is fitted with a Bosch easy starting magneto, Rushmore electric head, side, and tail lamps. Another very speedy looking vehicle is the Newmarket-bodied car, this having the standard form of honeycomb radiator. Particularly striking is the 35 h.p. limousine in which the driver's comfort is well studied, and the interior of the back seat is finely finished in grey figured cord, the panelling and beading of the windows being in polished mahogany. The lower outer panels are finished in olive green and the upper part in black highly glazed. Rather striking mudguards with V-shape corrugations down the centre are fitted, and a similar central corrugation appears along the centre line of the car from bonnet to back panel. No important changes appear in the Vauxhall chassis design for 1914, though there are certain detail improvements which were outlined in *The Autocar* last week.

WHITE

Country of Origin: U.S.A.

White-Coleman Motors Ltd., Camden Town, N.W.1 (Stand 51).

Exhibit: One 20–30 h.p. cabriolet, one 20–30 h.p. limousine landaulet, one 20–30 h.p. open touring model, and one 20–30 h.p. torpedo phaeton, all 95 × 130 mm., with four cylinders, four speeds, and bevel drive.

Features: The chief feature of White petrol cars is the electric starting and lighting set which is fitted as standard. The generator and motor are combined and driven by silent chain from the timing gear. The crankshaft, which is of large section and exceptional material, runs on large ball bearings. Lubrication is by pump to a sight feed on the dash, whence the oil falls by gravity to each end of the crankshaft and having entered the latter, passes through ducts by centrifugal force to the big end bearings and lubricates the cylinders and pistons by splash. The gearbox contains a direct third and an indirect fourth speed, and the propeller-shaft is unenclosed, being provided with two universals and a plunging joint. Both brakes follow the usual American practice and apply to drums on the rear wheels, one being of the contracting and the other expanding type. All the bodywork shown is by Cann Ltd., and is of an exceptionally high order of merit, being in all cases among the best examples of bodywork in the Show.

From *The Autocar*, November 15, 1913

PART SEVEN

SPEED AND PURSUIT

This book is not much concerned with motor racing, although competition—both authorized and unauthorized, amateur and professional, from the traffic lights as well as the starter's flag—has been with us since 1895. In the United States, and in many European countries outside Britain, racing took place on the open roads, and heroic and dreadfully dangerous it was, too. In England racing was prohibited, except on private land, and it was not until June 1907 that a track for competition, testing and record-breaking became available. The man responsible for its rapid construction was a rich Surrey landowner and motor enthusiast, H. F. Locke King. It was a remarkable achievement. On the morning after its opening The Times *reported: 'The face of the landscape has changed completely, since ground was first broken last October—and in the opinion of the majority of Weybridge residents, for the worse. The fact remains, however, that there is in existence a track for motor racing that from a theoretical point of view is as nearly perfect as human ingenuity can conceive. . . . Those who saw the site of the track last October and again yesterday could not but be struck with the enormous amount of work which has been accomplished.'*

This concrete oval saucer set amid the Surrey pines was 2 miles 1350 yards in circumference, with an additional finishing straight, and with two steep bankings over twenty feet high. For thirty-two years Brooklands remained the centre of British motor racing, and the exploits of drivers and cars are lovingly and comprehensively detailed in W. Boddy's The History of Brooklands Motor Course.

Brooklands aroused local resentment from the beginning, and it did not diminish with the passing years, when this area of Surrey became more built up. Regulations designed to reduce the noise level, and to prohibit driving at night, were introduced. One of those present on opening day was Mary, Lady Monkswell, whose comments (some of which appear in Mr Boddy's book) made in her diary evidently represented those of many of Mr and Mrs Locke King's neighbours.

The motoring press, however, reflected the passionate interest of the contemporary automobilist in this eighth wonder of the world, and pages of photographs and columns of enthusiastic editorial were devoted to it. Following Lady Monkswell's references of distaste there follows an extract from The Autocar's *description of the same opening day.*

The Horrid Motor Track

BY MARY, LADY MONKSWELL

Saturday, July 13th. We went down to the Barnes's at Fox Holm near Weybridge. Mr and Mrs Locke King came to dinner. They have been building this awful motor track and are so hated by their neighbours, many of whose houses they have simply ruined, that hardly anyone will speak to them. I was rather uncertain whether I had better go and see this horrid motor track, but as they offered to take me in the Fox Warren motor I thought it would be stupid of me not to go. I was well rewarded for going by having a nice talk with Mrs Wilfred Ward, the clever Roman Catholic (formerly Miss Hope Scott) who has written novels (*One Small Scruple*, *Out of Due Time*, and others). I made her acquaintance, first at Mrs Cave's, at Ditcham, long ago.

The motor track is a perfect nightmare. It has cost more than £150,000 to construct; a great oval of cement 60–100 yards wide and more than 2½ miles round. It is for motor races. Within it stands a ruined farm and cut down trees, mere desolation. A more unenjoyable place to come to on a hot Sunday afternoon I cannot imagine. The beautiful Surrey landscape looks down into this purgatory of motor stables and everything that motors require, seats for thousands of spectators cut in the side of the hill. There were some twenty of these snorting beasts, and Mr and Mrs Locke King were there looking most depressed. But as she offered to drive me round in her motor I got boldly in and sat by her on the 'box'. She put it to 43 miles an hour—I felt my eyes pressed in by the air at that terrific speed, and I could hardly breathe. I went round again in the Fox Warren motor, much slower. I find I don't care to 'go round'—what I like are the lanes and roads and views, and the getting to one's destination so quickly and easily. The enormous size of the arena, almost like a great Roman work, and the controlled strength of the motors, prevents this great horrid place from being vulgar. I might have felt differently last week when 20,000 spectators arrived, and 1,200 motors. No wonder the neighbours thirst for Locke King's blood.

From *A Victorian Diarist: later extracts from the journals of Mary, Lady Monkswell*, edited by the Hon. E. C. F. Collier, 1946.

First Day at Brooklands

IN THE enclosure and garage we found Mr E. de Rodakowski, the racing manager of the Brooklands Automobile Racing Club, presiding over a varied collection of cars from 80 h.p. racers down to modest 10 h.p. touring cars. These were marshalled in a long line, and their drivers enjoined not to pass each other, but the track proved to be too much temptation for them, and the line soon tailed out. As the cars stood in two rows before starting, from our point of vantage on the hill near the bridge, and looking down into the finishing straight, the whole thing appeared almost unreal. The cars themselves looked mere toys, and only the best-known makes and drivers could be recognized. At the head of the line was Mrs Locke King's old Siddeley car. Then we saw Mr Warwick J. Wright's 80 h.p. skeleton racer, Mr Hutton's 80 h.p. Berliet, Mr Weigel with his two eight-cylinder Grand Prix racers, and Mr Rawlinson with about the sportiest touring Darracq we have ever seen. It was one of the high-powered cars with a low four-seater body and a conning screen to match. Then there were a number of Daimlers, a Tourist Trophy Arrol-Johnston, and a Rolls-Royce (last year's winner), driven by the the Hon. C. S. Rolls, he having borrowed it specially for the occasion. Mr Coleman stole along on his White, with Mr Claude Johnson on a near relative of the 'Silver Ghost' hard on his wheels. We saw, too, Mr S. F. Edge on his six-cylinder Napier voiturette, Mr Siddeley on a car of his own name, Mr Okura on his huge Fiat, which rivalled Mr Jarrott's big de Dietrich for downright outspokenness of its exhaust. There they all stood, below the cliff, a double row of pygmies—some big and some small, some quiet, some noisy, some enveloped in the haze of oil, and one in a scarlet racing suit. Besides these notables were a large number of other cars down to quite small-powered machines. As we have said, from the bank sixty-odd feet above the course, these cars looked like toys. When they had moved off and the faster cars began to come away from the bunch, the procession appeared but a blur on the landscape. The racing Darracq could be seen far away high up on the banking, probably at the moment doing about sixty miles an hour. Mere pottering touring cars which were roaring along at forty to fifty miles an hour were lost on the vast track. They appeared to be scarcely moving at all—much the same as one watches a crack express train which is doing its seventy miles an hour, apparently creeping across the landscape. After the general procession, the cars were called in, and two or three one-design laps indulged in. For instance, three of four Daimlers went out together, when Mr Rendle's white car showed that it had the heels of the lot. Next came a trio of Rolls-Royces, which did not appear to race, but

Opening day at Brooklands

proceeded steadily at somewhere about forty miles an hour, and consequently gave one the impression that they were going about fifteen. After them came a batch of Ariels, and so on. Then the two eight-cylinder Weigels and the 80 h.p. flying Darracq were let loose. The Weigel cars went fast, but the Darracq simply flew. It made a lap at about ninety miles an hour, and went high on the banking, running at its greatest speed. The sight as it came under the bridge was well worth seeing.

A TRIAL OF THE TRACK

Mr E. M. C. Instone, who had his 35 h.p. Daimler in the enclosure, invited us to take a trial trip. We had driven down to Brooklands, but as our car was not in speed form on Monday, we had decided not go on the course. Mr Instone's invitation was therefore accepted with alacrity, and in less time than it takes to tell we were on the course. Upon it its vastness is even more realized than when taking a general view of it from the clubhouse or the high bridge. In a way it is more like being at sea than anything else. There is nothing but the interminable expanse of track in front; cars are overtaken as ship overtakes ship. The fact that they are proceeding at speeds from forty-five to sixty miles an hour is forgotten. Nothing but the rush of the wind and the bite of the concrete dust indicate speed at all. As the bends are negotiated one is unconscious of them. The great curve was taken without the faintest sensation of any sort of deviation from the straight line. The smaller one under the bridge could just be felt. There was that indescribable sensation of flying from the centre of the circle which the car was describing, but we were proceeding at something over fifty miles an hour, and Mr Instone was purposely holding the inside to see whether it required any effort to hold the car down. Having satisfied himself that it did not, he went higher up the banking, and at once the sensation of being on a curve was lost. An even better proof of the correct way in which the track had been laid out is in the way the banking begins and ends. As one strikes the curves or leaves them one does so almost unknowingly. There is no feeling of relief that the curve is done with, and the speed is not affected either way. As one rounds the curves the great bank shuts off the rest of the world just as one is shut off in the trough of the sea. However, the most interesting part of the whole trial on the Track was when the Darracq passed us.

A RACER ON THE CORNICE

We were on the larger curve and running at about fifty-five miles an hour well inside, when there was a crack as of musketry in the air above, and, looking up, we saw the racer, and heard it too. There it was twenty feet above us on the cornice making its eighty miles an hour. For the moment we had an absolute plan view of the car as it went by and above us. At high speed the cement dust from the track was particularly stinging, much more so than ordinary road dust. In fact, considering that the track looked absolutely dustless, there was more dust than might have been expected, though, of course, a mere nothing to what it would have been on a dry road. So far as could be judged, there are one or two places which are rather rough, though really nothing compared with the average road inequalities. When coming round the great bend there seems a slight inclination to turn into the finishing straight rather than to take the outer course. This, however, is an impression which might be entirely removed by a little practice. There seemed to be a very general opinion among the drivers of the fast cars that the pull-up was not sufficiently·long. That is to say, supposing the finish of a race was, as it usually would be, made in the long straight, the cars would have to slow down before passing the judge's box, otherwise at the very highest speeds of the racing cars it was feared they could not be pulled up, and that they would shoot right through the 'pull-up' across the track and over the ridge of its saucer sides. This, however, is not in the least likely, as the pull-up is somewhat sharply inclined. At the same time, it must be remembered that it would be necessary in many cases that the cars should pull up without going on to the track proper at all; otherwise they would come out at right-angles to any machines which might still be running in the race. No doubt the defect, if it exists, can be remedied comparatively easily by widening the pull-up in such a way that cars can rejoin the track proper at even higher speeds than is now possible. As to the banking of the track, there is no question that it is sufficient for the racing speeds of any cars at present made, and in this respect it is unquestionably a triumph for Colonel Holden and the accuracy of his calculations. In the struggle for speed supremacy someone will probably make a car which is too fast for the track, or, at any rate, too fast for it unless it can have the whole track to itself. So far as ordinary competitions are concerned between touring cars the course is absolutely safe. The only possible dangers are those of careless or bad driving, of which there were one or two examples on Monday, though luckily no harm resulted. Leaving out this element, the one danger is the failure of some vital part of a car at speed. This would probably spell disaster for the occupants of the car in any case, but if a spill were to occur close in front of another car or cars there would probably be a very bad smash indeed. With the exception of these two causes of danger the track is unquestionably as safe as it can be made, and we wish it the success it deserves. It is no small thing that private enterprise has conceived and executed a work which has been deemed worthy of copying by that most energetic of rulers, the Emperor of Germany. On the very day of the opening of Brooklands track it was announced that the Kaiser had determined that Germany should have a motor track which would be suitable for the highest speeds and free from the dangers of courses such as the Taunus, the race which His Majesty had followed from start to finish.

From *The Autocar*, June 22, 1907

The first Race Meeting took place three weeks later, on July 6, 1907. Attracted in part by the big prize money offered (2,100 guineas, or say £15,000 or $40,000 in modern money) for one event alone, top cars and top drivers appeared in numbers. The practices and customs of the turf were closely followed. Racing colours were worn by the drivers: J. E. Hutton, winner of the T.T. the following year, wore 'a blue coat and sleeves and primrose hat', with second colours of 'primrose coat, sleeves and blue cap'. 'There is some adverse comment,' wrote The Times, 'over the apparent efforts to follow too closely in the new kind of racing the rules, and even the phraseology, of the turf.' Contemporary reports suggest that the opening meeting was hardly the success it should have been. Only the Byfleet Plate, in which Jarrott on a Lorraine-Dietrich fought Newton on Edge's Napier hub-to-hub aroused 'some of the enthusiasm that it must be admitted had previously been lacking'.

The Times concluded: 'There were various opinions expressed as to the chances of a successful future for track racing of motors. It was impossible to judge of it from its first day, though the management claim that the attendance exceeded their expectation by at least 2,000.'

For the next meeting, on August Bank Holiday, prices for the enclosure were lowered from 2s 6d to 1s. Unhappily for the Locke Kings, horse racing still won. The meeting clashed with Sandown, and only 3,000 turned up.

247

However, as The Times *concluded, 'it will, they say, naturally take time to popularize it as a sport in the same manner as horse racing'. In a short time Brooklands became an accepted* venue, *and special trains had to be run from Waterloo to carry the crowds. Until the outbreak of war in 1939 these few miles of concrete provided splendid entertainment for hundreds of thousands, and invaluable technical information to automobile designers and manufacturers.*

Early American Auto Racing

BY W. F. BRADLEY

No one has a longer memory nor greater knowledge of motor racing in its formative years than W. F. Bradley. Here he describes the highly hazardous, hectic and rugged form of racing indulged in in America in the years before Brooklands was opened in Britain.

IN THE first decade of the twentieth century the United States presented vivid contrasts in the realm of motoring. On the Atlantic seaboard, and particularly in the New England states, highways were in a sufficient state of development to justify the use of an automobile. Cars were just toys for wealthy and idle New Yorkers, declared the Mid-Westerner, who looked with pride on the rapid growth of the railroad, right on the heels of the covered wagon, and who considered expenditure on highways to be a waste of money.

These remarks regarding the 'easterners' were not without justification. New York had a powerful club which took to itself the name of 'Automobile Club of America', although in reality it did not represent the United States: its members were all men of great wealth; its magnificent clubhouse was modelled on a château in the Loire valley; it had a modern garage and an expensive dynamometer; if it organized the Vanderbilt Cup races, it was for the love of the sport and because it had the means of indulging in this expensive pastime. The ownership of a foreign car—a Panhard and Levassor, a Brasier, a Darracq, a Delaunay-Belleville, a Hotchkiss, a Fiat or a Mercedes —seemed almost indispensable adjuncts to membership. Many of its members made annual trips to Europe and came back with the latest type of car, accompanied, if they were lucky and had the means, by a French chauffeur. It was in this way that Albert Champion, racing cyclist and then chauffeur, was introduced to the United States, where he founded the Champion Spark Plug Co., and later the A.C. concern.

There was some police opposition to the movement, but it was almost of a friendly, sometimes sporty, nature, as witness a scene in one of the New York police courts, where the entry of W. K. Vanderbilt was greeted by the presiding magistrate with the remark:

'Hallo, W. K., what's the trouble?'

'Speeding.'

'Twenty dollars.'

'O.K.; see you at the club tonight.'

It is true that the professionals sometimes got out of hand and, if the State border was reasonably near when the motorcycle 'Cop' blew his whistle, they accelerated and raced for the safety of the adjoining territory in which the man of law had no authority. If the driver was overtaken, it was still merely a case of speeding; if he succeeded in getting away he knew he would rise in the esteem of his companions and, whatever the result, the chase provided him with much pleasure. Sometimes the sport was of a more violent nature, as when Louis Strang made a bet that he would drive down Sixth Avenue on a Sunday morning with the throttle wide open (taped in this position to prevent it being closed) and make a turn into Twenty-third street. He succeeded, but his car came to rest half-way down the steps of the subway and had to be extracted by the fire brigade.

Jogging along the highway to Poughkeepsie, in the wake of a minor reliability trial, we half-dozen journalists were vaguely aware that there was a motorcyclist somewhere in the rear. These scribes represented such important dailies as the *New York Times, Herald, Telegraph, Brooklyn Eagle*, etc. They were in no hurry, for the 'story' was not yet ripe. Presently the policeman accelerated, shot ahead and ordered the car to a standstill.

He admitted our story that we had not been driving fast; he accepted our statement that we represented some of the world's greatest newspapers, but he retaliated with:

'I guess that's O.K., but I got orders to catch some of these speeding autoists; I got up too late and they all got away from me except you. You'll have to come with me to the Court.'

Over the telephone the judge listened to and accepted the report of the policeman that we had been speeding and indulgently agreed to allow us to continue, on condition that one of the party agreed to appear the following day to answer the charge. A fine was imposed.

In country districts the Sheriff sometimes installed himself in the village street armed with a shot-gun and, if the car did not come to a standstill at the given signal, its rear tyres were copiously riddled—and the fine collected on the spot.

After all there was no real animosity. The motoring enthusiast admitted that cars were often a nuisance—they raised dust, they killed dogs and chickens, they scared horses. But he felt that these were conditions which would gradually disappear as roads were improved or created, and with the change the necessity for police interference would disappear.

The great necessity was for roads and until they were provided motoring must be confined to a few favoured districts. There was a highway between New York and Chicago; there was even a speed record for the run, held by some dare-devil driver, and broken only during the summer months. No one thought of making the journey in winter.

If the use of a car was limited by the absence of roads, if in some districts cars were built specially to meet the local conditions, such as the level, sandy surfaces of Long Island, where the high-wheeled buggy had special advantages, still the sporting spirit was strong among early American motorists. International races might be limited to a small patch on Long Island, just beyond Brooklyn; to a portion of Savannah; to the beach of Daytona, but practically every town possessed a fair ground and a trotting track for horses. These tracks might not be ideal for cars, they frequently were only a mile, a mile-and-a-half, a mile-and-three-quarters, or two miles round, but they existed and they could be used for car races with very little modification.

Somebody thought of running twenty-four hour races on these trotting tracks years before the idea had come to Le Mans, or even before Le Mans possessed a motor club. New York had two such tracks, one at Morris Park, the other at Brighton Beach, adjoining the famous Coney Island. There was a delightful freedom about the rules: practically anything on wheels was admitted. The cars had to carry two men, they had to be equipped with headlights, and the tail light must always be kept burning.

At the beginning, starts were made just after dark, because of the spectacular effect; and, indeed, the glare of eighteen pairs of headlights, the flashes of red and blue from the open exhausts as the contestants lined up for the massed start, provided everything that the sensation-loving spectator could desire. Later, with a view to safety, starts were made at 4 p.m., a system adopted by Le Mans.

These beaten-earth tracks, designed for light trotters, soon went to pieces under the friction of cars covering forty to fifty miles in the hour. Then the repair gangs rushed in with rake and shovel, hose and brush, and endeavoured to repair the damage in the brief intervals between the passing of cars. Rain might come, transforming the dirt track into a quagmire. Goggles were useless and were thrown away. Skidding wildly to avoid cars seen at the last moment, showers of mud shot into the air, enveloping men and cars, but there was no slackening of the pace.

Tail lights must be kept lit all the time, and the Official, Fred Wagner—'Wag' to the boys—made this his special duty. At the risk of being run down by one of the mud-squelching monsters, handled by a man who had no respect for his own life or that of other people, Wag would venture out a dangerous distance waving his flag. But would a full-blooded American twenty-four hour racer stop for a dirty flag waved desperately by Wag? Instead, he swerved violently at the last moment to avoid him and gave orders to the mechanic to attend to matters. Spread-eagled on the bare chassis, with a whirling chain to left and right, the intrepid mechanic would generally succeed in reviving the essential tail light.

Fred Wagner was the only man who could control these wild, fearless, undisciplined race drivers. Generally he could do it with his biting tongue, but his fists were always kept in reserve. His speech was incisive and despite all his efforts he could rarely moderate it. A lady had trespassed into forbidden quarters and it fell to Wag to ask her to withdraw. He began well, with:

'Lady, I sure am sorry, but it is painful to have to tell you that if you don't get the Hell out of here you sure will break your God-damn neck.'

The infield was marked by a white rail four or five feet high. Beyond the rail were the replenishment stations with stacks of tyres, spare units, supplies of petrol and oil, tents and mechanical workers. Petrol was handled in big drums and dumped into the tanks with more dash than skill. As a result a petrol mixture hung in the air ready to explode under even a feeble spark, or merely from the lighted end of a cigarette.

There was a dull thud, followed immediately by shrieks and groans and looking round the sight presented itself of a score of bodies lying on the ground with gesticulating arms and legs and a car on three wheels running to a standstill.

'That's a fine batch for the hospital, Louis,' I remarked to the driver.

He answered almost angrily, 'Did I ask those birds to come and sit on the rail?' Then, ignoring the human wreckage to his rear, he yelled, 'Hi, beat it to New York, you Guys and get me a new axle.'

Relieved of immediate duties, Louis explained that he had tied the throttle in the fully open position to overcome a tendency it had to close, and when the front wheel detached itself from the axle a few seconds followed before he could release it; during those seconds the car dashed ahead out of control, carrying with it the rail and the rail birds.

Several fires had broken out during the night. There were obviously many people on the infield who had no legitimate business there, and to restore order the management decided to call on the Pinkerton men. Lining up shoulder to shoulder, right across the infield, the private Big Stick police moved forward with drawn truncheons in an irresistible line. If the person encountered was doing some obviously indispensable work, such as filling petrol drums or stacking tyres, he was not molested, otherwise he had to make the choice of running for the track and crossing it, or going down with a whack on the head. A reporter's notebook and pencil afforded no protection against the attack of these unofficial police.

'Beat it, Pinkerton men,' I cried to Paul Lacroix, Renault representative for the United States, who was present as holder of the track record and had challenged the others to better his performance.

Paul began to explain, but perhaps his knowledge of English failed him at this critical moment, for before half a dozen words had escaped him, he went down stunned by a blow on the head.

The race came to an end with less than 1,000 miles covered, leaving the record of 1,079 miles unbroken. Heavy rain had fallen during the last few hours, making it necessary to fit chains, even on the front wheels. An outside front tyre came partly off the rim of an American car, leaving the driver without control and causing him to collide with the outer rail, used for carrying water in the horse days, with fatal results.

With the end of the twenty-fourth hour, the promoter rushed forward to greet Ceirano, the winner. Standing in the persistent rain, the promoter pumped the arm of the mud-coated figure that had just dropped from the Fiat car, expressing his admiration and pouring forth his congratulations. Unaffected by this display of enthusiasm, the winning driver passed the cleanest portion of his free hand across his mouth and remarked: 'Say, Boss, guess I'll take the dough right now.'

The promoter looked offended, but without a word he drew a wad of greenbacks from his hip pockets and counted them out carefully in the pitiless rain. In more than one case, race promoters had been called away on urgent business during the last half-hour of a race. To put a stop to this inconvenience —for the winner at any rate—the American Automobile Association had made a rule that prize money should be deposited before the start of the event. But how could prize money be gathered together before the gate receipts had been collected? Thus the winner was too often the victim.

The only races which attracted attention outside the United States were those for the Vanderbilt Cup. W. K. Vanderbilt and his wealthy friends were thoroughly acquainted with all the developments in the Old World, they took part in races in France, Italy and Germany, they were seen at hill-climbs, they established records on French roads and, inevitably, they took European cars home with them.

Thus, when it was announced that there would be a road race in October 1904, for a cup presented by W. K. Vanderbilt Jr., no leading European maker could afford to be absent. Of the eighteen cars entered for this contest, only five were of American make: a Royal, a Packard, a Simplex and two Pope-Toledos. France sent six cars, Germany five and Italy two. Some of the world's best drivers were present, including Gabriel, George Heath, Werner, Albert Clement, Teste and Tart. The organization was copied on what the promoters had seen in Europe, but the copy was a poor imitation of the originals, for American law, based on that of England, forbade the closure of roads to the general public and the use of Federal troops was an impossibility. However, the powerful influence of the Vanderbilts, the Brokaws and other supporters made it possible to secure a circuit on the western end of Long Island and to assure the presence of a small number of local police. It was known, however, that had any stubborn farmer declared that he had the law on his side and that he would amble along the road with Old Dobbin on race day, nothing could have stopped him. Except, of course, that his cart would have immediately been overturned in the ditch. Upon this he would

Wagner in his Darracq winning the 1906 Vanderbilt Cup race at 61·43 m.p.h.

have brought a legal action, the result of which would have been compensation for the damage he had sustained, which compensation would have gladly been paid by the motoring enthusiasts. Dealing with private motorists presented greater difficulties. The night before the 6 a.m. start, they parked their cars as near the edge of the road as possible and after the race had started they had an exasperating habit of wandering over the highway. Add the fact that even the Vanderbilts had no power to stop the electric trains which crossed the course, and there were all the elements of danger and excitement the most intrepid driver could wish for.

From a technical standpoint, the race was a triumph for France, George Heath finishing first on his Panhard and Levassor at 52 m.p.h., nearly twelve minutes ahead of Albert Clement with a car built in his father's factory near Paris. Five others, two Mercedes and three Americans, were running when it became necessary to stop the race because the crowd had got out of control.

The second Vanderbilt race was won by Hemery, driving for Darracq, at 61·49 m.p.h., with George Heath second and Joe Tracy winning third place with an American Locomobile. The third race, in 1906, was a clean sweep for the Europeans, Louis Wagner finishing first on a Darracq, with Lancia second on Fiat, Duray third on Lorraine-Dietrich, Albert Clement fourth on Clement Bayard and Jenatzy fifth on Mercedes. Again it was necessary to stop the race because the crowd had got out of control while five cars were still running: a Thomas, driven by Le Blon, Heath's Panhard, Harding's Haynes, Nazzaro's Fiat, and Walter Christie's front-wheel drive model. The race was allowed to lapse in 1907. The following year, George Robertson captured the cup on a Locomobile and America again won in

1909, in the absence of foreign competition, with Grant on a six-cylinder Alco.

The lack of roads, and the legal restrictions against the use of those which did exist, were a real handicap to American motorists in the early years of the century, but there was one excellent outlet in the beach at Daytona, Florida. Here, long-distance races, sprints and short-distance records were carried out annually for a number of years, and always attracted European manufacturers interested in maintaining their position on the American market. If the foreigners could usually more than hold their own in the longer races, they were not supreme in sprints. The Stanley Steamer, for instance, could always beat the gasoline engines on a standing start half-mile run. Henry Ford's '999', a freak car built for short runs, was a match for the Darracqs, the Mercedes and the Fiats under special conditions. In the years from 1904 to 1908, Ford had not conceived his car for the people, and spent not a little time and money in stunt racing.

Walter Christie sent his front-wheel drive racer to Daytona, where he either drove it himself, entrusted it to his nephew, Louis Strang, or to the most fearless of all drivers, Barney Oldfield. Christie's front-wheel drive was never taken seriously in Europe: but fifty-three years after it was built, all its essential features—transverse engine and drive to the front wheels—were incorporated in an English mass-production car, and that car bore the imprint BMC.

From *Motor Racing Memories 1903-21*, 1960

Pursuit on the Dover Road

BY IAN FLEMING

I have deliberately omitted accounts of specific motor races from this volume: many racing anthologies are available for those, like myself, who enjoy them. But I did want to include several fictional pursuits. In spite of diligent search, however, I found it difficult to discover any that combine excitement, brevity, good prose, accuracy and a real sense of feeling for the motor car at speed. Only Bond qualified. And even the many who will have read of his race down the Dover Road after Drax and Gala will enjoy again this classic piece of pursuit.

THE MERCEDES was a beautiful thing. Bond pulled his battered grey Bentley up alongside it and inspected it.

It was a Type 300 S, the sports model with a disappearing hood—one of only half a dozen in England, he reflected. Left-hand drive. Probably bought in Germany. He had seen a few of them over there. One had hissed by him on the Munich Autobahn the year before when he was doing a solid ninety in the Bentley. The body, too short and heavy to be graceful, was painted white, with red leather upholstery. Garish for England, but Bond guessed that Drax had chosen white in honour of the famous Mercedes-Benz racing colours that had already swept the board again since the war at Le Mans and the Nurburgring.

Typical of Drax to buy a Mercedes. There was something ruthless and majestic about the cars, he decided, remembering the years from 1934 to 1939 when they had completely dominated the Grand Prix scene, children of the famous Blitzen Benz that had captured the world's speed record at 142 m.p.h. back in 1911. Bond recalled some of their famous drivers, Caracciola, Lang, Seaman, Brauchitsch, and the days when he had seen them drifting the fast sweeping bends of Tripoli at 190, or screaming along the tree-lined straight at Berne with the Auto Unions on their tails.

And yet, Bond looked across at his supercharged Bentley, nearly twenty-five years older than Drax's car and still capable of beating 100, and yet when Bentleys were racing, before Rolls had tamed them into sedate town carriages, they had whipped the blown SS-Ks almost as they wished.

Bond had once dabbled on the fringe of the racing world and he was lost in his memories, hearing again the harsh scream of Caracciola's great white beast of a car as it howled past the grandstands at Le Mans, when Drax came out of the house followed by Gala Brand and Krebs.

'Fast car,' said Drax, pleased with Bond's look of admiration. He gestured towards the Bentley. 'They used to be good in the old days,' he added with a touch of patronage. 'Now they're only built for going to the theatre. Too well-mannered. Even the Continental.'

Without noticing what he was eating Bond wolfed down some food and left the restaurant at 8.45. His car was outside waiting for him and he said good-night to the driver from Headquarters and drove to St James's Street. He parked under cover of the central row of taxis opposite Boodle's and settled himself behind an evening paper over which he could keep his eyes on a section of Drax's Mercedes which he was relieved to see standing in Park Street, unattended.

He had not long to wait. Suddenly a broad shaft of yellow light shone out from the doorway of Blades and the big figure of Drax appeared. He wore a heavy ulster up round his ears and a cap pulled down over his eyes. He walked quickly to the white Mercedes, slammed the door, and was away across to the left-hand side of St James's Street and braking to turn opposite St James's Palace while Bond was still in third.

God, the man moves quickly, thought Bond, doing a racing change round the island in the Mall with Drax already passing the statue in front of the Palace. He kept the Bentley in third and thundered in pursuit. Buckingham Palace Gate. So it looked like Ebury Street. Keeping the white car just in view, Bond made hurried plans. The lights at the corner of Lower Grosvenor Place were green for Drax and red for Bond. Bond jumped them and was just in time to see Drax swing left into the beginning of Ebury Street. Gambling on Drax making a stop at his house, Bond accelerated to the corner and pulled up just short of it. As he jumped out of the Bentley, leaving the engine ticking over, and took the few steps towards Ebury Street, he heard two short blasts on the Mercedes' horn and as he carefully edged round the corner he was in time to see Krebs helping the muffled figure of a girl across the pavement. Then the door of the Mercedes slammed and Drax was off again.

Bond ran back to his car, whipped into third, and went after him.

Thank God the Mercedes was white. There it went, its stop-lights blazing briefly at the intersections, the headlamps full on and the horn blaring at any hint of a check in the sparse traffic.

Bond set his teeth and rode his car as if she was a Lipizaner at the Spanish Riding School in Vienna. He could not use headlights or horn for fear of betraying his presence to the car in front. He just had to play on his brakes and gears and hope for the best.

The deep note of his two-inch exhaust thundered back at him from the houses on either side and his tyres screamed on the tarmac. He thanked heavens for the new set of racing Michelins that were only a week old. If

R

only the lights would be kind. He seemed to be getting nothing but amber and red while Drax was always being swept on by the green. Chelsea Bridge. So it did look like the Dover road by the South Circular! Could he hope to keep up with the Mercedes on A.20? Drax had two passengers. His car might not be tuned. But with that independent springing he could corner better than Bond. The old Bentley was a bit high off the ground for this sort of work. Bond stamped on his brakes and risked a howl on his triple klaxons as a homeward-bound taxi started to weave over to the right. It jerked back to the left and Bond heard a four-letter yell as he shot past.

Clapham Common and the flicker of the white car through the trees. Bond ran the Bentley up to eighty along the safe bit of road and saw the lights go red just in time to stop Drax at the end of it. He put the Bentley into neutral and coasted up silently. Fifty yards away. Forty, thirty, twenty. The lights changed and Drax was over the crossing and away again, but not before Bond had seen that Krebs was beside the driver and that there was no sign of Gala except the hump of a rug over the narrow back seat.

So there was no question. You don't take a sick girl for a drive like a sack of potatoes. Nor at that speed for the matter of that. So she was a prisoner. Why? What had she done? What had she discovered? What the hell, in fact, was all this about?

Each dark conjecture came and for a moment settled like a vulture on Bond's shoulder and croaked into his ear that he had been a blind fool. Blind, blind, blind. From the moment he had sat in his office after the night at Blades and made his mind up about Drax being a dangerous man he should have been on his toes. At the first smell of trouble, the marks on the chart for instance, he should have taken action. But what action? He had passed on each clue, each fear. What could he have done except kill Drax? And get hanged for his pains? Well, then. What about the present? Should he stop and telephone the Yard? And let the car get away? For all he knew Gala was being taken for a ride and Drax planned to get rid of her on the way to Dover. And that Bond might conceivably prevent if only his car could take it.

As if to echo his thoughts the tortured rubber screamed as he left the South Circular road into A.20 and took the roundabout at forty. No. He had told M. that he would stay with it. He had told Vallance the same. The case had been dumped firmly into his lap and he must do what he could. At least if he kept up with the Mercedes he might shoot up its tyres and apologize afterwards. To let it get away would be criminal.

So be it, said Bond to himself.

He had to slow for some lights and he used the pause to pull a pair of goggles out of the dashboard compartment and cover his eyes with them. Then he leant over to the left and twisted the big screw on the windscreen and then eased the one beside his right hand. He pressed the narrow screen flat down on the bonnet and tightened the screws again.

Then he accelerated away from Swanley Junction and was soon doing ninety astride the cat's eyes down the Farningham by-pass, the wind howling past his ears and the shrill scream of his supercharger riding with him for company.

A mile ahead the great eyes of the Mercedes hooded themselves as they went over the crest of Wrotham Hill and disappeared down into the moonlit panorama of the Weald of Kent.

Bond's face was a mask of dust and filthy with the blood of flies and moths that had smashed against it. Often he had had to take a cramped hand off the wheel to clear his goggles but the Bentley was going beautifully and he felt sure of holding the Mercedes.

He was touching ninety-five on the straight just before the entrance to Leeds Castle when great lights were suddenly switched on behind him and a four-tone windhorn sounded its impudent 'pom-pim-pom-pam' almost in his ear.

The apparition of a third car in the race was almost unbelievable. Bond had hardly troubled to look in his driving-mirror since he left London. No one but a racing-driver or a desperate man could have kept up with them, and his mind was in a turmoil as he automatically pulled over to the left and saw out of the corner of his eye a low, fire-engine-red car come up level with him and draw away with a good ten miles an hour extra on its clock.

He caught a glimpse of the famous Alfa radiator and along the edge of the bonnet in bold white script the words *Attaboy II*. Then there was the grinning face of a youth in shirt-sleeves who stuck two rude fingers in the air before he pulled away in the welter of sound which an Alfa at speed compounds from the whine of its supercharger, the Gatling crackle of its exhaust, and the thunderous howl of its transmission.

Bond grinned in admiration as he raised a hand to the driver. Alfa-Romeo supercharged straight-eight, he thought to himself. Must be nearly as old as mine. 'Thirty-two or 'thirty-three probably. And only half my c.c. Targa Florio in 1931 and did well everywhere after that. Probably a hot-rod type from one of the R.A.F. stations round here. Trying to get back from a party in time to sign in before he's put on the report. He watched affectionately as the Alfa wagged its tail in the S-bend abreast of Leeds Castle and then howled off on the long wide road towards the distant Charing fork.

Bond could imagine the grin of delight as the boy came up with Drax. 'Oh, boy. It's a Merc!' And the rage of Drax at the impudent music of the windhorn. Must be doing 105, reflected Bond. Hope the damn fool doesn't run out of road. He watched the two sets of tail lights closing up, the boy in the Alfa preparing for his trick of coming up behind and suddenly switching everything on when he could see a chance to get by.

There. Four hundred yards away the Mercedes showed white in the sudden twin shafts from the Alfa. There was a mile of clear road ahead, straight as a die. Bond could almost feel the boy's feet stamping the pedal still further into the floorboards. Attaboy!

Up front in the Mercedes Krebs had his mouth close to Drax's ear. 'Another of them,' he shouted urgently. 'Can't see his face. Coming up to pass now.'

Drax let out a harsh obscenity. His bared teeth showed white in the pale glimmer from the dashboard. 'Teach the swine a lesson,' he said, setting his shoulders and gripping the wheel tightly in the great leather gauntlets. Out of the corner of his eye he watched the nose of the Alfa creep up to starboard. 'Pom-pim-pom-pam' chirped the windhorn; softly, delicately, Drax inched the wheel of the Mercedes to the right and, at the horrible crash of metal, whipped it back again to correct the slew of his tail.

'Bravo! Bravo!' screamed Krebs, beside himself with excitement as he knelt on the seat and looked back. 'Double somersault. Jumped the hedge upside down. I think he's burning already. Yes. There are flames.'

'That'll give our fine Mister Bond something to think about,' snarled Drax, breathing heavily.

But Bond, his face a tight mask, had hardly checked his speed and there was nothing but revenge in his mind as he hurtled on after the flying Mercedes.

He had seen it all. The grotesque flight of the red car as it turned over and over, the flying figure of the driver, his arms and legs spreadeagled as he soared out of the driving seat, and the final thunder as the car hurdled the hedge upside down and crashed into the field.

As he flashed by, noting the horrible *graffiti* of the black skid-marks across the tarmac, his mind recorded one final macabre touch. Somehow undamaged in the holocaust, the windhorn was still making contact and its ululations were going on up to the sky, stridently clearing imaginary roads for the passage of *Attaboy II*—'Pom-pim-pom-pam.' 'Pom-pim-pom-pam . . .'

So a murder had taken place in front of his eyes. Or at any rate an attempted murder. So, whatever his motives, Sir Hugo Drax had declared war and didn't mind Bond knowing it. This made a lot of things easier. It meant that Drax was a criminal and probably a maniac. Above all it meant certain danger for the Moonraker. That was enough for Bond. He reached under the dashboard and from its concealed holster drew out the long-barrelled ·45 Colt Army Special and laid it on the seat beside him. The battle was now in the open and somehow the Mercedes must be stopped.

Using the road as if it was Donington, Bond rammed his foot down and kept it there. Gradually, with the needle twitching either side of the hundred mark he began to narrow the gap.

Drax took the left-hand fork at Charing and hissed up the long hill. Ahead, in the giant beam of his headlights, one of Bowaters' huge eight-wheeled

AEC Diesel carriers was just grinding into the first bend of the hairpin, labouring under the fourteen tons of newsprint it was taking on a night run to one of the East Kent newspapers.

Drax cursed under his breath as he saw the long carrier with the twenty gigantic rolls, each containing five miles of newsprint, roped to its platform. Right in the middle of the tricky S-bend at the top of the hill.

He looked in the driving-mirror and saw the Bentley coming into the fork. And then Drax had his idea.

'Krebs,' the word was a pistol shot. 'Get out your knife.'

There was a sharp click and the stiletto was in Kreb's hand. One didn't dawdle when there was that note in the master's voice.

'I am going to slow down behind this lorry. Take your shoes and socks off and climb out on to the bonnet and when I come up behind the lorry jump on to it. I shall be going at walking-pace. It will be safe. Cut the ropes that hold the rolls of paper. The left ones first. Then the right. I shall have pulled up level with the lorry and when you have cut the second lot jump into the car. Be careful you are not swept off with the paper. *Verstanden? Also. Hals und Beinbruch!*'

Drax dowsed his headlights and swept round the bend at eighty. The lorry was twenty yards ahead and Drax had to brake hard to avoid crashing into its tail. The Mercedes executed a dry skid until its radiator was almost underneath the platform of the carrier.

Drax changed down to second. 'Now!' He held the car steady as a rock as Krebs, with bare feet, went over the windscreen and scrambled along the shining bonnet, his knife in his hand.

With a leap he was up and hacking at the left-hand ropes. Drax pulled away to the right and crawled up level with the rear wheels of the Diesel, the oily smoke from its exhaust in his eyes and nostrils.

Bond's lights were just showing round the bend.

There was a series of huge thuds as the left-hand rolls poured off the back of the lorry into the road and went hurtling off into the darkness. And more thuds as the right-hand ropes parted. One roll burst as it landed and Drax heard a tearing rattle as the unwinding paper crashed back down the one-in-ten gradient.

Released of its load the lorry almost bounded forward and Drax had to accelerate a little to catch the flying figure of Krebs, who landed half across Gala's back and half in the front seat. Drax stamped his foot into the floor and sped off up the hill, ignoring a shout from the lorry-driver above the clatter of the Diesel pistons as he shot ahead.

As he hurtled round the next bend he saw the shaft of two headlights curve up into the sky over the tops of the trees until they were almost vertical. They wavered there for an instant and then the beams whirled away across the sky and went out.

Bond's car—4½-litre supercharged Bentley.
At the wheel, 'blower' designer Amherst Villiers
Courtesy Montagu Motor Museum

A great barking laugh broke out of Drax as for a split second he took his eyes off the road and raised his face triumphantly towards the stars.

Krebs echoed the maniac laugh with a high giggle. 'A master-stroke, *mein Kapitan*. You should have seen them charge off down the hill. The one that burst. *Wunderschön!* Like the lavatory paper of a giant. That one will have made a pretty parcel of him. He was just coming round the bend. And the second salvo was as good as the first. Did you see the driver's face? *Zum Ktozen!* And the *Firma* Bowater! A fine paperchase they have got on their hands.'

'You did well,' said Drax briefly, his mind elsewhere.

Suddenly he pulled into the side of the road with a scream of protest from the tyres.

'*Donnerwetter,*' he said angrily, as he started to turn the car. 'But we can't leave the man there. We must get him.' The car was already hissing back down the road. 'Gun,' ordered Drax briefly.

They passed the lorry at the top of the hill. It was stopped and there was no sign of the driver. Probably telephoning to the company, thought

262

Drax, slowing up as they went round the first bend. There were lights on in the two or three houses and a group of people were standing round one of the rolls of newsprint that lay amongst the ruins of their front gate. There were more rolls in the hedge on the right of the road. On the left a telegraph pole leant drunkenly, snapped in the middle. Then at the next bend was the beginning of a great confusion of paper stretching away down the long hill, festooning the hedges and the road like the sweepings of some elephantine fancy-dress ball.

The Bentley had nearly broken through the railings that fenced off the right of the bend from a steep bank. Amidst a puzzle of twisted iron stanchions it hung, nose down, with one wheel, still attached to the broken back axle, poised crookedly over its rump like a surrealist umbrella.

Drax pulled up and he and Krebs got out and stood quietly, listening.

There was no sound except the distant rumination of a car travelling fast on the Ashford road and the chirrup of a sleepless cricket.

With their guns out they walked cautiously over to the remains of the Bentley, their feet crunching the broken glass on the road. Deep furrows had been cut across the grass verge and there was a strong smell of petrol and burnt rubber in the air. The hot metal of the car ticked and crackled softly and steam was still fountaining from the shattered radiator.

Bond was lying face downwards at the bottom of the bank twenty feet away from the car.

From *Moonraker*, 1955

The Journey

BY ALDOUS HUXLEY

It is well known that every motorist is two people, and certainly the bolder is the one behind the wheel; also, very often, the more unscrupulous and beastly. Not that Lord Hovenden was a bad hat, in fact he was a rather nice spineless ass—until he climbed into the driving seat of his 30/98 Vauxhall. Total euphoria then consumed him. There was nothing in the world of which he was not capable —great orator, great lover. This little tale is about the pursuit of love, of Irene, round Lake Trasimene in Italy, until, under the same intoxicating influence of a Velox's speed that had emboldened her lover, she yielded. . . .

LORD HOVENDEN detached from his motor car was an entirely different being from the Lord Hovenden who lounged with such a deceptive air of languor behind the steering-wheel of a Vauxhall Velox. Half an hour spent in the roaring wind of his own speed transformed him from a shy and diffident boy into a cool-headed hero, daring not merely in the affairs of the road, but in the affairs of life as well. The fierce wind blew away his diffidence; the speed intoxicated him out of his self-consciousness. All his victories had been won while he was in the car. It was in the car—eighteen months ago, before he came of age—that he had ventured to ask his guardian to increase his allowance; and he had driven faster and faster until, in sheer terror, his guardian had agreed to do whatever he wished. It was on board the Velox that he had ventured to tell Mrs Terebinth, who was seventeen years older than he, had four children and adored her husband, that she was the most beautiful woman he had ever seen; he had bawled it at her while they were doing seventy-five on the Great North Road. At sixty, at sixty-five, at seventy, his courage had still been inadequate to the achievement; but at seventy-five it reached the sticking-point: he had told her. And when she laughed and told him that he was an impudent young shrimp, he felt not a whit abashed, but laughed back, pressed the accelerator down a little further, and when the needle of the speedometer touched eighty, shouted through the wind and the noise of the engine: 'But I love you.' Unfortunately, however, the drive came to an end, sooner or later. The *affaire* Terebinth went no further. If only, Lord Hovenden regretfully sighed, if only one could spend all one's life in the Velox! But the Velox had its disadvantages. There were occasions when the heroic, speed-intoxicated self had got the timorous pedestrian into awkward scrapes. There was that time, for example, when, rolling along at sixty, he had airily promised one of his advanced political friends to make a speech at a meeting. The prospect, while one was doing sixty, had seemed not merely unalarming, but positively attractive. But what agonies he suffered when he was standing on solid earth again, at his journey's end! How impossibly formidable the undertaking seemed! How bitterly he had cursed himself for his folly in having accepted the invitation! In the end he was reduced to telegraphing that his doctor had ordered him peremptorily to the south of France. He fled, ignominiously.

Today the Velox had its usual effect on him. At Vezza, when they started, he was all shyness and submission. He assented meekly to all the arrangements that Mrs Aldwinkle made and remade every five minutes, however contradictory and impossible. He did not venture to suggest that Irene should come in his car; it was through no good management of his own, but by the mere luck of Mrs Aldwinkle's final caprice before the actual moment of starting, that he did in fact find her sitting next to him when at last they moved off from before the palace doors. At the back sat Mr Falx, in solitude, surrounded by suit-cases. To him Lord Hovenden had even dutifully promised that he would never go more than five-and-twenty miles an hour. Pedestrian slavishness could hardly go further.

Heavily loaded, Mrs Aldwinkle's limousine started first. Miss Elver, who had begged to be granted this special favour, sat in front, next to the chauffeur. An expression of perfect and absolute bliss irradiated her face. Whenever the car passed anyone by the roadside, she made a shrill hooting noise and waved her handkerchief. Luckily she was unaware of the feelings of disgust and indignation which her conduct aroused in the chauffeur; he was English and enormously genteel, he had the reputation of his country and his impeccable car to keep up. And this person waved handkerchiefs and shouted as though she were on a char-a-banc. Miss Elver even waved at the cows and horses, she shouted even to the cats and the chickens.

In the body of the car sat Mrs Aldwinkle, Mrs Chelifer, Chelifer and Mr Cardam. Calamy and Miss Thriplow had decided that they had no time to go to Rome and had been left—without a word of objection on Mrs Aldwinkle's part—at the palace. The landscape slid placidly past the windows. Mr Cardam and Mrs Chelifer talked about traditional games.

Meanwhile, a couple of hundred yards behind, Lord Hovenden disgustfully sniffed the dusty air. 'How intolerably slowly old Ernest drives!' he said to his companion.

'Aunt Lilian doesn't allow him to do more than thirty miles an hour,' Irene explained.

Hovenden snorted derisively. 'Firty! But must we eat veir filthy dust all ve way?'

'Perhaps you might drop back a bit,' Irene suggested.

Lord Hovenden's car, 30/98 Vauxhall Velox
Courtesy Vauxhall Motors

'Or perhaps we might pass vem?'

'Well . . .' said Irene doubtfully. 'I don't think we ought to make poor Aunt Lilian eat our dust.'

'She wouldn't eat it for long, if old Ernest is only allowed to do firty.'

'Well, in that case,' said Irene, feeling that her duty towards Aunt Lilian had been done, 'in that case. . . .'

Lord Hovenden accelerated. The road was broad, flat and straight. There was no traffic. In two minutes Mrs Aldwinkle had eaten her brief, unavoidable meal of dust; the air was clear again. Far off along the white road, a rapidly diminishing cloud was all that could be seen of Lord Hovenden's Velox.

'Well, fank God,' Lord Hovenden was saying in a cheerful voice, 'now we can get along at a reasonable rate.' He grinned, a young ecstatic giant.

Irene also found the speed exhilarating. Under her grey silk mask, with its goggling windows for the eyes, her short lip was lifted in a joyful smile from the white small teeth. 'It's lovely,' she said.

'I'm glad you like it,' said Hovenden. 'Vat's splendid.'

But a tap on his shoulder reminded him that there was somebody else in the car besides Irene and himself. Mr Falx was far from finding the present state of affairs splendid. Blown by the wind, his white beard shook and fluttered like a living thing in a state of mortal agitation. Behind the goggles, his dark eyes had an anxious look in them. 'Aren't you going rather fast?' he shouted, leaning forward, so as to make himself heard.

'Not a bit,' Hovenden shouted back. 'Just ve usual speed. Perfectly safe.' His ordinary pedestrian self would never have dreamed of doing anything contrary to the wishes of the venerated master. But the young giant who sat at the wheel of the Velox cared for nobody. He went his own way.

They passed through the sordid outskirts of Viareggio, through the pinewoods beyond, solemn with dark green shadow, and aromatic. Islanded in their grassy meadow within the battlemented walls, the white church, the white arcaded tower miraculously poised on the verge of falling, the round white baptistery seemed to meditate in solitude of ancient glories—Pisan dominion, Pisan arts and thoughts—of the mysteries of religion, of inscrutable fate and unfathomed godhead, of the insignificance and the grandeur of man.

'Why ve deuce it shouldn't fall,' said Hovenden, as the Leaning Tower came in sight, 'I can't imagine.'

They drove past the house on the water, where Byron had bored himself through an eternity of months, out of the town. After Pontedera the road became more desolate. Through a wilderness of bare, unfertile hills, between whose yellowing grasses showed a white and ghastly soil, they mounted towards Volterra. The landscape took on something of an infernal aspect; a prospect of parched hills and waterless gulleys, like the undulations of a petrified ocean, expanded interminably round them. And on the crest of the highest wave, the capital of this strange hell, stood Volterra—three towers against the sky, a dome, a line of impregnable walls, and outside the walls, still outside but advancing ineluctably year by year towards them, the ravening gulf that eats its way into the flank of the hill, devouring the works of civilization after civilization, the tombs of the Etruscans, Roman villas, abbeys and mediaeval fortresses, Renaissance churches and the houses of yesterday.

'Must be a bit slow, life in a town like vis,' said Hovenden, racing round the hairpin turns with an easy virtuosity that appalled Mr Falx.

'Think if one had been born there,' said Irene.

'Well, if we'd both been born vere,' replied Lord Hovenden, flushed with insolence and speed, 'it wouldn't have been so bad.'

They left Volterra behind them. The hellish landscape was gradually tempered with mundane greenness and amenity. They descended the headlong street of Colle. The landscape became once more completely earthly. The soil of the hills was red, like that from which God made Adam. In the steep fields grew rows of little pollard trees, from whose twisted black arms hung the festooned vines. Here and there between the trees shuffled a pair of white oxen, dragging a plough.

'Excellent roads, for a change,' said Lord Hovenden. On one straight stretch he managed to touch eighty-eight. Mr Falx's beard writhed and fluttered with the agonized motions of some captive animal. He was enormously thankful when they drew up in front of the hotel at Siena.

'Wonderful machine, don't you fink?' Lord Hovenden asked him, when they had come to a standstill.

'You go much too fast,' said Mr Falx severely.

Lord Hovenden's face fell. 'I'm awfully sorry,' he apologized. The young giant in him was already giving place to the meek pedestrian. He looked at his watch. 'The others won't be here for another three-quarters of an hour, I should fink,' he added, in the hope that Mr Falx would be mollified by the information.

Mr Falx was not mollified, and when the time came, after lunch, for setting out on the Perugia road, he expressed a decided preference for a seat in Mrs Aldwinkle's limousine. It was decided that he should change places with Miss Elver.

Miss Elver had no objection to speed; indeed, it excited her. The faster they went, the more piercing became her cries of greeting and farewell, the more wildly she waved her handkerchief at the passing dogs and children. The only trouble about going so fast was that the mighty wind was always tearing the handkerchiefs from between her fingers and whirling them irretrievably into receding space. When all the four handkerchiefs in her reticule had been blown away, Miss Elver burst into tears. Lord Hovenden had to stop and lend her his coloured silk bandanna. Miss Elver was enchanted by its gaudy beauty; to secure it against the assaults of the thievish wind, she made Irene tie one corner of it round her wrist.

'Now it'll be all right,' she said triumphantly; lifting her goggles, she wiped away the last traces of her recent grief.

Lord Hovenden set off again. On the sky-line, lifted high above the rolling table-land over which they were travelling, the solitary blue shape of Monte Amiata beckoned from far away. With every mile to southward the horns of the white oxen that dragged the carts became longer and longer. A sneeze—one ran the risk of a puncture; a sideways toss of the head—one might have been impaled on the hard and polished points. They passed through San Quirico; from that secret and melancholy garden within the walls of the ruined citadel came a whiff of sun-warmed box. In Pienza they found the Platonic idea of a city, the town with a capital T; walls with a gate in them, a short street, a piazza with a cathedral and palaces round the other three sides, another short street, another gate and then the fields, rich with corn, wine and oil; and the tall blue peak of Monte Amiata looking down across the fertile land. At Montepulciano there are more palaces and more churches; but the intellectual beauty of symmetry was replaced by a picturesque and precipitous confusion.

'Gosh!' said Lord Hovenden expressively, as they slid with locked wheels down a high street that had been planned for pack-asses and mules. From pedimented windows between the pilasters of the palaces, curious faces peered out at them. They tobogganed down, through the high Renaissance, out of an arch of the Middle Ages, into the dateless and eternal fields. From Montepulciano they descended on to Lake Trasimene.

'Wasn't there a battle here, or something?' asked Irene, when she saw the name on the map.

Lord Hovenden seemed to remember that there had indeed been some-thing of the kind in this neighbourhood. 'But it doesn't make much difference, does it?'

Irene nodded; it certainly didn't seem to make much difference.

'Nofing makes any difference,' said Lord Hovenden, making himself heard with difficulty in the teeth of a wind which his speedometer registered as blowing at forty-five miles an hour. 'Except'—the wind made him bold—'except you.' And he added hastily, in case Irene might try to be severe. 'Such a bore going down-hill on a twiddly road like vis. One can't risk ve slightest speed.'

But when they turned into the flat highway along the western shore of the lake, his face brightened. 'Vis is more like it,' he said. The wind in their faces increased from a capful to half a gale, from half a gale to a full gale, from a full gale very nearly to a hurricane. Lord Hovenden's spirits rose with the mounting speed. His lips curved themselves into a smile of fixed and per-manent rapture. Behind the glass of his goggles his eyes were very bright. 'Pretty good going,' he said.

'Pretty good,' echoed Irene. Under her mask, she too was smiling. Between her ears and the flaps of her leather cap the wind made a glorious roaring. She was happy.

The road swung round to the left following the southern shore of the lake. 'We shall soon be at Perugia,' said Hovenden regretfully. 'What a bore!'

And Irene, though she said nothing, inwardly agreed with him.

They rushed on, the gale blew steadily in their faces. The road forked; Lord Hovenden turned the nose of his machine along the leftward branch. They lost sight of the blue water.

'Good-bye, Trasimene,' said Irene regretfully. It was a lovely lake; she wished she could remember what had happened there.

The road began to climb and twist; the wind abated to a mere half-gale. From the top of the hill, Irene was surprised to see the blue waters, which she had just taken leave of for ever, sparkling two or three hundred feet below on the left. At the joyous sight Miss Elver clapped her hands and shouted.

'Hullo,' Irene said, surprised. 'That's odd, isn't it?'

'Taken ve wrong road,' Hovenden explained. 'We're going norf again up ve east side of ve lake. We'll go right round. It's too much bore to stop and turn.'

They rushed on. For a long time neither of them spoke. Behind them Miss Elver hooted her greetings to every living creature on the road.

They were filled with happiness and joy; they would have liked to go on like this for ever. They rushed on. On the north shore of the lake the road straightened itself out and became flat again. The wind freshened. Far off on their respective hills Cortona and Montepulciano moved slowly, as they rushed along, like fixed stars. And now they were on the west shore once more. Perched on its jutting peninsula Castiglione del Lago reflected itself complacently in the water. 'Pretty good,' shouted Lord Hovenden in the teeth of the hurricane. 'By the way,' he added, 'wasn't it Hannibal or somebody who had a battle here? Wiv elephants, or somefing.'

'Perhaps it was,' said Irene.

'Not vat it matters in ve least.'

'Not in the least.' She laughed under her mask.

Hovenden laughed too. He was happy, he was joyful, he was daring.

'Would you marry me if I asked you?' he said. The question followed naturally and by a kind of logic from what they had been saying about Hannibal and his elephants. He did not look at her as he asked the question; when one is doing sixty-seven one must keep one's eyes on the road.

'Don't talk nonsense,' said Irene.

'I'm not talking nonsense,' Lord Hovenden protested. 'I'm asking a straightforward question. Would you marry me?'

'No.'

'Why not?'

'I don't know,' said Irene.

They had passed Castiglione. The fixed stars of Montepulciano and Cortona had set behind them.

'Don't you like me?' shouted Lord Hovenden. The wind had swelled into a hurricane.

'You know I do.'

'Ven why not?'

'Because, because... Oh, I don't know. I wish you'd stop talking about it.'

The machine rushed on. Once more they were running along the southern shore. A hundred yards before the forking of the roads, Lord Hovenden broke the silence. 'Will you marry me?' he asked.

'No,' said Irene.

Lord Hovenden turned the nose of his machine to the left. The road climbed and twisted, the wind of their speed abated.

'Stop,' said Irene. 'You've taken the wrong turn again.'

But Hovenden did not stop. Instead, he pressed down the accelerator. If the car got round the corners it was more by a miracle than in obedience to the laws of Newton or of nature.

'Stop!' cried Irene again. But the car went on.

From the hill-top they looked down once more upon the lake.

'Will you marry me?' Lord Hovenden asked again. His eyes were fixed on the road in front of him. Rapturously, triumphantly he smiled. He had never felt happier, never more daring, more overflowing with strength and power. 'Will you marry me?'

'No,' said Irene. She felt annoyed; how stupidly he was behaving!

They were silent for several minutes. At Castiglione del Lago he asked again. Irene repeated her answer.

'You're not going to do this clown's trick again, are you?' she asked, as they approached the bifurcation of the roads.

'It depends if you're going to marry me,' he answered. This time he laughed aloud; so infectiously that Irene, whose irritation was something laid on superficially over her happiness, could not help laughing too. '*Are* you going to?' he asked.

'No.'

Lord Hovenden turned to the left. 'It'll be late before we get to Perugia,' he said.

'Oo-ooh!' cried Miss Elver, as they topped the long hill. 'How lovely!' She clapped her hands. Then, leaning forward, she touched Irene's shoulder. 'What a lot of lakes there are here!' she said.

On the north shore Lord Hovenden asked again. Cortona and Montepulciano presided at the asking.

'I don't see why I should be bullied,' said Irene. Lord Hovenden found the answer more promising than those which had gone before.

'But you're not being bullied.'

'I am,' she insisted. 'You're trying to force me to answer all at once, without thinking.'

'Now really,' said Hovenden, 'I call vat a bit fick. Forcing you to answer all at once! But vat's exactly what I'm not doing. I'm giving you time. We'll go round ve lake all night, if you like.'

A quarter of a mile from the forking of the road, he put the question yet once more.

'You're a beast,' said Irene.

'Vat's not an answer.'

'I don't want to answer.'

'You needn't answer definitely if you don't want to,' he conceded. 'I only want you to say vat you'll fink of it. Just say perhaps.'

'I don't want to,' Irene insisted. They were very close, now, to the dividing of ways.

'Just perhaps. Just say you'll fink of it.'

'Well, I'll think,' said Irene. 'But mind, it doesn't commit . . .'

She did not finish her sentence; for the car, which had been heading towards the left, swerved suddenly to the right with such violence that Irene had to clutch at the arm of her seat to prevent herself from being thrown sideways bodily out of the machine. 'Goodness!'

'It's all right,' said Lord Hovenden. They were running smoothly now along the right-hand road. Ten minutes later, from the crest of a little pass, they saw Perugia on its mountain, glittering in the sunlight. They found, when they reached the hotel, that the rest of the party had long since arrived.

'We took ve wrong turning,' Lord Hovenden explained. 'By ve way,' he added, turning to Mr Cardan, 'about vat lake we passed—wasn't it Hannibal or someone. . . .'

'Such a lot of lakes,' Miss Elver was telling Mrs Chelifer. 'Such a lot!'

'Only one, surely, my dear,' Mrs Chelifer mildly insisted.

But Miss Elver wouldn't hear of it. 'Lots and lots.'

Mrs Chelifer sighed compassionately.

Before dinner Irene and Lord Hovenden went for a stroll in the town. The huge stone palaces lowered down at them, as they passed. The sun was so low that only their highest windows, their roofs and cornices took the light. The world's grey shadow was creeping up their flanks; but their crests were tipped with coral and ruddy gold.

'I like vis place,' said Lord Hovenden. In the circumstances he would have liked Wigan or Pittsburg.

'So do I,' said Irene. Through the window in her thick hair her face looked smiling out, merry in its childishness.

Leaving the stately part of the town, they plunged into the labyrinth of steep alleys, of winding passage-ways and staircases behind the cathedral. Built confusedly on the hill-side, the tall houses seemed to grow into one another, as though they were the component parts of one immense and fantastical building, in which the alleys served as corridors. The road would burrow through the houses, in a long dark tunnel, to widen out into a little well-like courtyard, open to the sky. Through open doors, at the head of an outside staircase, one saw in the bright electric light a family sitting round the soup tureen. The road turned into a flight of stairs, dipped into another tunnel, made cheerful by the lights of a subterranean wine shop opening into it. From the mouth of the bright cavern came up the smell of liquor, the sound of loud voices and reverberated laughter.

And then, suddenly emerging from under the high houses, they found themselves standing on the edge of an escarped slope, looking out on to a huge expanse of pale evening sky, scalloped at its fringes by the blue shapes of mountains, with the round moon, already bright, hanging serene and solemn in the midst. Leaning over the parapet, they looked down at the roofs of another quarter of the city, a hundred feet below. The colours of the world still struggled against the encroaching darkness; but a lavish municipality had already beaded the streets with yellow lights. A faint smell of wood-smoke and frying came up through the thin pure air. The silence of the sky was so capacious, so high and wide, that the noises of the town—like so many small, distinctly seen objects in the midst of an immense blank prairie—served but to intensify the quiet, to make the listener more conscious of its immensity in comparison with the trivial clatter at its heart.

'I like vis place,' Lord Hovenden repeated.

They stood for a long time, leaning their elbows on the parapet, saying nothing.

'I say,' said Hovenden suddenly, turning towards his companion a face on which all the shyness, the pedestrian's self-depreciation had reappeared, 'I'm most awfully sorry about vat silly business of going round vat beastly lake.' The young giant who sat at the wheel of the Vauxhall Velox had retired with the machine into the garage, leaving a much less formidable Hovenden to prosecute the campaign which he had so masterfully begun. The moon, the enchanting beauty of the face that looked out so pensively through its tress-framed window, the enormous silence with the little irrelevant noises at its heart, the smell of wood-smoke and fried veal cutlets—all these influences had conspired to mollify Lord Hovenden's joyous elation into a soft and sugary melancholy. His actions of this afternoon seemed to him now, in his changed mood, reprehensibly violent. He was afraid that his brutality might have ruined his cause. Could she ever forgive him for such behaviour? He was overwhelmed by self-reproach. To beg forgiveness seemed to be his only hope. 'I'm awfully sorry.'

'Are you?' Irene turned and smiled at him. Her small white teeth showed beneath the lifted lip; in the wide-set, childish eyes there was a shining happiness. 'I'm not. I didn't mind a bit.'

Lord Hovenden took her hand. 'You didn't mind? Not at all?'

She shook her head. 'You remember that day under the olive trees?'

'I was a beast,' he whispered remorsefully.

'I was a goose,' said Irene. 'But I feel different now.'

'You don't mean . . .'

She nodded. They walked back to their hotel hand in hand. Hovenden never stopped talking and laughing all the way. Irene was silent. The kiss had made her happy too, but in a different way.

From *Those Barren Leaves*, 1925

PART EIGHT

MAKING YOUR CHOICE

Your Choice in 1930

Engineering progress in the motor car moved slowly in the two decades between the world wars. The emphasis lay more in mass-production, marketing, 'packaging' and refinement than in radical mechanical development. Only a handful of small-production Continental manufacturers, and even fewer British and American manufacturers, offered their designers free rein. In 1939 the vast majority of mass-produced motor cars were technically less advanced than, say, Birkigt's 37·2 Hispano-Suiza of 1919 or Dr Fiedler's 1200 c.c. B.M.W. of thirteen years later. The export of cars was not taken very seriously by any of the major producers, and their characteristics met mainly national needs. The big American corporations led the way in styling, gimmickry and in measures designed to safeguard and add to the comfort of driver and passengers, and to reduce the labour of driving. By 1930 there still remained for the American buyer a wide range of makes and models; confusing in their similarity both in appearance and their balance of merit and demerit. As the following brief chapter makes clear in its résumé of exhibits at the New York Show, the customer had a perplexing task.

WHEN YOU come to the task of selecting your new car this year, you will find that you have taken upon yourself a more difficult job than heretofore —unless, of course, you are partial to a particular make. Practically all the better known cars have refinements that will appeal to your desire for speed, for safety, for appearance, etc.; but, in general, many of these features balance each other in different makes so that, to a large extent, you will have to guide you only the limitations of your purse and the knowledge you already have as to car performance and reliability.

And yet with all the refinements that have been made, mechanical improvements this year are not numerous. Some outstanding ones, however, indicate the intention of the manufacturers to build for you an ever finer, safer, more powerful, or more attractive car.

Mr C. F. Kettering* has outlined this development problem and describes the constant research that it is necessary for the manufacturer to conduct, but he does not stress the fact that whatever improvements are made come very gradually and almost unknown to the average motorist. We shall therefore outline briefly what appear to us to be the most noteworthy

* Technical research engineer at General Motors, who contributed an article included in the same issue of this magazine.

L29 Cord (*courtesy Warren Fitzgerald*)

refinements and improvements that have been made recently and others that are to be announced shortly.

In general, it may be said that improvements are limited to such details as spring shackles, carburettors, rumble seat doors, and the more general adoption of four-wheel brakes, of safety glass, and of other safety features. Several manufacturers, however, have greatly increased engine power. A few cars have been equipped with newly developed devices which add much to engine capacity, to riding comfort, or to ease of driving.

The desire for colour, fostered by the judicial use of it for several years and by almost a sunburst effect in the cars of 1929, is proving to be no fad but a method of expressing the car owner's individuality. In 1930 there will be a marked increase in colour used on many cars. In fact, colour has become such an important factor in the production of automobiles that manufacturers have employed colour directors—artistic experts who know how to harmonize colour combinations with individual designs.

Before going into further detail, we wish to refer you to the article on the Cord front-drive automobile.* This is the most radically new design in American passenger automobiles for 1930. Besides this car, several makers of sixes have recently announced production of new eights and it is rumoured that others will come into the market soon. Also, it has been stated authori-

* See Part 3, Chapter 2.

tatively that a new sixteen-cylinder passenger car will be announced in March or April by a manufacturer of cars in the higher price range.

New Packard eights announced in the fall, characteristically Packard in appearance but with subtle changes that add much to their already famous beauty, have several outstanding improvements. Both the driver's seat and the steering wheel are adjustable. Unusual vision is given in the front compartment by a front body pillar that has been narrowed, yet retains the same body strength. All windshields and windows are of non-shatterable glass. The left front spring trunnion, developed by this company a year ago to eliminate 'shimmy' and wheel 'whip', has been retained. The chassis lubricating system has been extended to include 43 points on the chassis which are oiled every day by turning a pump handle mounted within easy reach at the base of the steering column.

Packard has also developed a new carburettor which is said to have many advantages in smoothness of operation, acceleration, safety, quietness, economy, and easy starting. Steel-backed bearings and several other features found by the company to be of advantage in building airplane models are incorporated in the new engines. As in previous Packards, the pistons are automatically lubricated when the choke rod of the motor is pulled out, an arrangement which pumps oil on to the cylinder walls at the time it is most needed.

With three complete lines, each comprising eleven different types, and an almost unlimited choice of individual custom bodies by the best body builders, Packard may now be said to cover completely the fine car field.

One of the eights recently announced by a maker of sixes is the Nash twin-ignition straight-eight which the Nash Motor Company claims is the first of its kind in the world. Included in the announcement were details of a twin-ignition six and a single six. The new eight is powered by an eight-in-line twin-ignition, valve-in-head, nine-bearing motor with an integrally counterbalanced, hollow-in crankshaft; with aluminium alloy Invarstrut piston and aluminium alloy connecting rods capped at the crankshaft with case-hardened steel. It develops 100 h.p.

New features of the Nash eight include: steel-jacketed lifetime-lubricated springs, individually tailored to the weight of each car; cable-actuated internal-expanding four-wheel brakes which are self-energizing forward and backward; thermostatically controlled radiator shutters; Bijur centralized lubricating system to oil, by pressure on a foot pedal, twenty-one chassis points, including shackles; dash-bottom starting controls, etc.

Various mechanical and body refinements have been incorporated in the Nash eight. These include aircraft-type spark plugs, positive fuel-pump gasoline feed, solid chain-operated camshaft, improved clutch, and road-shock insulator. Most of these features will be found also in the two sixes

First deliveries of the fabulous Model J Duesenberg had been made about eight months before the 1930 New York Show. This is a later model, with Murphy convertible bodywork
Courtesy Warren Fitzgerald

while both the eight and the sixes have non-shatterable glass in windows and windshield.

Hupmobile is another producer of a new eight in the medium price class. This car is manufactured in five body styles, one of which, the cabriolet, has a patented top construction. The new eight develops 100 h.p., is said to attain an 80 mile an hour speed, and accelerates rapidly.

In these new Hupmobile eights, the radiator is higher and narrower, has built-in shutters, a new emblem, and a narrow chromium-plated shell. Among other improvements, this car has also adopted the road-shock eliminator attached to the rear end of the left front spring, and force-feed lubrication to all main, connecting rod, and piston pin bearings—forty-six points in all.

A third new eight is the Gardner with an eight-in-line motor and optional four-speed transmission. This new car comes in two series, in each of which there are eight models. Information concerning mechanical details of this new eight are not available but it is said to have several improvements.

Several features of the 'Great Line Ninety', an eight by Jordan, with a 75 horsepower, eight-in-line motor, reflect this company's claim of 'scientific engineering'. This eight has a crankshaft that is both statically and dynamically balanced and is therefore free from periodic vibration; it has pressure lubrication of main and connecting rod bearings, a double breaker ignition distributor, and other distinctly Jordan developments. Other features are: soft type chassis springs of special alloy steel, Houdaille shock absorbers, has a new style of ventilating rear side window. Exclusively a Kissel feature, this window swings on hinges like a residence casement window. The rear oval window of this model lowers the same as the door window glasses.

Duesenberg, Inc., displayed at the Chicago salon in November nine models built on the regular 265 horsepower Duesenberg chassis. Many new and luxurious features have been incorporated in these new bodies, three of which are by Murphy, two by Willoughby, and one each by LeBaron, Weyman, Derham, and Judkins.

Marmon has re-entered the fine car field with the production of the Marmon Big Eight. Powered with a straight-eight engine of 125 horsepower, this car is equipped with four-speed transmission and especially designed mechanical features such as: a double-dome cylinder head; invariable mechanical four-wheel brakes with cable linkage completely enclosed in lubricant-packed, sealed metal conduits; and mono-control windshield.

Addition of this car, built in nine body styles for the higher price class, enables the Marmon Company to blanket the price field since it already produces the Roosevelt in the low price range and the Marmon 66 and 78 in the medium price range. Further information concerning new models will be given out early in 1930.

The 1930 Buick will be offered in fourteen models in three series known s the 40, 50, and 60 Series. Longer wheel-bases; lower, longer, and more eautiful bodies; and many mechanical improvements and refinements aracterize these new Buicks. Additional power is given by the increase of nch in the cylinder bore of engines of all models. Other advances achieved : semi-elliptical rear springs; double-acting shock absorbers; sloping, -glare windshield; re-designed transmission and clutch; larger rubber r mountings; thermostatically controlled radiator shutters; and a wider e. The carburation system has been improved by a newly designed ne pump and the elimination of the low-speed carburettor adjustment.

radical changes have been made in the duPont. The eight models of w eight which were recently announced are distinctive in design, g as they do the French body style influence. They have a higher and cowl, with heavily crowned fenders brought to a point in front. new Chryslers, the 77, 70, and 66, were recently added to this well-ine. Noteworthy features in the 77 and the 70 are: multi-range, d gear shift; a down-draught carburettor; larger and more powerful Paraflex spring suspension; and chimney-type, rubber, shock

down-draught fuelization' system, the carburettor is mounted ngine instead of at the side, thus allowing a gravity flow of the ixture.

ew feature found in these two series is the de-carbonizer, a ying a new fluid called Carbosalve for dissolving the engine seat cushion springs which are said to be synchronized with the chassis springs, and new patented shackles, mounted in rubber to eliminate rattles and squeaks.

The Stutz Motor Car Company continues to stress the built-in safe features of Stutz and Blackhawk cars. The contribution to safety of the l slung bodies of these two cars—made possible by the worm gear driv the safety glass used in both; of side bumper running boards; of four-transmission; and of the vacuum booster on the hydraulic brakes Stutz, has been added to within the year by the Noback, an exclusi engineering achievement which is now on both the Stutz and the Bl

The Noback, which the writer considers one of the most impo tributions to car safety to be developed in recent years, is a br automatic actuating mechanism. Installed between the rear mission main shaft and the parking brake drum, this device preve backward rolling of a Stutz or Blackhawk when a stop is made so that it is entirely unnecessary to use the brakes for hold push one of these cars backward it is necessary to throw th into reverse and then throw it back into neutral. The car m or allowed to roll backward; but when a forward moti Noback again holds the car as before until the operatic company has also adopted, as optional equipment, t charger to be used on anything but racing cars and a

Stutz has just announced a new streamlined alu the Torpedo, in which are incorporated many of t Blackhawk. Four-speed transmission, Noback, t hydraulic brakes, and low centre of gravity, p safety for the occupants.

Balance and low centre of gravity have becom along with increase in engine power and spee Studebaker that the new President eight an are built with double drop frames, reveals a safety and balance for the Studebaker lin centre of gravity made possible by this d recently adopted non-shatterable glass f the most recent improvements in this

The Kissell Motor Car Company 95 and series 126 a four-speed trans result of two years of experiment a smoothness of operation and imp of engine and propeller-shaft spe The only other mechanical im Lovejoy shock absorbers. Th enlarged and body lines have

T

1930 Cadillac
Courtesy Montagu Motor Museum

carbon deposits. This device includes a fluid container mounted on the dash under the hood, a connection to the inlet manifold, and a plunger located on the dash. With the engine running, a quantity of the fluid is sent into the cylinders by means of the plunger. After the engine rests several hours and is then started up, the dissolved carbon particles are blown out of the exhaust. Chrysler has also adopted a rust-proofing process which is claimed to ensure a permanent finish and longer life for fenders and other exposed parts. An interesting Chrysler innovation is the rumble seat door which has been added to the Imperial roadster.

Pierce-Arrow, in 1930, will build three groups of cars, all of them straight-eights, although no changes will be made in general appearance or body design. In these cars will be incorporated several improvements over current production which, as a matter of fact, is new, since Pierce-Arrow's first straight-eight car was introduced early in 1929. Among the refinements are some which affect the manifolding; and the latest improvement—a very important one—is the adoption of stainless steel for more than 350 parts including small pieces, nuts and bolts which would ordinarily be subject to rust or corrosion.

Striking body designs will feature the exhibit of the Oldsmobile six at the New York Automobile Show. The body types on display will include the four-door sedan, two-door sedan, business coupé, sport coupé, convertible roadster, and phaeton, in standard, special, and de luxe models.

The Viking eight, companion car of the Oldsmobile six, will be seen in three distinctive models at this show. Designed by Oldsmobile engineers

283

with the resources of the General Motors research laboratories and proving ground at their command, the Viking has improved engine design.

A review of the automobile field gives the impression that manufacturers anticipate no great let-up in car buying in 1930 despite the recent disastrous stock market crash. It has been asserted that whatever effect it may have had will shortly be offset by a normal car sale and that the output in 1930 will be greater than ever.

Most of the 1930 cars, at least in the medium and higher price range, it will be noted, are finer, more luxurious, or so greatly improved as to indicate the belief of the manufacturers in the continuation of our general prosperity. In the low price field, the prices of the twenty models of Fords have been lowered by amounts varying from 15–20 dollars. To explain this, Edsel Ford is quoted as saying, 'It is our belief that, basically, the industry and business of the country is sound. We are reducing prices now because we feel that such a step is the best contribution that can be made to assure a continuation of good business throughout the country.'

On Running a Royce

BY LAURENCE POMEROY

Nothing could be more suitable than to close this volume with an account by the doyen of today's motoring writers of how he purchased an eleven-year-old Rolls-Royce, and his experiences with it during its first year under his ownership. It is a safe bet that every reader who has come this far through this book has at some time aspired to or actually possessed a Rolls-Royce motor car of some vintage or another. Laurence Pomeroy, much to the delight of his friends, eschewed some new, lush, 100 m.p.h. motor-car, and for the same amount of money bought a Silver Wraith with manual gearbox and almost six figures on the mileage recorder. The doubts that he so resolutely put behind him on signature of the delivery note never manifested themselves and he was able to show, as only Pomeroy can, that a year's driving of a Royce had provided not only satisfying nourishment of the soul, and an unsurpassed sense of comfort and well-being at the wheel, but also, if not an actual profit, at least a comparatively trivial loss. It is a little tale full of morals and lessons for all of us.

Let us rejoice, therefore, that L.P. did not lower himself to mere politics or potted meat; and instead lived to dignify certain paddocks and the streets of Marylebone, London, with a splendid Royce.

> A mature and deliberate conviction, not un-mingled with thankfulness, that Providence has placed us in a position which exempts us from the temptation to envy others, is neither selfish nor vain. . .
>
> *The Times*, June 23, 1867

WHEN SURVEYING thirty-five years of adult life the missed opportunities are all too clear. If in 1927, following a rather good report on the six-wheeler motor coach situation in Germany, I had taken the offered job with one of our leading heavy vehicle manufacturers I could by now be a director, and possibly the managing director, of one of Britain's leading industrial concerns; if I had followed the advice to stand as a National Liberal candidate in 1931 I might have possibly been in the Cabinet today; if I had pursued and married the heiress whom I met at the Conservative College at Ashridge in 1936 I should now be prominent in potted meat; most significant of all, if I

had not been excluded by a car accident from joining the Navy in 1920 I might today be one of their Lordships.

Mercifully there are credits as well as debits, and I count this day of writing, June 22, 1962, as the first anniversary of an indubitably wise decision. This was to spend £1,350 in the purchase of a 4¼-litre Silver Wraith Rolls-Royce, Chassis No. WFC 83, with an undivided H. J. Mulliner four-seater saloon body which was delivered to its first owner by Jack Barclay in 1950 and had since put 91,546 miles on the clock.

The vendor was Harry Martin, who assured me that the engine was not yet run in after a complete overhaul, and that the front suspension unit had been reconditioned. Despite this and the generally excellent external condition of the car I was aware that for this sum I could buy a new 3-litre car with disc brakes and an automatic gearbox, capable of 100 m.p.h., with ample enclosed luggage space and an all-round fuel consumption of 17–19 m.p.g. Bearing in mind that at least half my hourly motoring is in London, I was somewhat apprehensive about the driving of so large a car in London traffic and parking it in London streets. It could not fail to cross my mind that the running costs, after such a considerable mileage, could be expensive in terms of petrol, oil, maintenance and repairs.

Putting these prudent doubts resolutely behind me I had little hesitation in closing the deal after a two-mile road test round Regent's Park. Now, after twelve months, I can make a report which may be interesting to the general reader and of value to persons who contemplate following in my footsteps.

The main merit of the car has been its unfailing reliability. With 106,299 miles now on the clock the mileage in the past year has been 14,753, and the only mechanical failure a leaking exhaust manifold gasket, which, annoyingly enough, spoiled a 100 per cent record a week ago. The mechanical chassis lubrication system eliminates monthly maintenance and the only required service attentions, for items which have become less than 100 per cent, but which have left the car completely driveable, have been the replacement of a rather tired electric wiper mechanism; relining the brake servo; eliminating stickiness in the horn button; replacing the electric clock; and fitting a distributor arm of the right make in place of the foreigner mysteriously in its place when the car was bought.

There have been three regular service attentions and four new Dunlop tyres, which still have another year's use in them. The coachbuilt body has also needed attention from time to time, more especially in clearing the drain pipes from the sliding roof and in striking the right balance between doors tending to stick and others producing a slight rattle. During a day's work Mr Fred Connolly had his men bring the hide upholstery up to a condition barely discernible from what it had been twelve years previously.

In round figures the cost of maintenance and mechanical work has been £75; on the body £30; the electrics £15; and the tyres, say, £30. Total maintenance had thus amounted to £150.

This would have been less if a new car had been bought, but in their first 5,000 or 10,000 miles new cars can be subject to endless teething troubles, and it would have been exceptional to have had the use of such a vehicle for more than forty-nine weeks out of fifty-two. Even if all the work were done free under guarantee, there would still be a bill of £50 for hire of a substitute, a half worn-out set of tyres (around £20), so that in sum one has a figure for a new car of about £100, together with the misery of many minor ailments which it seems almost impossible to avoid.

A motor car is an assembly of 20,000 pieces, and if put together with an accuracy of 99·9 per cent will be delivered to the customer with twenty things wrong! In my youth it was commonplace for every chassis to be driven on the road with a soapbox body for a week or two before being fitted with its body, then for a further week in order to seek and rectify minor defects before the buyer had the car. Such procedure would be prohibitively expensive today and the owner of a modern car who complains of unreliability should bear in mind that he has paid a basic price of £1,000 for a car superior to one which in pre-war periods would have cost him £4,000 in terms of modern money.

In the Royce any journey, however long or short, is rewarding. Starting from rest, a slight whine on the first gear (belying the fact that the designed life is one and a half hours at full torque) soon changes to a barely audible hum on the two indirect ratios which are engaged with the utmost smoothness by small movements of the short right-hand gear lever. Clumsiness with the clutch or gear lever brings immediate protest, but reasonable skill gives superlative response. The driving position is as near perfect as can be and, although this is not a car intended to be hurled through corners at sports-car speed, the steering in itself is, from the hand-wheel to the road-wheel, made to such a pitch of efficiency that it constantly signals to the driver the equation of cornering force and road surface, and reflects without perceptible loss in time or effort every response of the driver.

Thus, whether one is threading one's way through traffic leaving bare inches on each side, or sweeping round a main road curve, the Royce sets an example which is rivalled by no more than half a dozen models of today, of which four are made in Italy.

From the viewpoint of the driver the elevated seating position is of value in evaluating the traffic as well as giving a good view of the surrounding country. On the open road, and since Sir Henry Royce adapted the Hispano-Suiza braking system for his cars in 1924, the stopping power of these vehicles has been rightly renowned for low pedal pressure, even response and absolute consistency; but minimum stopping distance has been less remarkable, and it would be absurd to pretend that my 1950 car can equal the all-round merit of a 1962 design with disc brakes on all four wheels. This notwithstanding, in city work the braking system must be rated excellent, and on the open road it is more than adequate in relation to a true maximum speed of around 80 m.p.h. and a normal cruising speed of 70 m.p.h.

There may be many who would regard road speeds of this order, with an inability to out-accelerate a Minx or Victor, a genuine deprivation, but this is something which is 'all in the mind', and a level of performance acceptable on a car which is running safely, silently and smoothly might be a misery on a low-priced production car which was short, brutish and nasty.

Compared with a new car of comparable price one must, in given circumstances, be prepared to sacrifice 5–7 miles in each hour of running time, so that if you were to start on a new car at 9 a.m. and stop for luncheon at 1 p.m. I and my old Royce would be twenty miles or so away, and would arrive about half an hour later. To offset the depressing prospect of thus missing two or three aperitifs is the fact that the Royce is not just a restful car; it is a positive therapeutic. I have often (truthfully) said that certain cars could be driven 400 miles in a day without physical exhaustion, but the Royce is the only one I know in which I can start in the morning physically exhausted (from causes into which we need not enter) and finish the day's run wholly revived.

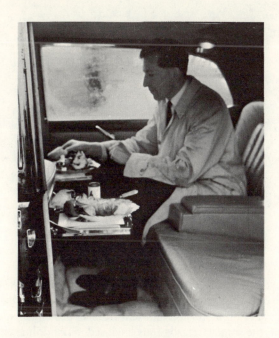

This thaumaturgy I explain by the fact that cruising at 70 in silence is restful; the steering and brakes combine to give a sense of continuous security; the succession of views from the high placed seats is intellectually stimulating; and the general respect that is paid to the car is emotionally satisfying. The music from the Radiomobile transistor radio is reproduction of a very high order and the comfort of the seats is at least the equal of the armchair from which I am now dictating this article.

These pleasures on the journey are greatly fortified by the practical picnic equipment. The pull-down tables are sufficiently big to permit a tablecloth with plate, knife and fork, and a glass, with a bottle of fizz placed upon a supplementary shelf which opens up below. Sunshine and fresh air can pour in through the sliding roof and can be enjoyed both when stationary and at any speed. It has well been said that every gentleman's house should have a gallery in which he may walk in the afternoon should it rain. I feel that no car is complete without some form of opening head.

A further joy of the Mulliner body of WFC 83 is the ease with which one may move, I had almost said walk about, inside it. A matter of moment is that the 'B' pillar is sufficiently behind the front seats to make possible the insertion of parcels between them and the rear bootrest without opening the rear doors.

Only when picnicking, and taking an occasional nap by the side of the road, have I myself had cause to appreciate the exceptional legroom in the rear compartment, but my adult passengers have waxed enthusiastic at being

able fully to extend their legs, and when visiting my daughter's school I have found it quite easy to take her and four friends to make a seven-seater load. For the most part of motoring this exceptional passenger space is more important than the somewhat exiguous enclosed, *lockable* luggage space, but if one has any faith in human nature it is possible to divide the load by an ingenious Mulliner refinement. Having first stowed any delicate personal effects or tender luggage, these can be isolated from wind and weather by pulling down a roll-top after which a full-sized cabin trunk can be strapped on to the nearly horizontal luggage platform, distance pieces being swung up so that the bodywork cannot be harmed, and the tail itself held at an angle for added security.

In this fashion it is probable that more luggage can be carried on the car than with a current design, but, taken all round, I do not pretend that the efforts of the engineers at Crewe in the past dozen years have been wholly in vain.

The latest cars enjoy power steering and can sustain far higher road speeds; they are immune from the small draughts which it is almost impossible to eradicate from an elderly car and they have an altogether higher standard of heating and ventilation.

Moreover, suspension has come a long way since the immediately post-war period. A wheel encountering a manhole cover sends a shock through the relatively flexible frame of WFC 83, which is in turn followed by shake through the hand-made structure of the Mulliner body, and certain kinds of wavy road surface will promote a strong pitching motion. The wise man will, with such a car, slow right down before traversing a *passage à niveau* in France; it is manifestly incorrect to translate this phrase by the English '*level* crossing'. However, the general behaviour of the 1950 car's suspension on rough French roads is far better than one might expect it to be from isolated examples of poor British roads. One thing remains common, irrespective of the country in which one is motoring, or the model one is driving. This is 'The Magic of a Name'. Very soon after I had bought WFC 83 a friend said that he assumed I had been animated mainly by the initials on the radiator. This is not true, but I agree that the prestige of the car is an added attraction, more especially as I conceive it to be *snob* in the French, but not in the British, meaning of the word. Certainly no car could be further removed from *presque cad*.

This instant and well-nigh universal recognition of top quality has many practical advantages as well as being an occasion for personal pride. Egress from side turnings is eased by the way in which other traffic halts; police assist; attendants at car parks which look full find that extra little space; when visiting factories one is waved on to the director's entrance. Also important to many people, including myself, is that a car of this kind is 'neutral' in the sense that one is not insulting any other manufacturer by failing to run a car of his make.

Last, but by no means least, is the attraction of first-class detail. The hand throttle, the ride control, a fuel gauge accurate to less than half a gallon, companions in the rear quarters, subtle interior lighting, and front seats which after being pushed back to ease exit subsequently latch on to a pre-determined position when moved forward, are minor items which in all give a major feeling of satisfaction. And all these good things are to be had for nothing even after allowing the extra £50 as compared with a modern car in respect of maintenance and using 100 gallons more fuel and 10 gallons more oil to give a total cash 'premium' of £80. For in fact this £80 is turned from a loss to a profit by the movements of the second-hand market. These fix the depreciation of the possible new Blank or Dash at £525 during the past twelve months, and for the Royce at £350, so that I emerge from the deal with a benefit of £95. Even friends who said that my purchase of the Royce was an extravaganza crowning a lifetime in which I have been con-tinuously suspended over the abyss of bankruptcy by the cantilever of credit, cannot deny this to be a good thing.

Thus with reason I drive this splendid memorial to a man who was one of the world's great mechanics, in a state of euphoria which enables me to reflect that perhaps all does turn out for the best in the long run. I do not have the instinct for profit which is the hall-mark of the first-class business man; since, in the words of the good Queen, 'we have gone sliding down into Democracy' politics have become a dreary, as well as a traditionally dirty game; zeal for potting meat might well have been short lived; and an alternative to Admiralty could well be lying full fathom five, my bones of coral made.

The Motor, July 18, 1962

EPILOGUE

MOTOR BUS

What is this that roareth thus?
Can it be a Motor Bus?
Yes, the smell and hideous hum
Indicat Motorem Bum!
Implet in the Corn and High
Terror me Motoris Bi:
Bo Motori clamitabo
Ne Motore caedar a Bo—
Dative be or Ablative
So thou only let us live:
Whither shall thy victims flee?
Spare us, spare us. Motor Be!
Thus I sang; and still anigh
Came in hordes Motores Bi,
Et complebat omne forum
Copia Motorum Borum.
How shall wretches live like us
Cincti Bis Motoribus?
Domine, defende nos
Contra hos Motores Bos!

A. D. GODLEY

One man's meat is another man's poison
My favourite car is an Avions Voisin

TRADITIONAL